Intersecting Lives

Intersecting Lives

HOW PLACE SHAPES REENTRY

Andrea M. Leverentz

UNIVERSITY OF CALIFORNIA PRESS

University of California Press
Oakland, California

Library of Congress Cataloging-in-Publication Data

Names: Leverentz, Andrea M., 1973- author.
Title: Intersecting lives : how place shapes reentry / Andrea M. Leverentz.
Description: Oakland, California : University of California Press, [2022] |
    Includes bibliographical references and index.
Identifiers: LCCN 2021061638 (print) | LCCN 2021061639 (ebook) |
    ISBN 9780520379411 (cloth) | ISBN 9780520379435 (paperback) |
    ISBN 9780520976733 (epub)
Subjects: LCSH: Prisoners—Deinstitutionalization—Social aspects—
    Massachusetts—Boston. | Prisoners—Deinstitutionalization—
    Massachusetts—Boston—21st century—Case studies. | BISAC: SOCIAL
    SCIENCE / Criminology | SOCIAL SCIENCE / Sociology / Urban
Classification: LCC HV9306.B7 L48 2022 (print) | LCC HV9306.B7 (ebook) |
    DDC 365/.60974461—dc23/eng/20220127
LC record available at https://lccn.loc.gov/2021061638
LC ebook record available at https://lccn.loc.gov/2021061639

Manufactured in the United States of America

31 30 29 28 27 26 25 24 23 22
10 9 8 7 6 5 4 3 2 1

CONTENTS

ACKNOWLEDGMENTS

First and foremost, I thank the people I, and my research assistants, interviewed for this project. People generously gave their time and shared their experiences, including joys, hopes, and pain. Talking to people and hearing their stories is the most rewarding part of this process, and reading through transcripts takes me back to those moments. Sometimes people ask how you can do research like this without becoming emotionally invested in the people you meet. My response is that you can't. Or, at least, I can't. Of course, I try to analyze and present data with honesty and fairness and some distance. But I am also genuinely fond of the people I've met along the way, and I take very seriously the trust they placed in me. I hope I have done justice to their experiences and perspectives.

This research was made possible because of funding from the National Science Foundation, Law and Social Sciences Program (Grant #1322965). In addition, I, along with Johnna Christian and Elsa Chen, received funding from NSF (Law and Social Sciences and Sociology programs, #1535615) to host a workshop at Rutgers University, Newark, on "Prisoner Reentry and Reintegration: Improving Data Collection and Methodology to Advance Theory and Knowledge." At the workshop, we brought together scholars working on issues related to incarceration and reentry from across field, method, institution, and rank. The whole workshop was generative and a great opportunity at which to present an early version of what became chapter 2. I thank all the participants for their engagement. That workshop was also the impetus for our edited volume, *Beyond Recidivism*. My contribution to that volume is a chapter on the methods and ethics of doing research among people returning from prison. I touch on some of those issues in appendix A here but develop some of the ideas and issues there. Some of the arguments here were first developed in articles in *Social Problems* 67(1), *City and Community* 17(4), and *Studies in Law, Politics, and Society* 77. Thanks to the reviewers and editors of those articles for their feedback.

Several research assistants conducted interviews, helped construct interview guides, and talked through data collection and analysis issues. Casey Ryan, David Copeland, Audris Campbell, and Eileen Kirk all interviewed men and women at the House of Correction. Adam Pittman, Jennifer Skinnon, Erin Allain, and Casey Ryan interviewed community members and attended community meetings. Adam and Jen deserve special thanks for doing the bulk of community member recruitment and interviewing and talking through many issues related to the analysis of these data. Some of this work is also reflected in our article in *City and Community*. Adam also undertook the Herculean task of coding and cleaning criminal history data.

Several friends and colleagues read the full manuscript. Johnna Christian, Jamie Fader, and David Kirk participated in a virtual workshop, providing excellent feedback, conversation, and encouragement. Sofya Aptekar read most, if not all, chapters and always provided fast and thoughtful feedback. Sarah Mayorga read pieces, answered questions, and shared in my book-writing anxiety. Audience members at several conference presentations and talks have asked guiding questions and gave much appreciated feedback and enthusiasm along the way. I am always grateful for the Racial Democracy Crime and Justice Network for fostering and supporting an impressive network of scholars and allowing me to take part. Being involved with RDCJN has been one of my most rewarding professional experiences.

A project like this cannot happen without the cooperation of correctional staff. Hallway conversations with Gerry Walsh first sparked my interest in the House of Correction, and he patiently answered my many questions about CORI codes. Gerard Horgan supported the project from the start, and Rachelle Steinberg came through in a major way to make sure it could go forward. In addition, she always facilitated access and answered questions. Christina Ruccio and Joanne White helped to coordinate the interviews with women and men, respectively. Several other staff members at the House of Correction facilitated the interviews by processing us into the institution and bringing people to us. Bill McNicholas and Mike Glennon patiently answered my questions about probation and sentencing practices.

Several people reviewed the manuscript at various stages. Venezia Michaelson has now provided generous, valuable, and thoughtful feedback on two of my books. I should be so lucky to get her feedback on future work.

She provided an excellent combination of validation and encouragement with critical suggestions; I am extremely grateful. Anonymous reviewers likewise were supportive and constructive. One reviewer wrote (paraphrasing), "I respect this decision, but let me try to save the author from herself." This made me both laugh and listen. I tried to follow your advice, and to the extent I did not: you tried! Maura Roessner has been an amazing support since this manuscript was a jumbled mess of data and half-baked ideas and working with Maura, Madison Wetzell, and everyone at the University of California Press has been fantastic. The feedback I received along the way improved the manuscript immeasurably. Of course, all remaining errors and limitations are my own.

The time that I was writing was a period of tremendous loss for everyone. Several important colleagues of mine passed away while I was writing. Patrick J. Carr, Xiaogang Deng, Richard P. Taub, and David Terkla all supported my career at various stages and in various ways, and for that I will always be grateful. I hope there will be time coming where we can collectively mourn all whom we have lost this past year. Two people who participated in this research, as far as I know, have also died. Quentin died during the data collection phase and Daniel died while I was writing.[1] I am glad I had the opportunity to get to know Quentin and Daniel and am heartbroken for them and their loved ones that they didn't have more time. I dedicate this to their memory and hope I have done justice to their (and others') experiences.

As always, I also thank my family for making sure I don't take myself too seriously and the friends who provided a welcome break from my own head.

PREFACE

In an earlier research project, interviewing women who had been incarcerated in Illinois, I was struck by the ways in which the women talked about their neighborhoods. They knew, from twelve-step programs they had been exposed to in prison and in a halfway house, as well as from broader cultural narratives on incarceration and reentry, that they were not "supposed" to return to their old neighborhood upon their release. Yet many did return to an old neighborhood or move to a similarly disadvantaged neighborhood. Partly this was out of necessity, either because they were staying with family, because these neighborhoods were relatively affordable, or because they were where supportive housing, such as single-room occupancy buildings, were located. In addition, however, the women had more positive reasons for living in these neighborhoods, as well as negative reasons to avoid living in more "desirable" neighborhoods. For example, Mary, who was living in Englewood in Chicago, where she had also grown up, said "crime is real bad in Englewood." She did not embrace the crime but felt safer there because "I don't have to worry about it . . . because I know people all around the neighborhood" (Leverentz 2014: 167). For her (and many others), the familiarity of the neighborhood and its people made her feel safe.

Other women embraced their agency, either to avoid drugs in high-drug-use areas or to find drugs even in new areas. For these women, neighborhood context was less important than their own will. If anything, the presence of open drug use could serve as a reminder of a past life to which they did not want to return. A few women took it even further and saw themselves as an asset to their neighborhood. Bennie said that she had been "part of the problem." Now, however, she was "part of the solution." She did not judge neighbors who were currently involved in prostitution or drug use—"everybody got a part to play in society; . . . that's their place in life at this time in their lives"—but she saw herself as a role model and an example that change is possible (Leverentz 2014: 170). Lisa S tried to negotiate between young men selling drugs in her West Side Chicago neighborhood and other residents. She said, "I asked them 'is that fair to us?' They said no" (Leverentz 2014: 171).

The idea of the women redefining their own role in their neighborhood and reframing their engagement with it was different than much of the "neighborhood context" research literature that found that returning to one's old neighborhood or returning to disadvantaged neighborhoods would increase reoffending among returning prisoners. A concentration of formerly incarcerated people in neighborhoods like Englewood and Lisa S's West Side neighborhood was a drain on community resources and placed those people squarely back within their criminogenic social networks. While the women's narratives are not statements of objective truth, they did seem largely consistent with their behavior in the time I knew them.

In addition to the different stories emerging from neighborhood context research and my interviews, these narratives of being an "asset" to a neighborhood also raised questions of how their neighbors perceived them. Did Bennie's law-abiding neighbors welcome her, despite her lengthy criminal record? Or were they wary? Did Lisa S's neighbors welcome her back after her time in prison and her attempts to negotiate drug selling in her neighborhood? I could not answer questions of neighbors' perceptions within that study, so I began exploring questions of neighborhood frames around crime and punishment in Boston-area neighborhoods. In the more stereotypically "high-crime" and Black neighborhoods, community leaders were more sympathetic to at least some people with criminal records and had more nuanced frames for understanding incarceration, reentry, and "former prisoners" (e.g., Leverentz 2011; Leverentz 2012; Leverentz and Williams 2017). Residents and community leaders were concerned about crime and violence in their neighborhood. They recognized, however, that while some incarcerated people may be a threat, many others were not. They also saw crime and violence as a community problem to solve, with wary cooperation, at most, with the police. In contrast, residents and community leaders in white-dominated neighborhoods adopted an insider/victim and outsider/criminal framework that lent itself to a law-and-order response to crime and fear of crime.[1]

It was from these two streams of earlier research that this project was conceptualized. I had narratives of women in Chicago who had been incarcerated and residents and community leaders in Boston-area neighborhoods. Were there contextual differences that explained the patterns? Or did these community patterns hold? To address this, I wanted data on the experiences of people who had been incarcerated and other residents in the neighborhoods to which they were connected (as current or former residents). Was there consensus in perspectives of the roles of formerly incarcerated people in neighborhoods? Did they even share similar senses of neighborhood life or neighborhood identity?

An added dimension was the county-level House of Correction system in Massachusetts. A majority of people sentenced to serve time in the Suffolk County House of Correction live within a few miles of it. They serve maximum sentences of 2.5 years per charge, with many cycling in and out. They were removed and returned to their communities, as with any incarceration-reentry pattern, but it was more local and the transitions more rapid. How did either of these dimensions shape the experiences of incarcerated people and of their communities? They also represented a majority of people sentenced to serve time in Massachusetts.

The central themes of this book are how people experience place and how this is shaped by their social position. A recent history of incarceration is one dimension of their positionality. So are race and racism, gender, socioeconomic status, length of time in the neighborhood, and one's engagement with and connection to their neighborhood. In addition to residential neighborhood, I also consider how people use and move about space, including the nonresidential places they go, how they get there, and whom they encounter along the way. This is a story of reentry from incarceration, but it is also a story of the importance of place and the importance of a contextualized and a social-interactional understanding of place.

Introduction

AFTER JOHN, a Black man in his 30s, was released from the Suffolk County House of Correction, he moved back to a small apartment in a poor, predominantly Black neighborhood in Boston that he shared with a cousin and several roommates. He spent most of his time within walking distance of his apartment. He walked, worked out in a nearby park, and carefully navigated his relationships with other young men in the neighborhood, "I don't want to be seen with them, 'cause I don't wanna be labeled. You know what I'm saying?" He avoided the temptation to return to selling drugs. He said, "because it was up to the point that's all I had left to do. . . . Post up on a block, nine times out of ten you're going to get an up. I just stood firm." John had most recently been incarcerated on assault charges after stabbing his son's mother's new boyfriend. As a result, they had a restraining order out on him, and so he also tried to avoid them. He complained about the difficulty of this, "First of all we live in the same neighborhood, so if I walk, we going to bump into them." John's experience illustrates why many criminologists argue for the dangers of people returning to an old neighborhood, or to a disadvantaged neighborhood, after incarceration. He was embedded in a neighborhood that included recent victims, people who knew him as someone who sold drugs, and other young Black men who might draw the attention of the police. Still, he had stable housing, which put him in a better position than many others leaving prison or jail.

In contrast, Sandy, a white woman in her 30s, spent her first few months after incarceration "bouncing" from place to place. After one night at her boyfriend Carl's father's house, they had a falling out with the father and had to leave. She and her boyfriend stayed in a motel, in several rented rooms, and on the street. A long period of addiction had strained her relationships with her family, and she could not count on them for support. Paying for rented rooms "obviously puts me in a position to do illegal stuff, because my family sucks." Sandy continued to acquire new charges related to shoplifting and to struggle with drug use. In several of the apartments in which they stayed, other residents used drugs, as did she and her boyfriend. Sandy did not consider halfway houses, shelters, or sober homes viable options, because many would not allow her and Carl to stay together, and the cost for the two of them was prohibitively high. She found new places to stay through chance encounters, such as running into people she knew at the bus stop. These fluid housing arrangements and chance encounters characterized Sandy's living situation for several months after her release from the House of Correction. Not only did she and her boyfriend move regularly, but they moved across the entire Boston region. In their case, even defining their "neighborhood" in a clear way is impossible.

John and Sandy are two of the individuals I and a team of research assistants interviewed about their return to the community after incarceration in the Suffolk County House of Correction in Massachusetts. The overarching premise of this book is that neighborhood and place are important dimensions of reentry from prison or jail. While few might disagree that place matters, we have a less clear sense of *why* or *how* it matters, and we rarely get a view of the lived social-interactional dynamics between returning prisoners and receiving communities. As Nikki Jones writes in *The Chosen Ones*, "The process of redemption is situated in social settings and social interactions" (Jones 2018: 4). Importantly, these interactions include "everyday" interactions, not just those with the formal criminal legal system. I argue that place matters through the interactions it fosters. These interactions include those with family, loved ones, and other ongoing relationships, but also with familiar faces and strangers on the street. These interactions, as shaped by both neighborhood and activity space—or the places a person goes as part of routine activities—shape outcomes, including offending, surveillance, relationship formation, and access to opportunities.

These interactions also are shaped by one's own social position, and how that shapes others' responses. For example, one theme that repeatedly came up in our interviews is that of Black and Latino men feeling profiled as "fitting a description." Everyone with a criminal record and a history of incarceration feels this to some degree, particularly when their records may be checked. Black and Latino men, especially younger men, experienced a more generalized assumption of guilt and suspicion. This too is shaped by location, as behaviors and people are more and less tolerated across places. As John Irwin argued in 1985's *The Jail*, "offensiveness" is a more important factor in arrest than is crime seriousness. Offensiveness is something that "conventional witnesses or their agents (the police) impose upon events; it is a summation of the meaning they attach to the acts, the context, and, above all, the character of the actors" (Irwin 1985: 23). Acts performed by people who are seen as "disreputable" are viewed very differently than those performed by "ordinary citizens," and acts performed in disreputable places may be more tolerated than those same acts in other places. Irwin argued that jails primarily house what he called the "rabble class"—people who are detached, or not well integrated into conventional society, and disreputable, or perceived as irksome, offensive, or threatening (Irwin 1985). People in positions of power use these arrests, detentions, and incarcerations to manage the less powerful.

Jailing and shorter-term incarceration, like in a House of Correction, continue to disproportionately impact people who are marginalized along several dimensions, including because of racism, sexism, and the criminalization of poverty. Policing policies like stop-and-frisk and order maintenance policing disproportionately impact low-income Black and Latinx communities (Western et al. 2021). In some cases, this takes the form of "recovery management," where law enforcement may try to coerce people into programs or services (Gowan and Whetstone 2012; Stuart 2013, 2016) or "banishment," where ordinances delimit zones of exclusion from which "undesirables" are banned (Beckett and Herbert 2009). While some of the strategies and frameworks have changed, the dynamics of cyclical arrest, incarceration, and release of marginalized populations remain (Sered and Norton-Hawk 2014; Comfort 2016; Kohler-Hausmann 2018; Ellis 2020).

This book makes several contributions. First, it presents a multifaceted analysis of how neighborhood context and place shape incarceration and reentry, from *both* returning prisoner and receiving community perspectives. While a growing body of research focuses on formerly incarcerated individuals and their experiences of reentry, few examine the community's perspective. Even more rarely are these two perspectives included in the same study. In addition to interviews with men and women returning from incarceration, we interviewed residents of three neighborhoods—parts of Dorchester, the South End, and South Boston—chosen because of their proximity to the House of Correction and their varying relationships with it and with crime and crime narratives. A second contribution is that it takes a comprehensive view of the role of locations and place. For example,

I also address experiences such as Sandy's—people with few if any ties to place. Often experiences like Sandy's are treated as missing data because of the difficulty of characterizing their residence, yet their stories are crucial in understanding neighborhood and place dynamics. In addition, I analyze the experiences of formerly incarcerated individuals who return to suburban or rural areas. Together, these experiences are key to understanding both the importance and limitations of neighborhood as a concept.

REENTRY AND SHORT-TERM INCARCERATION

A vast majority of people who are sentenced to incarceration will be released—in 2019, over six hundred thousand people were released from state or federal custody (Carson 2020). After several decades of dramatic increases, the prison population, including both admissions and releases, has been slowly decreasing since a high in 2009. In 2019, the state and federal incarceration rate decreased slightly for the eleventh consecutive year and the prison population has declined 11 percent since its 2009 peak (Carson 2020). In addition, the racial disparities in incarceration decreased somewhat in this period, as the incarceration rates for Black and Latinx men and women decreased faster than the white incarceration rates. While prison sentences in the United States are long by international standards, the mean time served for people released from state or federal prison in the United States in 2016 was 2.6 years and the median time served was 1.3 years (Kaeble 2018). Forty percent served less than a year (Kaeble 2018).

While much of the attention on prisoner reentry is focused on people being released from state and federal prisons, they represent only one dimension of the criminal legal system. County and city jails typically are used to hold people in pretrial detention and for shorter sentences (usually less than a year). While jail admissions have also declined in the past decade, 10.7 million people are admitted to a city or county jail, on average for stays of twenty-five days (Zeng 2020).[1] Much like prisons, our use of jails has increased dramatically in the past several decades (Subramanian et al. 2015). Rates of substance use disorders and mental illness are much higher in jail than in the whole population. As with prison incarceration, Black people are disproportionately jailed. People who are detained prior to their conviction often remain incarcerated because they cannot afford bail (Subramanian et al. 2015). The possibility of a faster release from detention is one factor in a decision to plead guilty. In many ways, jails reflect a criminalization of poverty and disadvantage more so than the protection of the public. As Reuben Miller recently wrote, "It is clear to anyone paying attention that the legal system does not administer anything resembling justice but instead manages the nation's problemed populations" (Miller 2021: 6). This dynamic is nowhere more visible than in jails and among those serving short sentences.

The system of incarceration in Massachusetts is relatively unusual in the United States. Rather than a two-tier system of county/local jails and state prisons, Massachusetts has a three-tier system, with county jails, for pretrial detainees, county Houses of Correction, for those sentenced to 2.5 years per charge or less, and state prisons, for those sentenced to more than 2.5 years per charge.[2] The House of Correction system is central to understanding incarceration in Massachusetts; it houses the majority of people sentenced to incarceration in the state. Judges in Superior Courts can sentence defendants to either state or county sentences, while judges in the much busier District Courts cannot sentence someone to state prison.[3] In fiscal year 2013, 91.4 percent of the 39,049 convictions in Massachusetts were seen in a District Court, and 8.6 percent were seen in Superior Court. Overall, in fiscal year 2013, 88 percent of incarcerated defendants were sentenced to a House of Correction and 12 percent were sentenced to a state facility.[4]

Black and Latinx people are overrepresented in the Massachusetts criminal legal system, at all levels. Much of the race/ethnic disparities can be explained in the nature and severity of the initial charges (Bishop et al. 2020). The picture of incarceration in Massachusetts is further complicated by the fact that not all counties have facilities for women, and so some women serve county sentences in the one state women's prison.[5] Suffolk County *does* have facilities for women; approximately 11 percent of their release population are women.[6]

Massachusetts experienced similar patterns of incarceration as the country in the past decade, with the number of people incarcerated peaking in 2010 and then slowly decreasing.[7] In the period we were recruiting (January 2014–June 2015), approximately fifteen hundred people were released from the Suffolk County House of Correction a year.[8] Most of these were released to Suffolk County. The average sentence for all people released from the House of Correction during our recruitment period (2014–2015) was about nine months, and their average time served was approximately six months.[9] The total release population was approximately 33 percent white, 43 percent Black, and 22 percent Hispanic or Latinx.

Approximately 35 percent of incarceration sentences in Massachusetts include a split or "from-and-after" sentence.[10] With a split sentence, the sentence is divided between time in custody and a sentence that is suspended for a period of probation. If the person violates the terms of their probation, they will be returned to custody for the suspended period. A from-and-after sentence links two charges, often with a custodial sentence on one charge followed by a period of probation on a second charge. Approximately 25 percent of those starting a probation sentence do so after a period of incarceration.[11] There are sixty-two district courts in Massachusetts, and the Boston Municipal Court has eight further divisions within the city. It is thus not difficult to pick up charges out of multiple courts. Occasionally someone in our sample was transferred after serving one county sentence to complete a sentence in another county. More common was the need to juggle several overlapping probation sentences out of multiple courts. Those with supervised probation should have their cases transferred to their jurisdiction of residence. Those with administrative probation only (a less intense supervision) remain in the sentencing court. In these cases, the person may have to report less frequently but maintain obligations to multiple courts simultaneously. Probation violations could result in more time in a House of Correction. These violations could reflect new arrests or criminal charges, but also things like not reporting a change of address, missing court dates, a positive drug test, or failing to pay required fines or fees.

Jails remain a way for cities to "manage" their disadvantaged and "disreputable" populations (Irwin 1985; Stuart 2016; Western et al. 2021). Many of the people who are housed in county facilities in Massachusetts, and many of the people in this sample, are serving time for relatively minor charges, like drug possession, shoplifting, public order offenses, and probation violations. The circumstances surrounding their arrests are often tied to disadvantages resulting from racism, poverty, and addiction. They also are often tied to local contexts. This highlights that arrest, incarceration, and reentry are all relational activities, not something limited to the individual incarcerated.

NEIGHBORHOOD CONTEXT OF REENTRY

Research documenting people's experiences upon exiting prison has demonstrated that many are concentrated in a small number of typically disadvantaged neighborhoods (La Vigne et al. 2003; Brooks et al. 2005; Simes

2018). For example, the men and women comprising Bruce Western's Boston Reentry Study sample moved to under half of Boston's census tracts, which tend also to have higher levels of disadvantage (Simes 2018; Western 2018). There are at least three dimensions through which scholars raise important questions about neighborhoods and prisoner reentry. The first is where people move upon their release from prison. To what extent are people with criminal records concentrated in a small number of neighborhoods? What is the distribution of people across urban, suburban, and rural areas? How do people's post-prison neighborhoods compare with their pre-prison neighborhoods? A second set of questions involve the influence of neighborhood context on offending or reincarceration. Do neighborhoods shape people's post-prison likelihood of offending or of reincarceration? How? What dimensions shape their experiences with offending and desistance? When we talk about recidivism, we often mean the likelihood that a person reoffends. But recidivism is usually measured by arrest, conviction, or incarceration. So, to what extent is a "neighborhood effect" of recidivism a measure of offending behaviors of people released from incarceration or of surveillance and control by law enforcement, probation, and parole officers? Third, how does neighborhood shape people's post-incarceration experiences? For example, can they access public transportation? Is their neighborhood walkable? Do they have existing or can they develop new social networks within their neighborhood? This book is primarily concerned with this third question, though it is helpful to situate it within the literature on the first two questions.

Both in terms of neighborhood attainment and outcomes related to neighborhood context, neighborhoods can be framed both as physical places and as an expression of social networks (Harding, Morenoff, and Wyse 2019). Perspectives on how and why neighborhoods matter in prisoner reentry are typically premised on social interaction within the neighborhood. For example, residential change is a potential turning point, in which a move sets a person on a new path, in this case, away from offending (Abbott 2001). One reason residential change is posited as an important turning point is because it can disrupt existing social networks that may contribute to offending (Laub and Sampson 2003; Kirk 2012). If people leaving prison move to a new neighborhood than they lived pre-prison, they presumably have less contact with their existing criminogenic social networks. For those living either in a neighborhood in which they have such networks, or in a high crime neighborhood, this might contribute to reoffending or to an intentional distancing of oneself from others in their neighborhoods, to avoid temptation, victimization, and surveillance (Harding et al. 2019; Leverentz 2020b).

Sociologists David Harding, Jeffrey Morenoff, and Jessica Wyse (2019) conducted an extensive study of reentry experiences in Michigan, involving analysis of administrative records and repeated interviews with a sample of men and women released from Michigan prisons. They divided their sample's neighborhoods and neighborhood engagement into four categories that incorporate both the relative level of crime and disorder in the neighborhood and a person's connection to place. "Chaotic detached" was the most widespread type of neighborhood engagement among their sample. Chaotic detached neighborhoods were high in crime and violence, but the person in question was new to the neighborhood, or all neighbors tended to keep to themselves to keep themselves safe. As a result, people living in chaotic detached neighborhoods felt little responsibility or connection to their neighborhoods and typically defined the neighborhood in negative terms. In contrast, those living in "chaotic connected" neighborhoods were also living in impoverished neighborhoods, but with family. Crime was prevalent, but people were familiar with others in the neighborhood, and they felt they could successfully navigate life in the neighborhood. In neighborhoods classified as "safe detached," people were relatively detached from others in the neighborhood, and it was quiet. Those living in "safe connected" neighborhoods were typically returning to live with middle- or upper-middle-class families and were at least tenuously connected to neighborhood organizations or otherwise connected to social networks in the neighborhood. Key to navigating life in the neighborhood were not only characteristics of the neighborhood itself, but also the level and nature of one's engagement with it.

In addition to neighborhoods as social networks, Harding and colleagues (2019) emphasize the role of neighborhood as a spatial location, including access to transportation, employment, and social services. Many returning prisoners have neither a driver's license nor the funds to afford a car. Only some have friends or family who can drive them, and driving without a license leaves them at risk of arrest and possibly reincarceration if on probation or parole. A spatial mismatch between people and jobs is exacerbated by a lack of access to transportation and is less of a concern for those who can travel to job-rich areas (Sugie and Lens 2017). For many recently incarcerated people, these jobs are low wage, and the hours involved in working and traveling to and from work leave little time to look for other work (or anything else). People also may face both individual and community deficits in transportation accessibility (Bohmert 2016). On an individual level, people may have poor physical health, making transportation less accessible. At the community level, they may live in inaccessible areas, making public transportation less accessible and making them more reliant on social supports for transportation.

Access to transportation also highlights another important dimension of neighborhood context: that people often do not spend all their time in a residential neighborhood. The concept of activity spaces can expand how we think about returning prisoners' navigation of space and how neighborhood and place matter. Activity spaces are the subset of all locations with which an individual has direct contact as the result of routine activities (Horton and Reynolds 1971; Browning and Soller 2014). Most people spent time outside of their residential neighborhood for daily activities, like work, socializing, and to access services (Cagney et al. 2020). These patterns of movement are shaped by individual characteristics and access to resources and transportation. It is thus important to consider how people move about space, and how they engage not only with their neighborhood but also other commonly traveled areas (Farrall et al. 2014). The people in this study have varying levels of connection to their residential neighborhood and have smaller and larger activity spaces that are shaped by where they live, what they need, and how readily they can travel.

Studies addressing the effects of the neighborhood context of people returning from prison suggest that those living in lower-crime, less disadvantaged neighborhoods have lower rates of reoffending or reincarceration, though there may be variation across offense types (Kubrin and Stewart 2006; Hipp et al. 2010). Individual factors do matter, and segregation patterns and the concentration of returning prisoners in some neighborhoods may mean that some neighborhoods experience higher levels of offending because of who lives in that neighborhood. However, neighborhood effects scholars (e.g., Kirk 2020; Harding et al. 2019; Kubrin and Stewart 2006) document that neighborhood also has an independent effect on reoffending and reincarceration. Daniel Mears and colleagues found that men released from prison to resource-deprived areas were significantly more likely to be convicted of violent crimes, but less likely to be convicted of subsequent property or drug crimes (Mears et al. 2008). There also were significant race and neighborhood segregation interaction effects. In part, Mears and colleagues speculated whether the lower likelihood of new drug convictions among "young minority males" in segregated neighborhoods reflected differential enforcement rather than differential behavior (Mears et al. 2008).[12] Access to resources also affects reincarceration. John Hipp, Joan Petersilia, and Susan Turner (2010) found that people on parole were less likely to be reincarcerated when they lived near social services; this effect was particularly pronounced for Black people. However, when the demand for those services went up, so too did reincarceration (Hipp et al. 2010).

Offending, reconviction, and reincarceration are central concerns to people coming out of prison, correctional agencies, and the public. While the public is concerned for public safety, people being released from prisons or jails also hope to stay out of prison. This desire shapes the behavior of people who have been incarcerated and affects multiple areas of their lives in both direct and indirect ways, including how they navigate life in their neighborhoods. In an earlier study of women being released from Illinois prisons to Chicago neighborhoods, I found that while some women were afraid to move back to their old neighborhoods because of possible "temptations," others wanted to, because of the social ties and familiarity they had for that neighborhood (Leverentz 2010). Some believed they could be an asset to others in the neighborhood because of their history of addiction and offending, demonstrating the possibility of change. Others emphasized their own agency in choosing to not use drugs, regardless of the context they were in. Some also had learned from previous experiences that "that's like they say in that book, that shit doesn't work.[13] Excuse my expression, but it don't work, that geographical thing. If you want to find it, you're going to get it" (Leverentz 2014: 165).

This may be particularly pronounced when one moves within a city or region, where returning to old neighborhoods and people is easier (Kirk 2009; Sharkey and Sampson 2010), but Abra, the woman quoted here, had moved across Illinois and still had the experience and knowledge to develop new networks. This leaves people to also learn how to manage temptations and to regulate movements to protect themselves. Among the Chicago women I interviewed, that often meant framing their neighborhood as a neutral force or as a positive place for redemption (Leverentz 2010). On the other hand, a response to feeling surveilled leads many people to stay indoors as much as possible and to be careful about whom they are seen with, not only to avoid any peer pressure to engage in illegal activity, but also to avoid the *impression* that they might be engaged in illegal activity or to otherwise draw attention of law enforcement (Leverentz 2018, 2020b; Fader 2021). Of course, other factors also shape people's engagement with neighborhoods and places beyond a fear of rearrest. People need to go to work (or look for work), go to medical appointments, seek out additional services and supports, and otherwise live their lives. Doing so involves navigating space, both in those activities and in transit. And again, both physical spaces and how they shape and are shaped by social networks are important.

MOBILITY AND NEIGHBORHOOD ATTAINMENT

Beyond characteristics of neighborhood context, moving to a new neighborhood upon release may also shape neighborhood engagement and reentry experiences. Moving, and sometimes moving frequently after release, are common experiences among returning prisoners. Approximately a quarter of the Boston Reentry Study (BRS) sample moved back to their pre-prison census tract (Simes 2018). Claire Herbert, David Harding, and Jeffrey Morenoff (2015) found that, according to administrative records, the average person on parole in Michigan moved 2.5 times per year for their first two years post-release and nearly all (over 90 percent) of the people they tracked moved at least once. These moves included—in decreasing order of frequency—moving to an intermediate sanction (e.g., drug treatment facility), to a different private residence, to go on the run from parole, to treatment, to prison, or to the street. Forced moves accounted for over half of the moves (Herbert et al. 2015). Similar patterns occurred in the Boston Reentry Study. A large proportion of the BRS sample moved frequently and sometimes had no stable address to provide. Over 60 percent of the total sample lived in more than one place in their first-year post-release, nearly 40 percent lived in more than one place in their first week, and approximately 16 percent either lived in institutional settings or stayed in different places every few days (Simes 2018).

The frequency of moves and the neighborhoods to which people return reflect both the impact of incarceration and larger patterns of inequality. Herbert, Harding, and Morenoff conclude that while the predictors of housing insecurity among a general population (e.g., mental illness, drug use, prior experiences with incarceration and homelessness) also predict housing insecurity among people on parole, so too does involvement with the criminal legal system. Using the National Longitudinal Survey of Youth (NLSY79), sociologists Michael Massoglia, Glenn Firebaugh, and Cody Warner (2013) found that those who had been incarcerated lived in more disadvantaged neighborhoods than those who had not. There also is significant racial variation in the impact of incarceration on neighborhood attainment. White people who had been incarcerated lived in more disadvantaged neighborhoods post-release, while Black and Latinx people did not. They argue that this reflects general neighborhood inequality in the United States and that white people then "have more to lose" from a prison sentence because they tended to live in more advantaged neighborhoods prior to incarceration (Massoglia et al. 2013). Similarly, in Michigan, people released from prison were released to highly disadvantaged neighborhoods and stayed in highly disadvantaged neighborhoods. Only about 10 percent of the Michigan sample (Harding et al. 2019) experienced upward *or* downward mobility in the first twenty-four months after release. Racial differences in neighborhoods that people returned to reflected larger patterns of segregation and poverty (Harding et al. 2019). Black releasees lived in significantly more disadvantaged neighborhoods than white releasees, but they were no more likely than any other Black Michigan resident to live in a high-poverty neighborhood (Harding et al. 2019). Similar patterns were found in Boston, with Black and Hispanic respondents living in neighborhoods with the greatest levels of disadvantage, controlling for pre-prison neighborhood disadvantage (Simes 2018).

People may move to a new neighborhood or neighborhoods after incarceration for several reasons. Family members they were staying with previously may have moved, or other family members with whom they can stay may live in a different neighborhood (Simes 2018; Harding et al. 2019). Researchers at the Urban Institute found that 45 percent of men returning to Chicago moved to a new neighborhood upon release, and most commonly to avoid trouble or because their families had moved (La Vigne et al. 2004). Almost two-thirds were living with family upon their release (La Vigne et al. 2004). Staying with family may reflect a permanent housing situation, as when someone moves home to live with his or her spouse and children. In other cases, it may be a temporary situation that leads to additional stress and strain in that household (Western 2018). Post-release moves also may include stays in programs or shelters or a desire to start over upon release. These moves often reflect limited choices and opportunities for people being released from prison, and a high level of financial and social instability. They also often happen within an urban area or region and are moves between similarly disadvantaged areas (La Vigne et al. 2004; Massoglia et al. 2013; Herbert et al. 2015).

Some moves may place former prisoners in closer or more distant relationship to programs and services, like drug treatment and reentry programs (Hipp 2010). They also may be nearer or farther from accessible jobs for which they are likely to be hired (Pager 2007) or to transportation that might allow them to travel to those jobs (Sugie and Lens 2017). They may experience varying levels of stigma in different community contexts (Leverentz 2012). In addition, sociologists Patrick Sharkey and Robert Sampson (2010: 670) emphasize the importance of taking a "contextually conditioned" perspective on the impact of residential mobility. In other words, we should not assume all moves function in the same way. They found that adolescents who moved within the city of Chicago were more likely to commit violent acts, while those who moved from Chicago to outside the city were less likely to engage in violence (Sharkey and Sampson 2010). They attribute this both to a physical distance from the city and the cessation of ties to city institutions, like the public school system. The gap in violence is explained by the racial/ ethnic composition of destination neighborhoods, the quality of the school context, adolescents' perceived control over their new environment, and fear (Sharkey and Sampson 2010).

Similarly, sociologist David Kirk found that distance moved mattered, suggesting the importance of a stronger break with former ties (Kirk 2009). He found that people who moved to a new parish (county) upon release were significantly less likely to be reincarcerated than those who returned to the same parish. Kirk was able to leverage the "natural experiment" of Hurricane Katrina in New Orleans and the surrounding region to control for the selection effects of moving (Kirk 2009, 2012, 2020). Given the widespread impact of hurricane damage in the New Orleans area, there was less reason to believe that people who did move were fundamentally different in key ways (e.g., motivation) than those who did not. After the hurricane, people were also significantly more likely to move to a different parish upon their release (50.1 percent compared to just under 25 percent for two years prior) (Kirk 2009).

People may experience significant tensions and constraints when moving, including a sense of physical and social isolation when moving to "good" neighborhoods. Moving to a new neighborhood may impede one's ability to negotiate violent or criminal situations because of a lack of familiarity with neighborhood norms and networks (Anderson 1999; Sharkey 2006; Harding 2010; Clampet-Lundquist et al. 2011). In an analysis of boys and girls in the Moving to Opportunity experiment, a sizable minority of teen boys who stayed in their neighborhoods had developed navigational strategies to avoid trouble in those neighborhoods, including avoiding being in the neighborhood or altering their routines within it (Clampet-Lundquist et al. 2011).[14] Boys who moved to a new neighborhood did not have such strategies, which the authors attribute to the boys living in low-poverty neighborhoods, often without same-age or slightly older peers, at key developmental stages (Clampet-Lundquist et al. 2011; see also Harding 2010). This meant they lacked knowledge of the "geography of danger," did not develop necessary navigational skills, and so were unprepared when they moved to higher-poverty neighborhoods later. This may be particularly pronounced among young men of color, and so reflect gender, race, and stages in the life course.

A residential change may influence reoffending or reincarceration through its influence on social networks and supervision. In addition, moving may reflect or contribute to a shift in identity and the meanings placed on offending and living a law-abiding life (Giordano Cernkovich, and Rudolph 2002; Giordano, Schroeder, and Cernkovich 2007; Maruna and Roy 2007). Maruna and Roy (2007) argue that a geographic change is one of several possible sources of self-change, but that it is unlikely to be successful without a corresponding cognitive self-transformation. Without this cognitive shift, they argue, a geographic change alone is unlikely to have long-term effects on recidivism. Someone whose networks are disrupted, for example, might develop new connections if they choose. They also may become known to a new group of law enforcement officers over time. Residential change frequently fails to foster desistance, leading to cynicism about its potential to do so (Leverentz 2014). However, if a geographic change supports a change in identity, such a move immediately upon release may be a key moment to encourage longer-term changes in self-conception and behavior (Kirk 2012).

As with questions of neighborhood context, understanding where and why people move to different neighborhoods is important for understanding questions of desistance, reoffending, and reincarceration, and for understanding social lives more broadly post-incarceration.

THE IMPACT OF CRIME AND INCARCERATION ON NEIGHBORHOODS

Other residents of neighborhoods are also impacted by a concentration of returning prisoners. Todd Clear (2007) documented that neighborhoods impacted by incarceration experience disruptions to family financial support, damages to the neighborhood economic and political structure, and a destabilization of the community. The coercive mobility of incarceration, in which people are forcibly removed and then later returned to communities, affects crime rates in impacted neighborhoods. Clear and colleagues found that when neighborhoods experienced a moderate level of removal of people to prison, crime rates declined. However, after a certain level, additional prison admissions increased the crime rate (Clear et al. 2003). Large numbers of people returning to the community from prison can also lead to an increase in crime, which may reflect challenges to neighborhood self-regulation that incarceration-induced residential instability creates (Clear et al. 2003). Black residents in Tallahassee primarily saw formerly incarcerated people as harmless to their communities; "they try to treat him [the formerly incarcerated person] better than residents believe people outside the community do" (Clear 2007: 127). They perceived stigma attached not only to the individuals who have been incarcerated but to the neighborhoods to which they are released. In addition, residents recognized the financial and relational costs of incarceration (Clear 2007).

Crime and narratives about crime are important dimensions of how residents, businesses, and the media understand place. As Girling and colleagues argue, "when people talk about *crime* they are often talking about *places*" (Girling Loader, and Sparks 2000: 5, emphasis in original). News and entertainment media highlight violent and sensational crimes, which are often linked, directly or through signaling, to poor, often Black and Latino neighborhoods, to men of color (as offenders or suspected offenders), and to white women (as victims) (Chiricos, Eschholz, and Gertz 1997; Gilliam and Iyengar 2000; Parrott and Parrott 2015). This media coverage shapes commonly understood narratives about crime, criminals, and urban places, telling media consumers who criminals are and where crime occurs. Within the context of these broader messages, crime narratives also shape the meaning attached to life in specific communities. For example, the media and residents often see crime as expected in poor neighborhoods of color and shockingly unexpected in middle-class and white areas. These narratives shape how people understand what it means to live in urban areas in general and what it means to live in particular places (Suttles 1972; Hummon 1990). In addition, respondents' race, length of residence in the neighborhood, and neighborhood racial composition all may shape how they perceive their neighbors and how they code threats (Small 2004; Tach 2009; Leverentz, Pittman, and

Skinnon 2018). Feelings of social integration into a local community reduces fear of crime and feelings of vulnerability (Adams and Serpe 2000).

Narratives about crime also illuminate public attitudes about crime, crime policies, and punishment, which reflect general concerns about crime or society more than direct experiences with victimization. General social anxieties, like a concern for general social values, take the form of racially coded crime rhetoric and punitive policies (Tyler and Boeckmann 1997; Cullen, Fisher, and Applegate 2000; Useem, Liedka, and Piehl 2003; King and Maruna 2009). Fear of crime research has demonstrated that fear of victimization is tied to both individual characteristics and neighborhood context. In addition, understandings of crime and disorder are racially and ethnically coded so that the presence of groups most associated with crime in the urban United States (i.e., Black and Latinx people) signifies to others that crime is more likely (Chiricos, Mcentire, and Gertz 2001; Quillian and Pager 2001; Sampson and Raudenbush 2004). Fear of crime and crime salience are, in turn, predictors of punitive attitudes (Warr 1980; Covington and Taylor 1991; Costelloe, Chiricos, and Gertz 2009). Concerns about the economy, "youth today," and racial and economic changes in the neighborhood all may increase punitive attitudes and support for punitive policies like increased sentence lengths, the use of chain gangs, and more serious penalties for juvenile offenders (Costelloe et al. 2009; King and Maruna 2009). Importantly, these dynamics vary by place. Residents of more diverse communities, communities with larger proportions of people of color, or communities undergoing racial transformation to greater proportions of people of color may express greater levels of punitiveness, as an expression of social threat (Baumer, Messner, and Rosenfeld 2003).

In my previous research on two Boston-area communities, both communities were primarily concerned with violent and drug offending (Leverentz 2011, 2012; Leverentz and Williams 2017). Yet the meaning of that, and the implicated offenders, in each area was quite different. In the pseudonymously named Urban Hub and Factory Town, community members understood crime through dominant metanarratives, but they translated these metanarratives through the lens of place identities (Merry 1981; Alkon and Traugot 2008). In both cases, narratives were racially coded and gendered, with offenders primarily seen as Black and Latino men. However, in Urban Hub, with an established identity as a Black neighborhood, rather than framing all young Black men as a threat, they saw most "criminals" as petty offenders who were not a major threat to the neighborhood. They saw a need for support and direction for many and a criminal legal response for few. Within the context of a history of strained relationships with law enforcement and broader patterns of mass incarceration, community members did not draw conclusions based on a criminal record, but rather focused on what they knew of the person. Occasionally someone was seen as intractable; more often, they were dumb kids or unlucky. In contrast, the dominant voices in Factory Town, with a sizable and growing population of color, framed crime and criminals as Others and as an "outsider" category in a white-dominated crime discussion. Many participating in public crime-related discussions in Factory Town drew clear lines between who was a member of the community and who was not. Criminals were outsiders, both literally and figuratively, and were referred to with racialized language. Criminals were both physically and socially distant from the law-abiding residents and were excluded as part of the community, even when they lived in Factory Town. In both places, residents, law enforcement and criminal legal system officials, and social service representatives all used similar crime-place-based narratives.[15]

REENTRY IN BOSTON

This book focuses on the experiences of people being released from the Suffolk County House of Correction and on the experiences of living—for those being released from incarceration and for other residents—in three Boston neighborhoods. In this section, I briefly detail the four focal places and how I went about learning about the experiences of people in them.

House of Correction

The first key place in this study is the House of Correction. It opened in late 1991, replacing a century-old facility on Deer Island, a peninsula and now part of the Boston Harbor Islands National Recreation Area. The Deer Island facility, first an almshouse then a House of Correction, replaced a facility in South Boston. The current House of Correction has just under two thousand beds across 674 cells.[16] The complex includes twenty-seven housing units, with three floors in the main tower for women. It is located in the center of Boston, roughly where the South End, South Boston, Dorchester, and Roxbury meet. The complex is just off Interstate 93, between the Greater Boston Food Bank and the Boston Medical Center, Boston's public hospital. Nearby are several methadone clinics, a needle exchange, and a homeless shelter that opened in early 2015. The area surrounding the House of Correction is called the Newmarket District, Mass-Cass (for the nearby intersection of Massachusetts Avenue and Melnea Cass Avenue), Methadone Mile, or Recovery Road, each with its political implications (Vivant 2020).

People who serve time at the House of Correction often experience periods of homelessness and addiction. Until 2014, Long Island, an island in Boston Harbor, was home to a large campus of drug treatment, homelessness, and other social services that was commonly used by people exiting the House of Correction.[17] A bridge connected Long Island to Moon Island, which connects to Squantum Peninsula in Quincy (a suburb just south of Boston) via a causeway. The bridge was not adequately maintained and in October 2014, Boston's mayor abruptly closed it.[18] This also meant closing all services that were located on the island, throwing the homeless and recovery communities of Boston into a tailspin. Boston's mayor said at the time, "This was a difficult, but necessary, decision that was made in the interest of public safety. This bridge has been a source of grave concern for many years, and I was not willing to risk the possibility of disaster for one more night, with the data presented to us about the serious condition of the bridge."[19] The city scrambled to find temporary housing for people who relied on Long Island programs, and eventually opened the Southampton Shelter in early 2015, with beds for approximately four hundred men, a block away from the House of Correction. In 2017, the Boston Public Health Commission opened a daytime engagement center behind the shelter to provide a space off the street for people who stay at area shelters or use area recovery services.

Reentry from a House of Correction is primarily a local phenomenon. A majority of people are incarcerated from and return to within a few miles of the facility, and disproportionately to disadvantaged communities of color (Forman, Van Der Lugt, and Goldberg 2016). For most of the people we interviewed, the House of Correction—and incarceration more broadly—was a specter in the background once they were released. They feared reincarceration, and a few spent time in the immediate area at methadone clinics or nearby shelters or halfway houses. For the most part, they left it, as a place, when they were released. In chapter 1, I return to some of their experiences with the criminal legal system, for readers who want more background on their earlier experiences.

While most of the people sentenced to the House of Correction are released to the local area, there is significant variation in the neighborhoods that are adjacent to the facility. To look at the neighborhood context of reentry, I chose three neighborhoods that reflect some of this variation, including racial/ethnic composition, socioeconomic status, impact of incarceration and reentry, and neighborhood reputation. These three neighborhoods also highlight different themes and dimensions of the connections between neighborhood and reentry.

Dorchester

Dorchester is the largest neighborhood, in geography and in population, in the city of Boston, though I focus on a smaller area within it. The whole area is about six square miles, with approximately one hundred thousand residents. It originally was a separate town, founded in 1630, and was annexed into the city of Boston in 1670. Dorchester is racially and economically diverse, with substantial racial and economic segregation within it. In recruiting residents of Dorchester, we focused on the neighborhoods roughly between Codman Square, up along the Fairmount train line and roughly between Bowdoin Street and Blue Hill Avenue, to Upham's Corner. For simplicity's sake, unless stated otherwise, when I refer to Dorchester, I am referring to this area. While there is racial and economic diversity in this section, there are sizable Black and poor populations. The area is 63 percent Black, compared to 24 percent for the city. Twenty-four percent of the families are below the poverty level and the median household income is significantly lower than the city as a whole; only two of the area's seventeen census tracts have a median household income above the city's median. It is a high-crime area—over half of Boston's 2017 homicides were in the two police districts that cover this area—and bears the reputation of being one. While that reputation is often applied to all of Dorchester, crime and violence is concentrated in the area around the Blue Hill Avenue corridor. It is also these neighborhoods within Dorchester with the greatest concentration of people committed to the House of Correction and being detained in the Nashua Street Jail (Forman et al. 2016).

This area, then, is the stereotypical "high-crime" Black neighborhood that also receives a relatively high proportion of Boston's returning prisoner population. The people that we talked to who lived, or had lived, in Dorchester were aware of these stereotypes and realities of crime and incarceration in their neighborhood. At the same time, a key theme among them—both those who had been incarcerated and those who had not—was a strong sense of place identity. Those who were in, or closer to, crime-involved networks had to learn how to navigate space to minimize their involvement and their surveillance. But they felt comfortable in the familiar spaces of their neighborhood and often had strong and important ties to family and friends in the area. While there were risks and dangers of living there, it was also "home" to many. While a number of those we interviewed had strong affective ties to their neighborhood, it was also a place where they *could* live, because they had a family member who lived there and could allow them to stay.

South End

The South End is a gentrified section of the city, with bifurcated high- and low-income populations and racial/ethnic diversity. Gentrification, which began in the area in the early 1960s, led to an influx of white residents (Small 2004; Tissot 2015).[20] Based on the most recent census estimates, just over half the population is white. By the end of the twentieth century, the South End was also one of the wealthiest neighborhoods in the city (Small 2004). While the average median household income is above the city median, there is wide variation within the census tracts that make up the area, with half below the city median and half well above. Two of these census tracts also have above the city average of families in poverty (21 percent and 33 percent). The police district incorporating the South End has more index crimes than any other district in the city, largely driven by property crimes. A quarter of the city's larcenies in 2017 occurred in this area, far higher than any other district.

The South End has long had a connection to social service programming in Boston. It is home to the Pine Street Inn, one of the largest and most visible homeless shelters in the city, several public housing developments, and the public hospital. When programming was available on Long Island, buses transported clients from the South End to Long Island, further cementing the connection between social service provision and the South End. In addition, it borders the new Southampton Shelter, the Suffolk County House of Correction, and Roxbury, another high-crime neighborhood in the city and "the heart of Black culture in Boston."[21] The South End also contributes disproportionately to House of Correction admissions, with half of these coming from the Pine Street Inn (Forman et al. 2016).[22]

These characteristics make the South End an interesting site in which to look at neighborhood perceptions of incarceration and reentry and how they shape the experiences of returning prisoners. While the neighborhood has a large high-income population, it also has a history of celebrating diversity—"diversity is a defining feature of the South End's identity" (Tach 2014: 24)—including the neighborhood's low-income residents and social service recipients. This "diversity" identity remains strong among some long-term residents, though it is less central to newer residents. In addition, the closure of the Long Island bridge and the impact on the South End was a touchstone moment for many residents, challenging the limits of their tolerance of diversity. Interviewing a wide range of South End residents revealed the ways in which physical proximity did not translate into social proximity. Stark differences in the perceptions of life in the South End emerged between those who had been incarcerated in the House of Correction and other residents, as well as between higher-income white and lower-income residents and residents of color.

South Boston

South Boston is a peninsula between Dorchester Bay and Boston Harbor. It has a reputation as an insular, working-class Irish neighborhood, with significant racial and class tensions (Krysan 2003). In the past several decades, it has undergone significant gentrification: working-class white residents moved out as middle- and upper-class residents moved in. Today, the neighborhood remains predominantly white (85 percent of its residents are white). The average median household income among all but two of South Boston's census tracts is well above the city's median. Thirteen percent of families are below the poverty level; these are concentrated in the two low-income tracts (with 46 percent and 47 percent of families below the poverty line), which are home to public housing developments. The people of color in the neighborhood are also concentrated into these two tracts. It is a low-crime area, experiencing approximately 6 percent of violent crimes and 8 percent of property crimes in the city (of twelve districts). While there are a few halfway houses and social services, it has far fewer than the South End and the area near it and is not known as a "service destination." Overall, it receives an average number of people returning from the House of Correction, relative to their size of the city's population (Forman et al. 2016). Among the three target neighborhoods, it receives the smallest proportion of returning prisoners.

South Boston is the least obvious choice for inclusion in this study, and in some ways its contribution is as a comparison of a neighborhood where prisoner reentry, reincarceration, and related issues are less of an issue. Residents are more concerned about parking and negative consequences of development than they are about crime or incarceration. In this respect, it reflects a normative experience of many neighborhoods. The concentration of incarceration means that some neighborhoods are strongly impacted, while many are not. Still, South Boston was not immune to crime. It had recent ties to organized crime and drug use. Around the time of this research, several high-profile homicides happened in South Boston. These homicides were seemingly random attacks on "innocent" victims and drew widespread media and police attention. These crimes were framed as aberrations. In this sense, it also reflects a parallel to Dorchester, where news coverage of crimes and violence was normalized and rarely drew outrage or much attention from outside the neighborhood. While several of the people that we interviewed who were being released from the House of Correction had ties to South Boston, it was inaccessible to most. This reflects an inaccessibility, both socially and financially, of "good" neighborhoods for people exiting prison.

METHODS

To understand local and relational dynamics around prisoner reentry, I draw on four streams of data. First, I and a team of research assistants interviewed men and women being released from the Suffolk County House of Correction.[23] Respondents were recruited between late January 2014 and June 2015 (see table 1 for a summary of participants). Anyone being released during our recruitment period was eligible to be interviewed. The plan was to interview participants five times: once shortly before their release, once shortly after, and then every three to four months, covering about a year post-release. This time frame covers the immediate transition to the community, which often corresponds to high levels of instability and high rates of reincarceration. By interviewing people multiple times through this period, we could learn about how they navigated this transition, and how their prerelease attitudes and goals played out post-incarceration. In the analysis, I often highlight these narratives across interviews to reflect both what happened to them and how their perspectives shifted over time. While still limited in that it captures only approximately a year, it provides a glimpse into a key period of transition. Some interviews got off schedule if we temporarily lost touch. Of those we interviewed five times, the average time covered is just over

TABLE 1 Recruitment: All HOC Releasee Interview Respondents
and Total House of Corrections Releases during Same Period

	Men (N = 61)		Women (N = 39)		Total (N = 100)	
	Sample	HOC	Sample	HOC	Sample	HOC
White %	38	30	72	62	52	34
Black %	44	45	26	26	36	43
Latinx/Hispanic %	18	24	3	11	12	22
Asian/Pacific Islander %	0	1	0	1	0	1.3
Average age (years)	37.7	34.4	36.5	34.1	37.2	34.3
Average time served (months)	6.3	6.2	3.9	3.5	5.4	5.9

fourteen months, and ranged from nine to twenty-eight months. Interviews in the community took place at the person's home or a public place such as a coffee shop or public library branch that was convenient for them. Appendix A in this book and Leverentz (2020a) include more details on interview practices and dynamics.

Interviews were recorded and transcribed.[24] Each interview guide covered some of the same questions, including where they were living, if and where they were working, and how and with whom they spent their time. In each interview, respondents were asked where they lived and why and to describe their self-defined neighborhood. In addition, aspects of their engagement with the neighborhood, other areas in which they spent time, and their movements about space came up in many areas of the interview. Each interview also covered different information, including childhood experiences and more explicit questions about their activity spaces. New questions included those that were added to further emerging analysis.

Second, we had two "official" measures of criminal legal system involvement. With their permission, we collected official criminal record information on people being released. These provided another glimpse into people's involvement with the criminal legal system, often providing confirmation of what they told us, and sometimes gave us information about what happened with people we lost contact with. In addition, we received anonymized information on everyone who was released from the Suffolk County House of Correction during the time we were recruiting interview respondents. This provides a frame of reference and context to our interview sample as it compares to the overall release population.

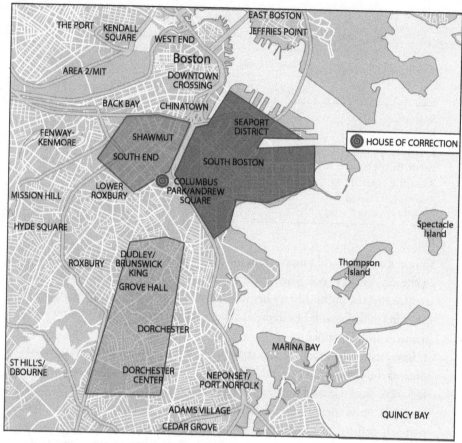

MAP I. Target neighborhoods. Source: Google Maps.

To learn about receiving communities, we took two additional approaches: interviews with residents and participant observation in three areas of Boston: parts of Dorchester (the neighborhoods roughly along the Fairmount commuter rail line and Blue Hill Avenue from Codman Square to Uphams Corner), the South End, and South Boston (see map 1). These three neighborhoods are geographically close to the House of Correction, but have very different relationships to it, along with different demographics and narratives around crime.

We interviewed eighty-four residents across these three communities (twenty-seven in Dorchester, thirty-eight in the South End, and nineteen in South Boston; see table 2). Residents were recruited through a variety of approaches (e.g., inviting people at community meetings, snowball sampling,

TABLE 2 Neighborhood Resident Recruitment

	Dorchester		South Boston		South End		Totals	
	N = 68,397	N = 27	N = 36,161	N = 38	N = 31,920	N = 19	N = 617,594	N = 84
	Neighborhood	Interview Sample	Neighborhood	Interview Sample	Neighborhood	Interview Sample	Boston	Total sample
Black %[1]	57.0	55.5	4.5	5.2	10.9	18.4	28.8	27.3
White %	9.1	29.6	81.5	94.7	54.9	64.8	57.2	61.9
Asian %	5.8	3.7	4.2	5.2	16.4	7.9	10.2	5.9
Latinx/Hispanic %	25.3	18.5	8.2	0.0	15.0	5.3	19.0	8.3
Women %	52.0	63.0	50.8	58.0	49.8	42.0	52.0	52.0
Men %	48.0	58.0	49.2	42.0	50.2	58.0	48.0	48.0
Homeowners %[2]	28.8	52.0	40.3	68.0	38.9	53.0	33.0	56.0
Renters %	71.2	44.0	59.7	32.0	61.1	42.0	59.4	41.0
Families below poverty line	24.0	—	13.0	—	12.0	—	16.7	—
Household income	$41,712.24	—	$89,734.40	—	$75,743.92	—	$58,516	—
Average house value	$355,775.00	—	$482,033.33	—	$741,601.79	—	—	—
Length of residency (mean years)	—	22.5	—	14.7	—	14.7	—	19.7
Length of residency (range)	—	1–3	—	.5–67	—	.5–53	—	.5–67
Median year move in	2008	—	2010	—	2009	—	—	—
Regularly attends community meetings	—	52%	—	74%	—	45%	—	53%

1. Race and ethnic categories are alone or in combination, and so might total more than 100 percent. Respondent race/ethnicity is self-report and may also include multiple groups. Three people in Dorchester identified as Latinx and Black and are counted in both categories. One person in South Boston identified as Black and White and is included in both. One respondent in Dorchester identified as a member of the "human race" and is excluded from the table.

2. These totals exclude one South End resident who is currently homeless and two people (in the South End and Dorchester) who did not answer this question.

drawing on our own networks, posting or distributing fliers). As the interviews went on, we continued to revisit what we perceived to be key categories of people in each neighborhood and adjusted recruitment as needed (Weiss 1994; Small 2009). For example, the South End and South Boston have experienced several waves of gentrification and we wanted to include residents from each of these waves. In other words, we adopted a case-based, rather than a sample-based, logic (Small 2009). While our sample is not statistically representative, it captures a range of experiences in each neighborhood and includes a diverse group of participants. For example, 53 percent attended community meetings regularly, and the rest did not.[25] Forty percent were renters, 55 percent were homeowners. Just over a quarter (27 percent) were Black, 62 percent white, 6 percent Asian, and 8 percent Hispanic or Latinx. Just over half were women, and just under half men. They had lived in their neighborhoods for an average of twenty years, ranging from six months to sixty-seven years. Some were living in neighborhoods where they grew up, and others were recent transplants, to Boston or to their current neighborhood. Interviews covered broad topics, like their perceptions of their neighborhood, connections within it, and their perceptions of crime, safety, and social control. We asked some questions explicitly about incarceration and reentry, including whether or not they would consider hiring or renting to people who had been incarcerated. Here, there was not much variation, with a majority of residents in all three neighborhoods reporting that "it depends," often on the nature of the conviction. More differences emerged in the ways they characterized neighborhood life, and how fears of crime and their neighbors played into that.

The research team also attended community-based meetings that focused at least in part on crime issues (e.g., crime task forces, resident associations, police-community meetings). This was targeted participant observation, to hear how residents and community leaders talked about the neighborhoods and about crime and safety in the neighborhood (Carr 2003; Leverentz 2012). There was significant variation in how crime and neighborhood life issues were framed in each of the three areas. For example, all three areas have neighborhood associations. In Dorchester neighborhoods, these always included police reports and discussions of incidents of crime, violence, or disorder. In the South End, there was significant discussion, and debate, over drug use and homelessness in the area and their association with several neighborhood institutions like shelters. In South Boston, drug use and violence both sometimes were brought up, but it was not uncommon for entire meetings to focus exclusively on issues related to development or parking. Gentrification and development were concerns in all three areas, but often dominated discussions in South Boston. Not everyone participates in community meetings, and these should not be taken as a singular voice for any community. However, they do reflect dominant narratives and illustrate key concerns of those communities, without being influenced by researcher questions (Leverentz 2012).

About half of the men and women we interviewed returning from the House of Correction had ties to our three target neighborhoods. Predictably, given patterns of incarceration and reentry in Boston, more people have connections to Dorchester than the South End or South Boston, but we talked to some with current or former ties to all three. In addition, the inclusion of people from or returning to places other than our target neighborhoods became analytically fortuitous. First, simple screening tools may well have eliminated people with some ties to our target neighborhoods (e.g., if they had lived there in the past, but weren't "from" there). As I develop in later chapters, the experiences of men and women living in suburban areas and small towns also provide key insights into reentry in ways that are often overlooked in research with an "urban" focus. In addition, a sizable number of people released from prison experience tremendous housing instability and centering their experiences is necessary to understand reentry as a process. While outside the initial scope of the study, these experiences were analytically very useful (and developed in chapters 2 and 6). These two chapters draw just on the interviews with people returning from the House of Correction.

It is not possible to fully do justice to the experiences of all the people we interviewed. I draw more extensively on the experiences of about a dozen people, who have a more prominent role in the chapters that follow. In most cases, these are people we interviewed five times and reflect a range of experiences along key dimensions (e.g., race/ethnicity, gender, neighborhood or town). In some cases, parts of their stories appear in multiple chapters, or I use a more extended example within a single chapter. This allows me to present a more holistic account of a smaller number of people, who reflect the diversity of participants and key aspects of their experiences, while supplementing their stories with those of others. In each chapter in which I quote someone, in the first reference, I include a few key details about them. With subsequent quotes or discussions of them in the same chapter, I include race and age in parenthesis. In addition, appendix B includes a list of quoted participants, and the index includes all references to each participant.

OVERVIEW

This book starts with the House of Correction. In chapter 1, I introduce the people who are experiencing reentry from the House of Correction, including their experiences navigating it and the criminal legal system, how their experience there compares to that of other correctional institutions, and their plans for release.

While neighborhood is one force shaping people's lives, few people exist solely within their neighborhoods. They move about space, often leaving the neighborhood in which they live, to work, to access services, and to maintain social ties. In addition, among people returning from prison, a sizable portion of people do not have a clearly distinguishable or stable neighborhood. They move frequently, often with large geographical jumps, stay in shelters, churn in and out of jail and treatment, and stay on the street. Social networks that might connect them to places are often attenuated. Both those who travel to different neighborhoods as part of their routine activities and those who have unstable, or no, housing spend much of their time in public spaces. They are often perceived to be among the more disorderly and disreputable, inspiring scorn or fear among other residents. In chapter 2, I detail the variation in activity spaces among this group of interviewees, with particular attention to those with limited ties or engagement with their residential neighborhood, including where and why they move about space, and how they engage with others. I also discuss what their experiences mean for the use of neighborhood as an analytic concept.

The next three chapters focus on life in the target neighborhoods both for those with a history of incarceration and those without, and how those experiences do and do not converge. In chapter 3, I focus on Dorchester, with its reputation of being a high-crime area, with sizable Black and low-income populations. What does prisoner reentry mean here? Drawing on participant observation and interviews with both returning prisoners and residents in Dorchester, I detail how crime and incarceration shape social life in the neighborhood and what it means to be a returning prisoner in Dorchester. Social networks are key. People returning from prison depend on their social networks for support, but also must navigate some of these relationships carefully, when they are tied to former offending and might draw attention from law enforcement. Other residents depend on knowing their neighbors, at least superficially, for a sense of safety and security.

In chapter 4, I turn to the South End. Not surprisingly for an economically bifurcated and racially and ethnically diverse neighborhood, there is also substantial variation in how people view life in the South End. For those whose frame of reference is Pine Street Inn, the Southampton Shelter, or any of the number of methadone clinics and halfway houses in the area, the neighborhood is "bad" and dangerous. The wealthy residents who gentrified the neighborhood primarily see it as a safe neighborhood of beautiful brownstones and destination restaurants. For a group of earlier gentrifiers, their place identities are also tied in with a tolerance of diversity and a welcoming—up to a point—of social services and low-income populations. These groups have cognitive maps that correspond to their framings and engagement with the neighborhood. The varying experiences and neighborhood frames also have led to different groups contesting control and access to the neighborhood. The returning prisoner population is a visible segment of the South End, particularly in its southeast corner, and how they are viewed by their neighbors depends largely on the social positionality of those neighbors. How then does this contestation impact the people who are returning from prison, and how are they viewed by these other groups? There is little evidence that they benefit from the area's diversity, but rather that both the presence of a large number of wealthy neighbors and a number of social services leads to greater scrutiny and efforts at social control.

In chapter 5, I turn to South Boston. South Boston has changed dramatically since it gained popular attention in the 1997 film *Good Will Hunting*. It is somewhat less insular and working class than it used to be, though still overwhelmingly white. Key battles among residents are around development and minor forms of social disorder. Crime is not unknown in South Boston, but it is also not an everyday concern for most. For those people returning from prison with ties to South Boston, it is now largely out of reach economically and socially, and the relative lack of services means they have few reasons to return. For the most part, even those with ties to South Boston see returning as both unattainable and undesirable, because they perceive themselves to be unwelcome. Long-time residents of South Boston remain close-knit, and it retains some of its insularity. South Boston serves to illustrate the possibilities and limitations of returning to low-crime neighborhoods with a low concentration of returning prisoners.

Not all of those in the returning prisoner sample were released to the three target neighborhoods or to Boston. In chapter 6, I discuss those who were released or moved to suburban or rural areas, and who have very different relationships to place than those in urban areas. Despite an urban focus in much of the research on reentry, suburban and rural reentry are growing in importance, and the people impacted face different sets of circumstances and constraints. By drawing on these experiences, I begin to develop an analysis of neighborhood and place in suburban and rural contexts. These participants' experiences highlight the importance of public transportation and the value of geographically concentrated services. A relative or total absence of public transportation in suburban and rural areas limits movement to walking distance, which, combined with lower density, also limits employment opportunities, services, supports, and social relationships.

Finally, in the conclusion, I return to the theoretical and policy relevance of neighborhood. In addition, I address how policies can better account for the needs of both people returning from prison and other residents.

ONE

Criminalizing Disadvantage

RACE, CLASS, GENDER, AND REENTRY IN BOSTON

My first option is to stay with my father and his step-wife, but to be honest, he's dealing with a lot of alcohol issues. So, I'm thinking more like a dry shelter, out on Long Island.

PABLO, Black man in his 50s

She let me stay the week, but it's like, it wasn't long enough. It was bad timing, because here it is. I'm right back to the same. I'm right back down to square one again.

BRUCE, Black man in his 30s

THE MEN AND WOMEN we met shortly before their release from the House of Correction were highly marginalized because of a lifetime of experiences with the criminal legal system and other institutions. While most were well intentioned and hopeful about their release, they were also worried about their ability to succeed at staying out of prison. Their reentry plans were often loose and unraveled quickly. Few had access to adequate support, and many made difficult and constrained choices. In this chapter, I provide some examples of how their earlier experiences with the House of Correction and the criminal legal system shaped their plans as they were being released.

RACE, CLASS, AND GENDER IN CRIME AND PLACE

People's experiences returning from prison—and living in neighborhoods—is shaped not only by place, but also by who they are and how they connect to place. Intersectionality provides a framework through which we can understand how race, gender, class, and other factors shape one's experiences, in

31

general, and particularly here in terms of experiences with incarceration, reentry, and neighborhood life. Intersectionality emphasizes that all people have intersecting socially constructed identities that are ordered into social strata and organized within a "matrix of power" (Crenshaw 1991). Theories of intersectionality emphasize the importance of analyzing the interconnected identities of individuals, and how these identities are perceived and responded to by others (Potter 2015).[1]

Young Black and Latino men adopt behaviors to minimize their risks and to navigate through space safely (Cobbina et al. 2008; Harding 2010; Fader 2021). For many young men, managing safety often means not leaving one's neighborhood, as they perceive their own neighborhoods as safe and others as potentially a site of retaliatory violence (Cobbina et al. 2008). For young Black men, the mere act of being in a public space might mark them as potentially delinquent or criminal and therefore at risk of both retaliation and police surveillance (Cobbina et al. 2008; Fader 2021). Boys in the Moving to Opportunity study who moved to new neighborhoods felt they were less accepted in their new neighborhoods and possibly more targeted by police surveillance. The boys who stayed in their neighborhoods and so were more familiar with them also developed navigational strategies to avoid trouble (Clampet-Lundquist et al. 2011). These boys knew what places to avoid, and when, to avoid trouble.

In contrast, girls in the Moving to Opportunity study were more likely to hang out in destination places, like malls or downtown shopping districts, rather than in the neighborhood (Clampet-Lundquist et al. 2011). They also were more likely to hang out in places with adult supervision. Jody Miller (2008) found that young African American women used strategies like staying close to home and avoiding public spaces in their neighborhoods as ways to stay safe (see also Cobbina et al. 2008). These strategies can help African American girls avoid situations that will require them to fight, and thereby allow them to behave in ways that others perceive as "good" while remaining safe (Jones 2010). Some girls may embrace a tough "ghetto chick" identity to give themselves freedom and mobility in an unsafe world (Jones 2010).

Women who are involved, directly or indirectly, with prisons experience gendered and raced responses in the criminal legal system (Haney 2010; McCorkel 2013; Wyse 2013).[2] Legal scholar Kimberlé Crenshaw argues that Black women are "subject to the twin dimensions of hypervisibility and substantive erasure" (Crenshaw 2013: 31). They are a part of the stereotypical at-risk Black family, headed by a single mother, and yet absent from much programming directed at "saving" Black boys and families. In addition, there is growing awareness and attention to the problems of the *criminalblackman* stereotype (Russell-Brown 1998), and yet less attention to how raced and gendered stereotypes shape the experiences of Black women. Crenshaw writes, "Longstanding rhetorics that framed men as uniquely damaged by racism have primed Black communities to endorse neoliberal accounts of social life that subtly shift the focus from historically constituted relations of power to the failures of family formation and gender conformity" (Crenshaw 2013: 32). This framing both blames Black women, as inadequate mothers, wives, and girlfriends, for the criminal involvement and incarceration of Black men, and ignores their own disproportionate rates of incarceration. Women who engage in offending are often looked upon as "doubly deviant," violating both gender and legal norms (Owen 1998; Heimer and De Coster 1999). Black women face an additional layer of stigma. Women's responses to the messages they receive are also shaped by their own positionally—for example, as mothers, as community members, as Black women—and competing social messages about who they are and what they should aspire to (Leverentz 2014).

In her presidential address to the American Society of Criminology, Candace Kruttschnitt (2016) reminded us that the salience of gender varies by context and is shaped by other forms of stratification, including race, class, and sexuality. Rather than just asking "does gender matter?" we should be looking at situations and relational processes in which gender is foregrounded, or not. For example, the process of redemption may work similarly for men and women, but the specific hooks for change may differ across gender and be shaped by racialized gender ideologies (Giordano et al. 2002; Jones 2018). Black men who are trying to break free from the criminal legal system are encouraged to give up the "code of the street," while still being expected to be providers and protectors to their families (Anderson 1999; Jones 2018). The ways in which Black gender ideologies play out for Black men are consequential not only for these men, but also for women and girls because of how they reinforce gender-based hierarchies (Jones 2018). For Black women who are themselves being released from prison, racialized gender ideologies might mean resuming caregiving roles within families and communities, even when those same relationships might have been abusive and indirectly, at least, related to offending and/or drug use (Leverentz 2014). Jones argues that the solution, then, is "a framework for understanding how, for example, structural violence and interpersonal violence, police violence, and street harassment are *interconnected*" (2018: 168, emphasis in original).

STIGMA AND REPUTATION

People returning from incarceration face stigma because of these interlocking systems of oppression, each of which affects their lives. All experience the stigma of a criminal record. Young Black and Latino men also face racial stigma and profiling that identify them as likely suspects, even before their records are known. People who have been incarcerated and have a history of drug addiction are often alienated from family and extremely socially and economically marginalized.[3] Those who are well known in their communities are easily identified as likely offenders because of their known histories, regardless of their demographics. Particularly in an individualistic context like the United States, people often experience these dynamics as individual failures. Sociologists Susan Sered and Maureen Norton-Hawk (2014: 160) conclude "each person is led to believe that one's misery is one's alone, a stance that militates against the formation of group, race, or class-consciousness, and inhibits the desire and ability to work collectively to change the system." The women they followed most often believed in personal responsibility as well, blaming themselves for their "failures" and blaming line staff in organizations rather than political leaders and policy makers that created the policies that limited them and trapped them in an "institutional circuit." Historian Lawrence Vale, writing about stigma attached to public housing, made a similar point about the consequences of stigma, "The most devastating consequence of stigma, as [Erving] Goffman makes clear, is that its marks become internalized; stigma is more than a measure of societal distrust, it is a deeply destructive cause of self-doubt" (Vale 2002: 14).

Erving Goffman emphasizes that stigma is about relationships, not individual attributes (Goffman 1963). An attribute that can be stigmatizing is not inherently so and is not creditable or discreditable in itself. And yet the stigma is very real in its consequences. "By definition, of course, we believe the person with the stigma is not quite human. On this assumption we exercise varieties of discrimination, through which we effectively, if often unthinkingly, reduce his life chances" (Goffman 1963: 5). This happens at the individual level toward those with a criminal record through the punishment itself, including all its formal collateral consequences (e.g., Travis 2005; Pager 2007) and informal judgments that follow. These judgments may be directed to individuals who have been incarcerated, along with their families and communities (Clear 2007; Comfort 2008). We see it in the narrative around criminals and "high-crime" neighborhoods (Leverentz 2012). We also see it in responses to Black Lives Matter and protests against police brutality that ask, "why don't they care about Black-on-Black crime?" that ignores extensive community activism in these neighborhoods and the systemic failures that foster differential rates of violence across neighborhoods (Peterson and Krivo 2010; Boyles 2019).

Feeling stigmatized impacts how people approach help seeking. Sarah Brayne (2014) found that those with any level of criminal legal system contact (from a police stop to incarceration) are less likely than those without to interact with "surveilling institutions," including financial, medical, labor market, and educational institutions. "Going on the run" from court dates, probation, or parole also may reflect frustration over their treatment in those systems (Goffman 2014; Leverentz 2018). In her ethnography of women who use drugs in Massachusetts, Kimberly Sue (2019) relayed the story of Serenity, a woman with a history of both incarceration and drug use. When hospitalized with an eye infection, Serenity left after one night against medical advice because she felt like she was being treated like a prisoner, rather than as a person or as a patient. Serenity responded to the stigma she felt as an intravenous drug user, resulting in a reluctance and resistance to getting help from hospitals or social services. It also contributed to her drug use. Serenity was quoted, "The defense mechanism for that is to be that. OK, that's how you want to label me, that's what I'm going to be. I'm going to be the best goddamn junkie I can be. . . . It's easier to put up that front than it is to deal with those looks and things that people say about you" (Sue 2019: 18). This narrative parallels that of the "persistent offenders" Shadd Maruna (2001) interviewed in his influential study of desistance. The men and women who felt trapped by their circumstances had a harder time desisting from offending than those who could maintain a belief in their inherent goodness and their ability to change their lives. Others in similar circumstances may consciously try to "blend in" to their surroundings to avoid being stigmatized as an addict or homeless or a former prisoner, or they choose where to go and not go to avoid such judgments (Parker 2019; Pittman 2020).

Places also have reputations, both stigmatizing and not, which can shape responses to the residents of and visitors to those places. Historian Lawrence

Vale wrote about the stigmatizing nature of contemporary public housing (Vale 2002: 13). High rates of crime or incarceration, racial composition, residential income, housing stock, and land uses can all shape neighborhood reputation (Sampson and Raudenbush 2004; Quillian and Pager 2010; Drakulich 2013; Wallace and Louton 2018). Towns and neighborhoods often fight against the placement of locally undesirable land uses (LULU's) to avoid being stigmatized by those institutions. Elites' place-based narratives have material effects on places and can shape a place's ability to resist these locally undesirable land uses (Gans 1982; Alkon and Traugot 2008). Towns or neighborhood leaders also may engage in strategic self-presentation or public acknowledgment to try to diffuse stigma attached to places (Eason 2017). For example, the town of Ossining, New York, changed its name from Sing Sing to distance itself from the infamous prison located there (Conover 2010). In contrast, John Eason (2017) detailed the ways in which town leaders in Forrest City, Arkansas, lobbied *for* a prison placement in their town to try to improve the town's image. This demonstrates the fluidity of stigmatized identities and the power of narratives to shift impressions.

Looking at incarceration and incarcerated populations is not the same as looking at offending or any category of illegal behavior. Incarceration is not a straightforward measure of the behavior of the people incarcerated; rather, it also reflects differential enforcement and different levels of vulnerability to arrest, both because of individual characteristics and behaviors and because of characteristics of places in which they are located. Thus, both individual and place relationships matter in these definitions and shape the likelihood of arrest and incarceration.

CRIMINAL LEGAL SYSTEM EXPERIENCES

Most of the people we interviewed as part of the House of Correction release population had been incarcerated before, across a range of facilities, and had extensive experience in the criminal legal system. For many of the people in this study, incarceration was not their first involvement with government institutions. Many have histories that include social service and foster care involvement (including their experience both as children and as parents). These experiences both make them more vulnerable to future arrest and have taught them to be wary of public institutions (see Brayne 2014). Bruce, a Black man in his 30s, lived with his grandmother, until he was taken out of her house and put into residential placement when he was 7. He said, "I know that I was in it. I know that it was negative. I know that I've seen a lot of shit. A lot. I've seen a lot of trauma go on in those places. A lot." Some of this shaped their behavior at the time. As Charles, a Black man in his 20s said, "I was just bad. I didn't care. I didn't have my mother, I didn't have my real mother. I didn't even have one of my own siblings with me. I'm not respecting nobody. Screw this. I was just going off. Didn't care, don't give a shit anyways. . . . It's just a whole lot of shit." For men like Bruce and Charles, their anger over this early trauma continued to affect how they related to institutions and the world more broadly. Whether their traumas manifested externally (in anger or violence) or internally (in drug use), it often led to circumstances and behaviors that resulted in involvement with the criminal legal system.

Many of the people we interviewed had lengthy histories of court involvement. For this population, decisions about whether to plead guilty rarely correspond in any simple way to "guilt" or "innocence" (see Leverentz 2018). People satisfied their short-term desire to get out of jail or the House of Correction but were still left with the long-term consequences of having a (growing) criminal record. Their decisions reflected a vulnerability within the criminal legal system. They pled guilty when they were, or when they were not "100 percent innocent." It also, however, reflected a short-term desire to get out of jail, knowing that the charges were minor, and they were unlikely to win the case in court. In the longer term, this contributed to their legal vulnerability, as they acquired more charges and more convictions, and so became a "likely suspect," particularly when this was combined with being in certain places that triggered heightened surveillance or suspicion. Context matters, in addition to behaviors and people's positions in various systems of oppression (Irwin 1985; Beckett and Herbert 2009; Crenshaw 2013; Stuart 2016). For people who were homeless or unstably housed or were experiencing drug problems, they were a visible and "offensive" group that could be managed through frequent arrests, probation violations, charges, and short sentences. These criminal histories made it more difficult to break out of the cycle of arrest and incarceration, as they looked more and more guilty with growing records. These experiences, over time, bred cynicism and distrust of the law. Both their decision-making and the outcomes reinforced their position.

Once a person is involved in the criminal legal system, it can be hard to break out of it. Jackie, a white woman in her early 30s, was serving time for the first time, though she had charges going back to her teen years. She said,

I commit a lot of crimes and I trust and believe and I'm grateful that I haven't got caught for them, because I'd really be doing a lot of time and this ain't for me. . . . Once you get caught in the system, it seems like you get stuck in the system. So that's why I'm glad I don't have nothing here, over my head yet. I've a couple of guilties that I didn't have before because my whole record is continued without a finding, but I took a guilty on the possession of E and possession of C, just so I don't have to deal with no probation or in and out of jails. This is too depressing and overwhelming.

Many others' experiences illustrate Jackie's fear of getting stuck. James, a white man in his 40s who had charges going back to his childhood, said he had been incarcerated "a few" times before, in state and county facilities; "it mushes together. It's like Groundhog Day."

A number of people in this study preferred to serve time rather than be on probation. Probation was often experienced as more burdensome, risky, and lengthy than incarceration (Phelps 2013; Phelps and Ruhland 2021). In Massachusetts, a judge may impose a minimum length of supervision and program components, but may later modify the sanction, including an extension of the duration of probation.[4] For many, this led to a sense of never-ending punishment and legal vulnerability. Arturo, a Black man of Caribbean descent in his 30s, had violated his probation. He had been mandated to a recovery home and was "just rebelling." He was discharged from the house for disrespecting an employee. Then, "they informed my probation officer and I went on a run for, what was my little run for? I think about a week or two, and then I got caught up with my probation and they basically hit me with that eighteen-months suspended time, and that's how we met" [at our first interview].

Sometimes, violations were the result of "noncompliance" because they could not afford the fees associated with mandated programming (Harris 2016). Charles, a Black man in his 20s, said, "I had to do the domestic [violence] program Common Purpose. And the reason why I didn't do it, cuz I didn't have the money for it. And then I started to get the money and so I started going. But my PO [probation officer] wasn't trying to hear it. And so he gave me a lil' three months [incarcerated]. So, when I get out, I have to do it again." In all these examples, their "offenses" were not enough to result in incarceration on their own. But because they were on probation, they did. While none were happy about being incarcerated, there was a sense of relief that when they were released, they would not be under supervision and would be "free."

Probation violations often led to incarceration, either immediately or after a period of being "on the run." People sometimes skipped court dates or probation check-ins to delay the resulting penalty. For those who do go on the run, this typically means trying to avoid trouble and the attention of the police. It is not a dramatic experience, either on the part of those on the run or the police or probation officers, at least for those with relatively minor charges. They typically just existed, trying to avoid police contact for as long as possible. No one is likely actively looking for them, but if they are stopped for any reason, their name is run, and the warrants will come up. Netta, a Black woman in her 30s, said "there's no fun being on the run. . . . Just trying to stay away from trouble and trying to stay away from the police." Jarrod, a white man in his 40s, was incarcerated on forgery charges. "My case is from five years ago. I was on the run for five years, just didn't get in trouble, didn't get in any trouble at all, so they didn't pull me out. Nobody found me, nobody. The charges were so small that they weren't really looking for me, so I just ignored it and then somebody said, you know, my sponsor had said to me, 'Jarrod, you can't keep running from it.' And I said, 'You know what, you're right.'" Jarrod had been living out of state and doing well, but "I had these court cases over my head and I had to come back to clear them up." In doing so, he felt frustrated with the progress he lost in his years on the run. By our third interview, Alfredo, a Latino man in his 40s, had a probation violation and a new charge after an attempted shoplifting incident. For that, he said he felt "like a jackass, right there. That was really dumb of me. . . . I feel really dumb and really ashamed of myself over that." He was expecting to be incarcerated for about six months to finish his probation sentence. He said this could happen:

> Any day. I could be driving with you down the street, you get pulled over and they ask me for my name, I have to get my name and two warrants are going to come out and I'm going to get arrested. It can happen to me every day. I'm living day by day right now. I try to avoid riding in cars. I pretty much stay by myself. If I was to turn myself in, I'll do it in the winter. I'm not trying to go back in the summer. At least finish the summer out here. That's my plans.

None of the people who were, or had been, on the run expected this to last. They saw this as an attempt to keep some level of freedom as long as possible. Going on the run was often a reflection of frustration and a sense of being trapped in the system but being on the run often meant living a quiet life out of trouble for a time, yet always with the specter of possible incarceration.

The sense of being stuck is sometimes the result of lingering open cases (Kohler-Hausmann 2018). Netta was a Black woman in her late 30s who was serving time on a parole violation. She received the violation when she picked up new charges after being on parole for about a year. Those new charges remained an open case, without a conviction, for over two years. According to her official criminal history, she had acquired 240 charges from forty separate arraignments. These charges were overlapping cases out of multiple courts. At the time we requested her criminal record, approximately one-third of these charges remained unresolved, either because the cases did not yet have a disposition or because she had an uncompleted probation sentence. For example, probation for charges in 2010 had been extended several times after she failed to report, most recently until late 2017. Netta's experience was not unique—juggling cases out of multiple district courts, open cases that remained open for lengthy periods, and extended periods of probation were all common. All these also lent themselves to a sense of powerlessness and cynicism.

Open cases made people vulnerable, but so did any history of criminal legal system involvement, even when all cases were resolved. Many were acutely aware that they "looked guilty" by virtue of their criminal record, making them more vulnerable if they got arrested again. For example, in our third interview, Sarah, a white woman in her 30s, said, "Even though I'm not on probation, anything could happen. Getting pulled over or something. Me having drugs on me. Me walking out of a drug house and the cops are there. Things like that. Even though I'm not stealing and robbing stores and stuff, it doesn't matter. . . . I mean, I know just like anybody else, I'm just one bad decision away from picking up." Here Sarah took responsibility for her choices, but she was also acutely aware—from her personal experiences of having her probation violated—of the severity of the consequences of those choices for someone with her record. Sarah focused on what would happen should she commit a new offense. Netta experienced what could happen by virtue of her record when she was arrested for a charge that was similar to those she had admitted guilt to in the past. This time, she said "That is my M.O. . . . For the first time, I feel vindicated because I could actually say that I didn't do it. But it didn't help the fact that I am in handcuffs and now I'm going to go to jail because my past says this is something I could've done." Netta believed she was particularly vulnerable because she was a Black woman who had committed similar offenses in the past, so no one would believe she did not commit this new crime.

Most of the people who ended up in the House of Correction were coming from backgrounds reflecting poverty, trauma, and multiple forms of disadvantage. Once they became involved in the criminal legal system, this often became an ongoing problem that they struggled to fully exit from. This is reflected both in their histories, before we met them, and their experiences when we knew them.

VARIATION IN INCARCERATION EXPERIENCES

People regularly made a clear distinction between a House of Correction and a state prison, with the former typically the desired place if one had to be incarcerated. One motivating factor to pleading guilty for many was an attempt to avoid state prison. For many, the House of Correction represented not only a shorter sentence, but an easier place to serve time. Several people also had experiences with or opinions of other counties' facilities. Christine, a white woman in her 40s, was transferred from another county that was renovating their facilities. She first went to a second county facility, and then was transferred to Suffolk, which she said was "better. We got better good time, they had programming. I was on the job, the work release when I went out and cleaned the community. Just more offerings there than [her home county], where there's not even a window and you never go outside. I felt lucky to be there." John, a Black man in his 30s, also compared the House of Correction to his experience at Rikers Island jail in New York City and New York state prisons and tried to warn younger cell mates of the rough lives they were going to lead:

> And I said, this jail right here it's like—it's not the toughest jail I've ever been in. I've been in Rikers, Attica, and I tell them like "the jails that I've been in will eat you little guys for lunch." You know? And I was nineteen and I was skinnier than this. You know and I'm telling these dudes, the CO's will eat you alive and prison will eat you alive, you know so you better take advantage of this jail because they give you the programs. In New York they cut all these programs out. They stopped a lot of programs in New York. Massachusetts, I see they try to help you.

People could, and did, complain about their experiences in Suffolk County as well, though they often saw it as relatively tolerable compared to other facilities.

For a few, though, being at the House of Correction was a step up in terms of security level and/or length of sentence than they had previously experienced. Donna, a white woman in her 50s, for example, had previously been jailed in her central Massachusetts town before, but not in a facility as large as the House of Correction. Donna was transferred to Suffolk County because her sister-in-law is a correctional officer in her central Massachusetts county. When I first visited her town, she asked me if I lived in Boston, and then responded "So this is like a hick town here, right? . . . Boston is huge, man. I was in awe when I went there. I didn't even get to go on a T train or nothing." When she went to Suffolk County, "I was petrified at first because my roommate was a—she broke her mother's back and she was really mean to me, you know. . . . This was the real deal. I was a mess when I first got here. . . . It took me like six weeks to get the feel, but now I got everything under control." For Donna this was a much more serious incarceration than she had experienced before. She was overwhelmed by the size of the House of Correction and because she did not know anyone there. It was also her first time incarcerated so far from home, and for as long as her current eight-month sentence. George, a White man in his 30s, was also serving his longest sentence, after receiving an eighteen-month probation sentence with two and a half years suspended. When we met, he said, "I mean like I said, it's been fifteen months. This is the longest I have ever been down, so it's definitely kind of crazy." Like Donna, George had a lengthy record of criminal charges, but his typical penalties were a month or less committed, restitution, and probation. His longest previous commitment was for six months. Compared to some of the others, Donna and George's history of incarceration was minor, yet for them their current sentence was unsettlingly long.

Women who were familiar with MCI-Framingham, Massachusetts's only women's prison, had mixed opinions about whether they preferred it or Suffolk County. Framingham housed women who were convicted with state sentences, those who were convicted with county sentences but from counties that did not have facilities for women, or pretrial detainees from those counties. While pretrial detainees were housed separately, county- and state-sentenced women were housed together and had access to the same programming. Lillian, a Black woman in her 20s, was about to be transferred to MCI-Framingham from Suffolk County to serve another county sentence (from a county without women's facilities) there when we met. She said "I want to hurry up and go to the other jail" because there were more opportunities there. While there are programs at Suffolk County, Lillian said, "This [Suffolk County] is not a females' prison. This is a man's prison. So, they have more of the freedom than we do, you know. But there is classes, there's really good classes." When she was at Framingham, she said "everything is so much better here." She highlighted additional programming and greater movement at Framingham. This time, she was at Framingham for a little over a year and was then transferred back to the House of Correction because she was getting into conflicts with an ex-girlfriend and her new girlfriend. This time, Lillian described the House of Correction as "very laid back." Sarah, a white woman in her 30s, spent time at MCI-Framingham on state charges, pretrial detention, and civil commitments.[5] Like Lillian, she thought women had more opportunities at MCI-Framingham. She said that at Suffolk County they got no time outdoors between October and April. She said, "at least in Framingham, you can go to the yard if you want all year round. If you want to go out there and brave the cold, go ahead. You had an option. We [in Suffolk County] don't get any options. We can't do anything."[6]

In contrast, Lena, a white woman in her 50s, who had spent time in Suffolk County, MCI-Framingham, and federal prison, said:

> Framingham is a zoo, hectic. That's all I can say about Framingham, hectic. They have things there too. You can go to college. You can learn, but it's very hard to focus when you're in there. It's just crazy, hectic. In here [Suffolk County], I think, they do all right. They do good with their programs. . . . Federal is more lax. It just is. I mean, it's still prison, but there's a lot more movement and more to do. It's more organized, very organized. The social setting is better, less tension. I think the CO's [correctional officers] treat you with more respect. As far as Framingham, there's no respect. The women get treated terrible there. I've been enough places, so I can say that. I don't have no problem with it. I think it's disgusting, the way they talk to women there. It's really a disgrace, the things I've heard come out of their mouths and the way they treat women.

Lena attributed much of the problem at MCI-Framingham to male officers, who she said treated women in a degrading manner.

MAINTAINING CONNECTIONS WHILE INCARCERATED

One of the factors that first interested me about the House of Correction system was an assumption about the relative ease of maintaining connections to loved ones. Since the facilities were located within each county, and primarily housed those who had been living in the same county, loved ones would be more easily able to visit (see Christian 2005; Comfort 2008 for discussions of barriers to visiting state prisons). The Suffolk County House of Correction is located near the center of the city, at the intersection of South Boston, Roxbury, the South End, and Dorchester. It is accessible by public transportation. A few did get regular visits, usually from a mother or a girlfriend. Jamal, a Black man in his 20s got visits almost every week. He explained that they could have three people on their visitor list. "Of course, my grandmother is on the visiting list, because without her, I'd probably be stressing. I probably would have not been in this interview without my grandmother. You know, she is, like you know, she is my backbone in here and she's like my rock. She's something I can hold on to and you know, she's something I can think about so when I get out you know, I wouldn't be looney, you know, crazy or be mental health, and stuff like that, you know. She's very supportive." Jamal's experience, however, was relatively unusual among the people we talked to. For some, other responsibilities made visits difficult. For Kristina, a white woman in her 20s who was serving time for the first time, no one on her visit list could come. Her mother and sister were both on her approved list, but "I know my mom's got a lot right now, with—my sister has been like in the hospital. So, I know she's got a lot going on. I know she would like to go come up. . . . She takes my daughter on the weekends and I'd rather, I would personally rather her like be with the baby than come see me, you know?" Kristina wanted her outside life to be a priority for those who were in it.

Many did not get visits at all, because of the barriers and perceived downsides. While visiting a House of Correction might be easier than state prisons in terms of distance, many reported that the logistics and bureaucracy made it more difficult. The process of getting visitors on an approved list was cumbersome, and they were only allowed three visitors. People who had a criminal record would not get approved. Sarah, a white woman in her 30s, said "In Framingham, they are not as thorough with the check. . . . They are more relaxed about the rules there, I guess. But this is different. You have to get an application and wait for the reply in the mail and set up an appointment. So yeah. I'm going to get out of here anyway." In addition, Sarah said, "I wouldn't want [my daughter] to come here [Suffolk County]. It is just a different atmosphere. The visiting room is not, like in Framingham, they have a nice big playroom, and they are not really strict about rules as much with the children. There is no type of child environment here at all with the visits." James, a white man in his late 40s, did not get visitors at the House of Correction, as a mutual decision between him and those who might visit. He said, "First off, the process here is very tough to, you know, put so many people on the list and it's just more degrading, I think. In state prison, it's easier to get visits, believe it or not." When he was incarcerated at a maximum security state prison about twenty miles outside of Boston, he said he did get visits. George, a white man in his 30s, said, "You know what, I'm not even going to bother having anyone come up. I can always call them. I'll see them when I get out." The process of getting visits approved, combined with relatively shorter sentences that made the lack of visits more tolerable, led many to go without.

For some, their extensive history of incarceration and often drug addiction also meant attenuated ties with family and other loved ones. They may have received visits during earlier incarcerations, but no longer. Pablo, a Black man in his 50s, said,

> To be honest, I wish, I wish my father would come up to see me once in a while and we get to kick it, and you know, talk about some of the things, but no. And I wish I was in my girl's life, 'cause you know . . . I believe that, you know, a man should be with a woman, a woman should be with a man. I believe that it's like part of being well, being whole in life. I believe if you're not with someone, something is missing in your life, you know? And that's how I am now. Something is missing.

When Corey, an 18-year-old Black man, was incarcerated in a state prison about a year and a half after his release from the House of Correction, it took him six months to reach out to his mother. "I was mad at my mother. I just put the past behind me and spoke to her." He said she first learned that he had been arrested because it was on the news. The difficulty maintaining contact and sometimes strained relationships also meant that family did not always know where people were when they were detained or incarcerated. They might have heard that they were locked up, but they did not know where. Given that many of these were at the county level also meant that there was no centralized way of finding out where someone was being held.

Many also felt that visits were traumatic, for both them and their loved ones, and they did not want to subject their loved ones, or themselves, to that, particularly given their relatively short sentences (Hairston 2003). Sandy said, "I used to see my daughters in jail and I just, I don't think it's fair. For other people to have to go through such chaos just to get in here. It's crazy." Tom, a Black man in his 40s, said in our first interview that visits were too depressing. For our final interview, he had once again been incarcerated. He again said, "I don't get visits. I've been doing this, I'm not proud of this, but I've been doing time so long that a visit is just depressing, watching somebody walk out the door." Rebecca, a white woman in her 30s, said, "My mother will not come up here and visit me anymore. . . . She doesn't like to come up here because she doesn't like to see me like this. She gets real nervous." For others, Rebecca said, "I know the outside world goes on. Go live it. I'll be home." When asked if he got visits, Charles, a Black man in his 20s, said "I could've but I chose not to. I'm not here for long. Know what I'm saying. So, my mom asked me to put her down on the visiting list. I'd rather not see you while I'm in here. Know what I'm saying. So, I could get visits, but I choose not to put them down." Melissa, a white woman in her 30s, also did not want visits. She said, "'Cause, you know why? It's the worst. I'm in frickin' jail. It's like don't even come. I don't even want to talk on the phone to be honest with you. No, it's like, I'll see you when I get out. Because it's the worst feeling. I'm in jail, what do want me to say? I do the same thing over and over every day. I don't know. I might sound miserable, but it's a miserable, cold place to be, and there's nothing new happening." Similarly, Brittany, a white woman in her 20s, said, "It's too hard. . . . Like, before I used to, like, talk on the phone the whole time and get visits and stuff and every time I'd leave, I'd leave crying. Or I'd hang, or I'd cry on the phone and just this time, I'm like, you know what? I'm just gonna—I only got ninety days, so it's like I'm just trying to do, concentrate on me, not everything outside, for once, I guess." This stress involved in the visits, combined with the shorter sentences, made it easier for many to just do without.

A number of people talked about maintaining a separation between prison and their outside lives. Sharon, a Black woman in her 40s who was serving time on her only charges, said she was too embarrassed to communicate with anyone other than her husband. Others with more experience being incarcerated also preferred to maintain a separation. Adam, a Black man in his 40s, said, "I don't like visits. . . . I just don't. Once I'm here I want to concentrate about doing my time. I don't want to know what's going on with the outside world. I just pray that everything is OK with, like, my family members and stuff." Stephen, a Black man in his 20s, talked about both the stress of visits and made a clear distinction between his life in prison and his life outside. "Because I don't like the being stripped when I coming back from the visits. And then I do not, when I'm doing time, I want to stay doing time. I mean, I don't want nothing really to do with the outside world. I mean coming in, I mean that ain't got nothing to do with me when I'm in here. I mean I want to stay focused doing time in here, I mean, out of all my bids, I got one visit. I mean, my first time here, 2000, after that visit I told my peoples I don't want no more visits."

People were more likely to maintain contact with family and other loved ones through phone calls and letters than visits, though this was also challenging. When Tom was incarcerated again, he called me several times.[7] When I met with him, he said "I didn't want you to accept the call, I just wanted you to realize it was me. . . . I didn't want you to answer because it costs too much, just like seven dollars. I don't understand. In Concord and Old Colony [two state prisons], it's only two dollars and eighty-six cents for a phone call. Here it's out of control. I don't know what they're trying to do. What are they trying to prove?" At the same time, he had been trying to call his mother, but "my family has not been able to accept the phone call and I didn't know. When my mother wrote me a letter, she said in her letter that the phone calls are too expensive." Tom had strained relationships with his family. "When I'm on drugs, it's just like they don't want me around." Tom also had a friend who "used to accept my phone calls. I've been having problems with her phone calls too lately. I don't understand. Usually she would accept the calls, but now she doesn't accept the calls. I guess when they say how much the calls cost on the phone, seven dollars, six dollars is a lot of money for one phone call and you don't have much to say." Because phone calls were Tom's primary way to connect with people, when they did not pick up, he had no way of knowing why.

Despite my initial optimism about what "local" incarceration might mean for maintaining contact with those outside, this did not play out in the lives of most of the people I talked to. This also meant that for many their release felt abrupt and left them scrambling to find a place to stay and to reconnect with family and friends.

REENTRY PLANS

People were generally excited to be released. Many, however, had limited plans and often shaky confidence. For many, their doubts were related to a history of drug use and addiction, which was common among those we interviewed. While addiction was common among all racial and ethnic groups, it was nearly universal among the white men and women we talked to. Commonly, they perceived drug use to be the reason they were incarcerated and the greatest barrier to staying out. James, a white man in his 40s, planned to be released to a halfway house. He said he was ready because he was "sick and tired." Ready, for him, meant that he would give himself over to the help the halfway house could provide, to "not take that first drink and drugs. If I can do that, the rest will fall into place." While he thought this time would be different, he was also most worried about "coming back here [the House of Correction]. Just not here, just falling back into this, this trap." Similarly, Lillian, a Black woman in her 20s, felt that this time would be different because "I'm not comfortable here anymore." She said:

> I used to be comfortable here. Because I knew that I was safe. I knew that me being here meant that my mother was sleeping good at night. I knew that me being here was meaning, or meant, that I wasn't out there hurting myself or possibly hurting someone else. I was OK with being here. Free meals, free, free water, place to sleep, roof over my head and I was safe. I was sober and I was alive. But it's not OK anymore. I'm tired of this place. I'm not comfortable here. And it's only, if I'm not comfortable here there's only one other thing I can do and that's change. That's how I know that this time is going to be different. Because before, I do my time and I leave, and still go get high because I knew this was going to be the end result and I was OK here. Now I'm not OK coming here. Which means I have to do something different out there. I have to change.

Julio, a Puerto Rican man in his 30s, said that he was now "addicted to my sobriety. Once you're addicted, you'll always be an addict, but the stuff you're addicted to is the one that can change. And I want to be addicted to being sober." Being tired of being incarcerated or living a lifestyle that may have led to it, does not automatically translate to a successful return to the community. Not wanting to be incarcerated is not enough to make it happen, but it was one step and they hoped to make it true.

Many had learned the limits of wanting to change post-incarceration first-hand, contributing to their own insecurities about their most recent release. Gillian, a white woman in her 30s, said she couldn't wait to be released; "I just want to move on. I feel like I'm stuck here, like I can't better myself. I can't even worsen myself. I just feel like a hamster running on a treadmill. I'm not going anywhere here." She wanted to be released and she planned to get a job and to stay busy. She also had a condo to return to, so some of her immediate needs were taken care of. While she was enthusiastic about the possibilities, she also had doubts about her ability to avoid future drug use. In answer to the question of whether this release would be different than earlier times, she said:

> Yeah. I'm tired of running. I'm tired of running. I can't say I'm going to stay clean. I want to stay clean, but I'm tired of running. In other words, I'm just not going to run anymore. I'm just going to face the existence for what it is. Do you know what I mean? I feel like I want to stay clean, but I don't know what's going to happen when I get out there. I'm not trying to be negative. I'm just trying to be realistic. I don't want to go out and have this big crap, show myself off, all these expectations of myself and then I can't meet them and then I feel like a failure. Do you understand what I mean?

Gillian's doubts were common. Many wanted to stay out of prison and many wanted to change aspects of their lives that made incarceration more likely. Fewer were confident in their ability to do so, especially as they also typically had experienced similar moments of hope and optimism that ended in future incarcerations. Brittany, a white woman in her 20s, echoed Gillian's ambivalence. She planned to go to a program when she was released, "Like, it's not a thing that I'm being forced to do or not; I'm choosing to do it. So, like, I feel like that's like a step in the right direction. Like, usually I come to jail and I leave and within twenty minutes of leaving, I'm getting high. But I leave with that intention. This time, I'm leaving with different intentions, so I'm hoping for the best, expecting the worst, I guess." A few people stated openly that they would use drugs when they were released, and more relayed tales of others who did, often resulting in an overdose. Most with a history of drug use hoped to resist the temptation of further use, though many doubted their ability to do so.

Some were also ambivalent about their chances because they were not sure they wanted to, or could, change. In our first prerelease interview, Kevin, a white man in his 20s, said, "I'll be honest with you, that's what they [his family] want. I mean, I have reservations. I want to get high, I'm a drug addict. I want to get high. I know it's not the best choice for me and I can't . . . I mean I do want to stay sober, and I know it's the best opportunity for me to move forward with my life, but at the same time, it's hard to imagine my life without, not even the cocaine, but the alcohol. Like, I love drinking." Kevin was most worried about the impact of using drugs or drinking on his relationship with his uncle, who had been trying to help him, but whom Kevin did not think understood addiction.

While the House of Correction does have caseworkers and reentry planning, people rarely felt this provided enough information, guidance, and support. During our first post-release interview, Theresa, a white woman in her 40s, and I tried to decipher the reentry programming information she had been given upon her release. She said,

> I've been trying to get them on the phone and can't. I'm having no luck doing anything. I really am not having any luck. I went to Chauncey Street, and I was sure they could help. . . . They had nothing to offer, which is odd. . . . I came up here to go to Chauncey Street, and I thought they had everything in there. They couldn't offer me anything in there. Every month, I go in there, you have to be in this program, and you have to have this many days, and also live in there.

I looked up addresses on my phone to give her a sense of how far away places were from the coffee shop we were sitting in. She was frustrated but trying to maintain her resolve. This came with significant inconvenience, as she took public transportation from her mother's house to downtown Boston, and then walked between places.

Many others had similar experiences of seeking services. Donald, a Black man in his 50s, detailed his experiences:

> I been running around, man. Trying to take advantage of some of the benefits that they have up for us. You know? A lot of them, they [House of Correction staff] didn't even tell me about. You know what I'm saying? I found out from other guys. I went to a meeting downtown. It's a AA meeting. I was coming back, and I met this guy on the train that'd I'd known for years. We went through a program together called First Academy. He sat and tell me, he said, "Did you go down to the, ARC or ACT?" or something like that.[8] I said, "No, what is that?" He said, "Man that's a place they give you a bus pass, a full bus pass. They help you with clothing." I got to meet them tomorrow at four o'clock.

His friend also told him about a few more programs. Donald went on to describe the preparation he received for his reentry, and its limitation.

> They have a thing there that's called Reentry, which is supposed to get you prepared, and give you that type of information, but it's not. I don't think I slept through a class or missed anything. You know what I'm saying.

Matter of fact, I know I didn't. . . . Seems like that would be the place that they would pound you with information so that you have a running start when you get out of here. Instead of looking for stuff because, here's what happens, a lot of people get frustrated and aggravated on their first week out, first three days out. They pick up and they start using.

Donald attributed the problems to both staff and the people who are incarcerated. He acknowledged that for some, "they trying. But some of them care, and some try. The reality of the matter is that they don't prepare you at all for nothing." He emphasized the importance of even "small" things like bus passes, which otherwise took a significant amount out of very limited incomes. He also described how reentry should be approached:

DONALD: Don't hand me a piece of paper with a list of what places you can go. OK, great. Yeah. That's what they—you know. I read stuff like that, but the average dude in jail is not reading that shit. It's got to be something like you got to sit down. It's like with kids. You got to sit down and tell them, "Listen. On 95 Berkeley Street, you can go there, and you go to the second floor, and you go in there and you talk to such-and-such a person." This is what you tell them. You know what I'm saying? If you just give a guy an address and tell him where to go, go down there, nobody does that. There's so many programs with so much money that because they don't go and get it, and don't know about it. Seriously.

AL: You think that someone needs to sit down and explain why you're going there, and how it works?

DONALD: To hold their hand and walk them through the process. They've been going through their own process their whole life. Nobody's holding their hands in anything. That's why they're in jail. Nobody really showed them how to do anything. You know what I'm saying? The people that did, were doing it screwed up too. You know what I'm saying? That's why I'm here. You know what I'm saying? It's like that. They're all young dudes.

The limitations of existing programming and approaches seem to be illustrated with Theresa's experience. The small number of people who were connected to any program at all also suggested limitations. A number also described an experience similar to Donald's, of running in to key people with information—usually people with shared experiences of incarceration and often while riding the bus or otherwise traveling through the city—and learning both about resources and how to access them. These often chance encounters played a significant role for many, and were much more commonly mentioned as a key source of information and support than were any "official" attempts to connect them to resources. In contrast to the written materials, the people Donald ran into on buses could tell him how things actually worked.

HOUSING PLANS

One of the key needs people face when being released from prison or jail is housing. In addition, as the previous chapter discussed, mobility, neighborhood attainment, and neighborhood context are key dimensions to the reentry experience. A few people we interviewed were released to a stable housing situation, and they stayed there throughout the follow-up. Julio, for example, a Puerto Rican man in his 30s, moved back to the apartment he shared with his wife and children. While they had to move once during the year after their landlord sold their building, they stayed together as a family and maintained their Section 8 voucher to help with rent. Occasionally, someone with a tenuous reentry plan managed to reach stability fairly quickly. George, a white man in his 30s, planned to stay with a friend in his hometown. This fell through, but he spent the first several weeks staying with a friend's aunt and uncle and then with another friend. Approximately two months after his release he moved into an apartment he shared with roommates, where he stayed the rest of the time I followed him. While his roommates changed, he stayed there.

Most of the people we met did not have stable housing situations. About a third of the people we interviewed four or five times moved at least three times in the year after their release.[9] In most cases, this reflected ongoing instability and tenuous housing. These were often people who did not have family to rely on, often because of a history of addiction that had frayed relationships. In addition, even when we met with people a few days before their scheduled release, many had only tentative, at best, plans for where they would sleep when they got out. These plans sometimes hinged on key encounters, which could lead to positive or negative outcomes and could unravel easily. I met Kevin just before his release and just before Christmas. His mental health worker interrupted our interview to pass along the contact information for a sober house, since it was the last time they would both be there. After she left, he looked startled. I asked him what he was going to do. He said,

See one thing I didn't say was, I said to myself yesterday that even though she gave me the number and stuff she said she was going to get back to me. And I said well if she doesn't get back to me, I'm not going to tell my uncle [about the option to go to a sober house]. Since she got back to me, I'd feel like I was screwing her over because she went out on a limb for me. This isn't to do with the facility. She did this on her own. I kind of gotta.

This small moment with his mental health worker pushed him to take her advice and follow his uncle's wishes, despite his fears. In our next interview, a few weeks later, he enthusiastically said that everything was great. He said, "I went to the sober house that my therapist recommends, it's a great group of guys there. I leave every day; I do stuff that makes me productive. It's crazy, I'm not used to it, and at the end of the day I'm happy." He went there the day he was released and described it as: "I went from not having a home for the last five years, to having a home in thirty seconds; that's how this lady [the owner] made me feel." While he later ran into problems, his initial transition was a positive one because of this connection. Others similarly reported these seemingly small moments of connection as key to a positive trajectory. As Kevin's case illustrates, individuals could make a key difference in reentry plans and outcomes. Unfortunately, several others had these key moments fall through.

It was common for people to be released with tenuous plans, and for these plans to quickly unravel. Often the choice of where to live upon release from prison is a choice made with few options. Many stayed with family, both because it was affordable (often rent free to them) and because their family would support their efforts. Daniel, for example, a Black man in his 20s, described his decision to live with his mother upon release: "It was, first of all, because I lost my apartment, so I am not trying to do no shelter or anything like that. She gave me an opportunity to get on my feet, stay there until I get on my feet. I feel that's the safest place I can be. I can be away from everybody and it's strict. I can stay focused on myself and my daughter and then get out." Daniel wanted to stay away from the "same old nonsense." While he thought his earlier behavior would preclude him from staying with her, "I didn't think I was able to stay at my mom's house because I really, I burnt down the bridge. Now we're rebuilding it and I can try to walk on it." He said his mom saw his efforts to turn his life around and so supported him. Daniel's decision reflects limited opportunities, but also provided a chance for him to avoid old social networks and to further rebuild his relationship with his mother by proving his sincerity in changing. Several others moved back to a family home or apartment, with their parents, spouses, or other relatives.

Relationships with family could be fragile. Bruce, a Black man in his 30s, stayed with his sister for his first week out, before they got in an argument, and she asked him to leave. He said "She let me stay the week, but it's like, it wasn't long enough. It was bad timing because there it is. I'm right back to the same, I'm right back down to square one again. Back in Harvard [Square] at 33 years of age. I had to start like basically everything over from scratch and it can be rough. Last night, these last few days have been rough." His sister was worried about what her landlord would say about an additional tenant, and she wanted some of the money he was owed through Supplemental Security Income (SSI) that he was still waiting for. While they stayed in contact, and he stayed with her "off and on" after this, he spent most of his time elsewhere. Others could not stay with family, often because of strained relationships with them. Tom, a Black man in his 40s, considered Roxbury "home," because "just, it's where my mother lives. It's where I grew up and I know everybody around the area." While he said he was close to his mother, staying with family was not an option "it's just hectic, you know what I mean? It's just ain't good, a good environment. . . . We get along, but we don't get along that great. You know what I mean?" Instead, he was planning to go to the Pine Street Inn, a large homeless shelter in the South End, when he was released, because "I have nowhere else to go." He had also stayed there for about two years prior to his most recent incarceration. He described it as "all right. It's keeping me off the streets; keeping me out of trouble." He described the surrounding area as "it's good. It's just a lot of drugs and activity, but you just got to keep your head up."

Others had very limited connections to family, often after years of addiction (on both sides) or abuse. Jackson, a Black man in his 30s, described his family, "I have a large family, but they all suck. They're all a bunch of alcoholics, drug addicts, and child molesters. I don't want nothing to do with any of them." He instead hoped to stay with a friend; "she's an addict. Her being an addict, other people who are addicts are there and they, they're always scamming and that makes the boost . . . credit card scams, stuff like that. So, I always come across stuff like clothes or things like that I need. That makes it convenient for me because I need stuff coming out of jail." Jackson was disconnected socially, and his main release plan was to contact someone who he thought might let him stay and whom he wasn't embarrassed to ask. While he had stayed with this friend in the past, he had not talked to her for months and he did not have concrete plans to stay with her. He just thought she would allow it, and it was less awkward to ask her than to show up unannounced at the home of a cousin with whom he got along. Jackson was finishing a sentence for drug possession, and while he did not want to sell drugs again, he expected that he would in that environment. When I asked him how he felt about that as a place to go, he said "I hate it. I actually hate it, but I don't really have much options at this point." I did not manage to find Jackson when he was released and did not interview him post release. His official criminal record suggests that his release played out as he expected it to. When he left Suffolk County, he had to serve a few weeks' time in another county. He began acquiring new charges almost immediately upon his release, and about a year later was sentenced to serve time again. These charges continued to be primarily drug possession and shoplifting related.

Pablo, a Black man in his 50s, had a relationship with his father, but he was wary of staying with him. He said, "My first option is to stay with my father and his step-wife, but, umm, to be honest, he's dealing with a lot of alcohol issues. So, I'm thinking more like a dry shelter, out in Long Island." Pablo ended up dividing his time between the Long Island shelter and staying in Boston Common. He also began using drugs quickly upon his release. In our third interview, which took place in the House of Correction and over a year after our second interview, he described this process. "I was drinking a beer or two. I was still functionable. I wasn't on the drugs. I was just drinking a little wine coolers, a little beer. . . . I started using drugs right after the blizzard [February of 2015, about seven months after his release]." This also led him to withdraw from others, including me. He said "This is why I started hiding from everybody that was trying to help me. You, family, and friends. I was just hiding. I would only come out at night. . . . I was getting your letters.[10] I was like, wow, I've got to call her as soon as I go to detox. I never made it to detox."

It was common for people we interviewed to be unstably housed and to live in tenuous circumstances, including at shelters, temporarily with family or friends, or on the street. This is not unusual among formerly incarcerated populations (Massoglia et al. 2013; Herbert et al. 2015; Simes 2018). Few had many options or much choice in where to live, and many moved frequently. Many also adopted the strategy that Pablo talked about of cutting himself off from loved ones while using drugs or alcohol, out of guilt and shame.

CONCLUSION

This is primarily a study of reentry and neighborhood and place experiences. Yet reentry cannot be fully decontextualized from a particular jurisdiction, system, or past experiences that shaped one's incarceration. Everyone's experiences are socially and institutionally situated, and understanding some aspects of these prerelease experiences also helps us understand their decisions and experiences after release. The people we interviewed often were convicted of minor offenses either directly or indirectly related to addiction and/or poverty, and racism, sexism, and other dimensions of oppression shaped how they were perceived. These perceptions were evident not only in the narratives of the people released from the House of Correction, but also through interviews with other neighborhood residents and through discussions that unfolded in community meetings around safety. Their experiences were further shaped by where they lived and where and how they moved about, making them sometimes more, sometimes less vulnerable to arrest and stigmatization. Many were disconnected from their families and from mainstream society and institutions. This experience of disconnect followed them into their reentry from incarceration. Key experiences leading up to incarceration, during incarceration, and in preparing for release all shaped their reentry experiences.

Over the next several chapters, I detail how their experiences were shaped by neighborhood context and how they engaged with place as they worked to establish themselves post-release. In the next chapter, I discuss when and how the idea of "neighborhood" is a meaningful concept for this population, and when and how it is not. I then offer three in-depth case studies of neighborhoods that are near the House of Correction and yet offer very different examples of neighborhood life and engagement. These three neighborhood cases highlight some of the dimensions that shape life post-incarceration and some of the neighborhood frames used by differently positioned residents.

TWO

Bouncing and the Black Box of Reentry's Neighborhood Effects

> I was all over the place. Like a bouncing ball. I'm just bouncing
> ... different places every week. I would go here. Then there'd be
> arguments over drugs or money.
>
> PABLO, Black man in his 50s

> You be on a train or a bus allows you to meet people you really
> don't want to meet. Or people that you want to avoid. If you
> want to avoid a certain crowd, you getting on a train and a bus,
> especially when school hours are done, you're going to bump into
> some people that you didn't want to see. It's going to happen
> because you have to get public transportation.
>
> ANDRE, Black man in his 20s

THIS PROJECT BEGAN as a study of the neighborhood context of prisoner reentry. Yet, while neighborhood context shapes social life in important ways, few exist solely within a single neighborhood. Most people spend time outside of their residential neighborhood as part of their daily activities (Cagney et al. 2020). These patterns of movement are shaped by individual characteristics and access to resources and transportation. It is thus important to consider how people move about space, how they engage not only with their neighborhood but also other commonly traveled areas, and how this shapes and is shaped by their experiences with incarceration and reentry (Farrall et al. 2014). People in this project have varying relationships to neighborhood and place. Some are deeply embedded in a neighborhood. They spend most of their time in their neighborhood and a majority of their social ties are within the neighborhood. Others travel outside for work, social activities, and to meet personal needs. For some of these, their deepest connections are outside of the neighborhoods in which they sleep. For them, their residential neighborhood does not provide much insight into their lives or their social networks. In addition, people's residences are often fluid and unstable, particularly in the time immediately after release from prison, and they may not feel a connection to or have social networks within the area they live. One's "former prisoner" status also shapes their ability to navigate space, which in turn shapes their ability to reenter and successfully remain out of prison.

The concept of activity spaces expands how we think about returning prisoners' navigation of space and how neighborhood and place matter. Activity spaces are simply the subset of all urban locations with which an individual has direct contact as the result of routine activities (Horton and Reynolds 1971; Browning and Soller 2014).[1] The spatial structure of the city will differ from person to person. People have varying levels of knowledge and familiarity with certain places, different affective senses of these places, and different levels of mobility (Horton and Reynolds 1971). Activity spaces include a consideration of patterns of movement and allows us to better understand when and how a spatially defined neighborhood matters, when and why it does not, and how and why nonresidential neighborhoods are important in understanding reentry experiences. Doing so using narrative interview data allows us to consider the meaning attached both to residential neighborhood and other areas where people returning from prison spend their time.[2] It also allows us to take seriously other places that people frequent, and the meaning attached to those places. For a returning prisoner population, places like methadone clinics, reentry or other social service programs, twelve-step meetings, day shelters, reentry and welfare organizations, day labor organizations, and homeless shelters may be important parts of their daily movement patterns. People often learn in drug treatment programs, especially twelve-step programs, to avoid "people, places, and things" or "wet faces and wet places" (Leverentz 2010; Harding et al. 2019). These are then invoked by people trying to navigate the street, shaping where they feel comfortable going and how they engage with people in public spaces. This is often accompanied by a humility of not wanting to appear "above" others, leading people to "keep it moving" or say "hi and bye" when they encounter people on the streets that they want to avoid. Public places like parks and public transportation stops and lines are also important spaces in which people come together regularly.

Looking at activity spaces of returning prisoners, and others who may live in the same neighborhoods, lets us see what living in a neighborhood means (and does not mean) for people, how they engage in neighborhood life, and how that fits into their overall life. For some, activity spaces may overlap substantially with their neighborhood, while for others, residential neighborhood is little more than where they sleep. This also helps us see the ways in which people can exist in the same places while having vastly different interpretations of them (Small 2004). While I include a brief discussion of those with neighborhood-based activity spaces, this chapter primarily highlights the experiences of those people returning from the House of Correction who have less neighborhood-focused activity spaces, either because of daily patterns of movement or because of extreme housing instability. These examples also illustrate how activity spaces reflect inequality and varying experiences of neighborhood life in our target neighborhoods.

ACTIVITY SPACES

For people returning from prison, there are a few key reasons why activity spaces matter. First, some people are extremely unstably housed, so even defining their neighborhood is challenging. This existence is both theoretically and practically crucial to understanding reentry efforts. For others, they may have a stable place to sleep, but they spend significant time away from that place and they may have affective ties elsewhere. While their residential neighborhood is a measure of neighborhood, it may not be the most important place to understand their lives or key outcomes. Another reason activity spaces matter is because the mere act of moving about space is significant. It is often then that people meet acquaintances, friends, and romantic partners, and when they encounter temptations and surveillance.

People's activity spaces may change over time. For example, a person involved in drug selling, may have a different activity space than that same person when he or she is attempting to "go straight," and avoid offending, offending peers, or law enforcement. Activity space sizes and dimensions are shaped by individual characteristics and needs, including access to transportation, proximity to community resources, and taste preferences (Chan, Gopal, and Helfrich 2014; Browning et al. 2017b). If people need, or have reason, to travel further distances and they have the means to do so, their activity spaces will be larger. Dara Chan and colleagues found larger activity spaces among formerly homeless individuals in neighborhoods with fewer available resources, and smaller activity spaces in neighborhoods with nearby community resources (Chan et al. 2014). In a study of men returning from prison, sociologists Naomi Sugie and Michael Lens (2017) found that men could compensate for living in areas without jobs when able to travel to job-rich areas. Daytime locations of these men helped balance residential deficits among highly disadvantaged groups. Traveling about space is also significant, in terms of the time it takes, the expense involved, and what happens along the way.

Activity space size is also shaped by taste preferences and the flexibility that comes with higher income. For example, higher-income individuals may have more diffuse activity spaces because they do not face economic or transportation constraints (Browning et al. 2017b). In Los Angeles, those with larger activity spaces also had more racially diverse activity spaces (Jones and Pebley 2014). That partly reflects an African American population that has moved from their "traditional core" neighborhoods but maintained ties to key institutions that they continued to visit in those neighborhoods. They thus had larger activity spaces than other race/ethnic groups (Jones and Pebley 2014). Additionally, this highlights the potential importance of third places, places that create spaces for social interaction outside of home and work (Oldenburg and Brissett 1982; Williams and Hipp 2019). Third places are important not only for their potential in fostering neighborhood cohesion, but also for creating key destinations outside of one's residential neighborhoods.

Activity spaces reflect and reinforce inequalities. For example, activity spaces of respondents in Los Angeles were more racially and ethnically heterogeneous than their residential neighborhoods, but activity spaces still reflect high levels of segregation across respondents' range of daily activities (Jones and Pebley 2014). Material constraints and social distance shape neighbors' routine activities so that they may not share activity spaces even when living in spatial proximity (Browning et al. 2017b). Activity spaces reflect socioeconomic segregation; highly advantaged and highly disadvantaged people spend time in largely non-overlapping spaces (Krivo et al. 2013). Those who live in advantaged neighborhoods spend their time in more advantaged spaces. White respondents in particular demonstrate an isolation of privilege relative to other groups. African American respondents living in advantaged neighborhoods do access more advantaged areas for some activities but tend to work in more disadvantaged areas (Krivo et al. 2013).

BEING IN TRANSIT

Having regular access to a car was rare among people being released from incarceration in the Boston area. For those without a car, going anywhere meant navigating public spaces, either on foot or public transportation. This meant that their transportation paths were very public, and often through well-populated areas. Several frequented key programs and shelters that also put them in contact with others with shared histories of homelessness, addiction, and incarceration. They spent significant amounts of time in public and on public transportation, often traversing large sections of the city and region. Not uncommonly, they crossed paths with others that they knew—from the street, the House of Correction or state prisons, and law enforcement. These encounters served multiple purposes, including as a source of information, to develop relationships, and as surveillance.

Getting a bus pass, particularly if free or subsidized, was a valuable resource for those in and near Boston and living near a bus or train station was a key asset. As Christopher, a white man in his 40s who did not have stable housing in the time I knew him, said, "Thirty bucks will help me get the bus pass, get me back to Cleveland [Circle] so I can put my stuff somewhere. . . . That bus pass is very important for me." In a later interview, he said he often relied on finding discarded bus passes with rides left on them, which constrained where he could go and where he could sleep. He said, "Now I don't know where I am going to go because the Pilgrim Church [shelter in Dorchester]—a lot depends on how much I can walk, you know what I'm saying? . . . I might be good [walking] for a day or two but look at me at the end of the day. I'm not going to walk and I don't have a bus pass." Philip, a white man in his 30s, could borrow a car to get to his job hanging drywall in the suburbs, but it would be too expensive. Instead, he leaves at 4 a.m., "I pay seventy-five dollars for my bus pass, and I travel there. I go to Dudley, and I get on the number 1. I take three buses. It takes me about an hour to get to work. . . . There's an express bus for an extra two bucks. Instead of a dollar sixty, it's like four dollars. . . . I don't usually do that because it can get expensive." Similarly, Theresa, a white woman in her 40s, could sometimes borrow her husband's car, but typically used the train or the bus; "it's just so expensive. I'd use it [car] all the time if I had the money to do it, it's crazy." For most, being able to get a bus pass was the most reliable form of transportation they could hope for, and many could only afford a free or subsidized pass. This also meant that if they wanted to go somewhere a bus did not, they could not go.

Some had either limited access to buses or chose not to use them, and so relied on walking or rides. For most of those living further out of the city, public transportation was both very limited and prohibitively expensive. Occasionally someone would not take the bus, even if it was available. Lena, a white woman in her 50s who was living in Chelsea, said "I walk. I can take the bus, but I never do. I don't take buses or cabs much. I walk everywhere." Lena wanted to see old friends, but to do so, "I would have to take a bus, a train, and a bus. We plan on it. Probably when the weather breaks." Alfredo, a Latino man in his 40s, for example said, "I'm just a driver. Even to this day, I won't get on the bus, mind you. If I have to go to my mother's house, I'll walk to my mother's house. I didn't even know. Back then it was so easy, you drop your change in the bus, you do your change in there and it was all that." Because of his reluctance to take the bus, he could not take a job that his friend offered him in a nearby suburb because he had no way to get there.

Multiple buses and lengthy commutes meant that transportation was also a social activity. I saw this during my interactions with participants. For example, Michael, a Black man in his 30s who was introduced to me by Arturo, described running in to Arturo, "Whenever he vanishes for a month or two, there's a nine in ten chance he's back in the Bay [South Bay, the House of Correction]. . . . He'll be clean for a week or two, and then fall back into old habits. I saw him about a month ago, on Dorchester Ave. He looked high then."[3] People connected and reconnected with people as they moved about the region, to both good and bad effects.

The risks associated with navigating space are shaped by neighborhood, and one's connection to the neighborhood. For John, a Black man in his 30s, walking about his neighborhood in Dorchester put him in potential contact with his son's mother, who had a restraining order out on him, which in turn made him vulnerable to a probation violation. He also could have chosen to reconnect with people who could give him drugs to sell. For John, and others in similar contexts, this often meant that they limited the time they spent outdoors. An ex-girlfriend of Wallace, a white man in his 40s, continually made allegations against him, accusing him of stalking her. He denied all of those charges and tried to document all of his movements as evidence against these allegations. He voluntarily wore an ankle monitor to provide evidence of his whereabouts and kept a log of his movements.[4] The woman lived nearby, he said: "Like when I go to the bus stop, she crossed back. I have to, the cops, my probation and the cops told me, every time you see her, just call us so we can log it in." For people in similar situations, they would go where they needed to, but would not "hang out" outside. Donald, a Black man in his 50s, described how he managed potentially difficult encounters:

I tell you, I went through Dudley Station the other day, and I seen guys that I've seen down there from twenty years, still doing the same thing. Slinging drugs and standing up high just talking. I know a lot of them, and I didn't get stuck. I said, "Hey what's happening?" He asked me for a cigarette. I gave him a cigarette. Gave a couple cigarettes out and kept pushing up. Kept pushing. Yeah, I don't stick around that stuff. Man, you know. It's like molasses. You get feet, and then it gets harder and harder each time. You know what I'm saying? I don't stick around. . . . I'm tired of that mess.

At the time Donald had that encounter, he was living in a suburb with his daughter, but passing through Nubian Square in Roxbury.[5] These types of encounters are easy to miss in neighborhood-based studies or research that focuses only on residential neighborhoods, and yet they are key to these men and women's social worlds. They spend a significant amount of time walking and taking public transportation, and often encounter people they know along the way.

While others commonly described negotiations similar to Donald's, it did not always work. María, a Latina woman in her 30s, described her first day out of the House of Correction. She said, "It wasn't bad. I didn't get picked up, so I walked to Mass Ave, I jumped on the bus, the train, and then I jumped on the bus, and I, uhm, I went to go see my brother. Well, I did have seven months clean. That lasted a whole fifteen minutes or whatever it took going from A to B. It didn't last long." Andre, a Black man in his 20s, expressed his gratitude that he did not have to rely on public transportation. He said, "I was once gang related and you be on a train or a bus allows you to meet people you really don't want to meet. Or people that you want to avoid. If you want to avoid a certain crowd, you getting on a train and a bus, especially when school hours are done, you're going to bump into some people that you didn't want to see. It's going to happen because you have to get public transportation."

The threats were not only related to people who might be involved in gangs, drugs, or illegal activities. David, a white man in his 50s, described two men he observed at a train station while updating his transit pass: "There were these two guys across the hallway. . . . They are really undercover cops waiting for someone to try to go through the gate. . . . Of course if you read the paper, the MBTA [Massachusetts Bay Transit Authority] catches a lot of people for warrants that way. Because once they catch you trying to go through, they call your name. . . . If I had a warrant, I'd never ever step behind somebody, because that's like shooting yourself in the foot. . . . If

I got caught for a lousy train ride." For similar reasons, many people talked about also being careful riding in cars if they had a warrant in case the car got pulled over. Being in public, on public transit or in cars, increased the likelihood that they could be stopped for innocuous reasons that could lead to arrest.

It is not just threats that people face outside or in transit, however. A number of people met, or reconnected with, romantic partners or friends that they crossed paths with on public transportation. Lillian, a Black woman in her 20s, met both her best friend and a boyfriend on the street. She met the man she called her best friend three years earlier; "I was in Dorchester one day, walking across the street. I was so hungry. And we just started talking, and we've been friends ever since." Throughout the two years that I knew her, he continued to be a key contact, and could also update me on where she was and how she was doing. Two years later, in our final interview, she described how she met her current fiancé:

> I was walking down [the street] going to the liquor store actually. He pulled over and he asked me if he could take me out to dinner. We exchanged numbers. I took his number, but I didn't call him. I could just tell he wasn't about what I was about at that time. I was out there. I was working the streets and stuff. One day, one night, a couple weeks later I got stranded. I was walking from the south side going towards the north side. He just so happened to be driving by and he gave me and my friend a ride.
>
> He gave me and my friend a ride and when she got out the car, he asked me to sit in the car. He was like, "Listen. I know what you're doing. I don't want sex from you but I will pay you to go to sleep." He looked tired. He was like, "I know you're hungry. If you go to my house and rest, I don't care where you sleep. If you don't want me to sleep with you or next to you, I'll sleep in another room. I just want you to get some rest and eat something. In the morning when you're ready to leave, I'll give you some money.

From here, he became a dependable resource for her, and they developed a relationship. Both her friend and her fiancé were in recovery and understood her challenges with drug use.

Others similarly met romantic partners when in transit. Wallace reconnected with his girlfriend of seven years on the bus. He said, "I knew her for like twenty years 'cause her daughter went to school with my son and then, we just, we didn't see each other for a while, then we just, we met at, ah, when we were both in recovery. We met on the bus one day after." John

(Black, 30s) had a similar story regarding a woman with whom he was in a "friendship relationship." They were former coworkers, and "we ran into each other on the bus. I was going to sign up for food stamps, she was there too. We exchanged numbers. She used to always ask about me because my cousin used to work with her too." Michael (Black, 30s) also met a girlfriend in Park Street station, downtown. Lena (white, 50s) reconnected with a friend that she originally met in a halfway house years before. She said, "She was at a bus drop one day, and she's like, 'Hey, Lena.' And to be honest with you, I'd forgotten her name. . . . She's nice, she's trying. She's struggling and trying, like me, with the job thing. She lives in a studio [apartment], too, with her boyfriend. It's like we have a lot in common, kind of. She wants to do the right, so if we're getting work and then I can hang out with her and maybe go to meetings and stuff."

In addition to meeting friends, they learned about key resources and services. In chapter 1, I quoted Donald, from our second interview, telling the story of meeting an acquaintance on the bus, and learning how he could get a monthly bus pass, which in turn made everything else easier for him to access. This was one of the most valuable resources that he could get in that moment. The man he ran into told him about a few other organizations. He went to one of them and realized a friend of his worked there. His friend said, "'Man, we going to take care of you. You don't have to worry about it.' I was almost in tears. I was getting a little discouraged, you know? Not that I was going to give up, but I was getting discouraged." In contrast, Theresa, a white woman in her 40s, was exploring the list of organizations she had been given, but without the insider knowledge to make sense of it. Thus, a fleeting moment like running into an acquaintance on a bus could sometimes prove key to getting information or access to resources. These sorts of encounters were common. This means that those who are not engaging in these movements—because they were avoiding being in public or because public transportation was inaccessible—may lack information and networks that could help them.

Especially because their transportation paths were almost always public, whether they were walking down the street or waiting for or riding the bus or train, the actual process of getting from one place to another was a social activity and required a significant amount of their time. It also made them potentially vulnerable to temptation or surveillance. They could choose to spend free time indoors, but when they needed to go somewhere, getting there was unavoidably a public activity.

NEIGHBORHOOD-BASED ACTIVITY SPACES

While some tried to minimize the time spent outside of their house, all did leave sometimes. For some, their activity space overlapped almost entirely with their residential neighborhood. John (Black, 30s), for example, spent most of his time in his Dorchester neighborhood, especially before he started working. He spent time in his apartment, he walked to his aunt's apartment, he walked his dog and exercised in nearby Franklin Park, he did community service and reported to his probation officer in Dorchester District Court. Even when he did start working, he traveled to work and back, but most of his focus was on Dorchester and within walking distance of his apartment. Just over half of those in this study fall into this category. Most of their time is spent in their residential neighborhood, and their primary focus is there, both in terms of time and emotional and relational connections. This is true of some who lived in Boston and some living in suburban and rural areas. In the urban case, these activity spaces reflect social relationships and lifestyles. They could access all they needed to access on a regular basis within their neighborhoods. In the latter case, this was also dictated by a relative lack of access to transportation. I return to neighborhood-based activity spaces in subsequent chapters.

AFFECTIVE- OR UTILITY-ORIENTED ACTIVITY SPACES

For the remaining half of the sample, their most important connections to place were not in the neighborhoods in which they lived. Some had stronger ties to places outside of their residential neighborhoods, but they still had a predictable and patterned activity space. They slept in one place and regularly spent time in a few others. People returning from prison often have little control over where they go upon their release. Many stay, at least at first, with family or friends or at a halfway house or other residential program. Because of this, many of my interviewees also had stronger ties to neighborhoods other than where they were living. In these cases, their "neighborhood" was a place they slept, but not where they spent much time or where they felt a connection. While some of those with neighborhood-anchored activity spaces also had places they frequented outside of their immediate neighborhood, the emphasis was on the neighborhood. For a utility- or affective-anchored group, their focus was outside of their residential area.

This meant not only key time spent outside of a residential neighborhood, which was often spent in public spaces, but also time spent going to and returning from other neighborhoods.

For some, people and places were a draw. They returned to old neighborhoods even though they weren't living there because of the appeal of that neighborhood. Others were drawn to neighborhoods in which they had strong social ties, even when this also came with a sense of heightened police surveillance or temptations like those that had led to their incarcerations. Sometimes those temptations were the point. Richard, a white man in his 50s who lived with his mother in a suburb about ten miles from the city center, took the bus in to Boston fairly regularly when he was using drugs. He described his typical day, "Wake up in the morning, around five. Get downtown by six, down near St. Francis [a homeless shelter and day program]. Grab my two bags of dope, get high, try to hustle and make some money, panhandle, whatever. Make a few dollars, get my next bag, go get something to eat maybe. Enjoy the day, get a coffee, go home, I'll be in bed by eight, nine." Richard was unusual because he traveled so far so frequently. When he stopped using drugs, as he did several times over the year, he also stopped going to Boston. For Richard and others, returning to old haunts was a draw, though one that he tried to regulate when he was trying to stay out of trouble.

José, a Latino man in his 40s who lived with his mother in a nearby suburb but who spent much of his time in Boston, said he expected it to be hard adjusting to society, because "well, just getting out, it's always been like that. Heading toward SPAN (a social service organization that served former prisoners), running into old friends. You know, the trains are packed." These meetings were not planned or intentional, but the public nature of much of his life fostered them. Being on the train and going to SPAN reminded José of the tenuousness of his life and freedom. He, and others, worried about running into associates that might lead to trouble. When Donald, a Black man in his 50s, was first released, he stayed with his daughter in a suburb, but frequently came into Boston. Because he aspired to have his own apartment, Donald moved to a shelter downtown so that he would be classified as homeless and therefore eligible for housing assistance. While Donald waited for an apartment, he slept in the shelter, but spent much of his time elsewhere. In addition to his daughter's house, he frequented a friend's house and a sober club, relying on public transportation to travel around the city. Donald tried to avoid spending too much time with old acquaintances that were still involved in drug use or illegal activity. He said, "It's not like I cross the street when I see them coming, I just keep it real short. I don't avoid them; I just don't have anything really in common with them anymore. I still have love for them." The amount of time people spent in public and the paths many of them traversed put them into regular contact with acquaintances. For those who were struggling to avoid drug use or offending, these became relationships to manage. Unlike those who were largely bound by their residential neighborhoods, people with affective- or utility-oriented activity spaces were less physically isolated and often spent less time at home and more time in public places.

Often, common destinations were public spaces or those geared toward people who were homeless and otherwise disadvantaged. José (Latino, 40s) described a typical day. "Well, I go to SPAN. I'll go to the [day] shelter [with programs, mailboxes, and shared voice mail]. At the shelter there's a lot of people that I know there. They serve breakfast and lunch. I'll go hang out in the park. Feed the squirrels. The birds. Then go back. Have lunch and just hang around. Sometimes I go to the Fens and just sit down and just enjoy the weather."

In each of these places, he ran into people he's "known over the years." While José spent much of his time in his mom's apartment, when he left home, he traveled several miles to various Boston neighborhoods. This was part familiarity and part going to programs, doctors, and service providers. Since these programs were not located in his neighborhood, his activity space was large, but also concentrated well away from his mom's apartment, leading to significant time on the street and public transit (Chan et al. 2014).

Many of the programs geared toward formerly incarcerated, homeless, or addicted populations are in areas with concentrations of methadone clinics, shelters, drug treatment, and other social service programs; this also made them easy targets for law enforcement. In addition, police and security regularly cleared out "undesirable" populations (Irwin 1985) from public spaces where residents and tourists tended to congregate, like in or near Boston Common. José described feeling harassed by the police, "I'm walking down the street and I'm not bothering nobody and they want to call me. It's always because I fit the description, but nothing's happened. You know, I don't see no other cars running around or them looking for anybody. 'You fit the description.'" One day, when José was planning to go to a reentry program, and according to him, "just hanging out," he was arrested for trespassing. He said, "In downtown now, all the areas are all trespassing near Chinatown. They're making every corner, everything is trespassing and I guess they're

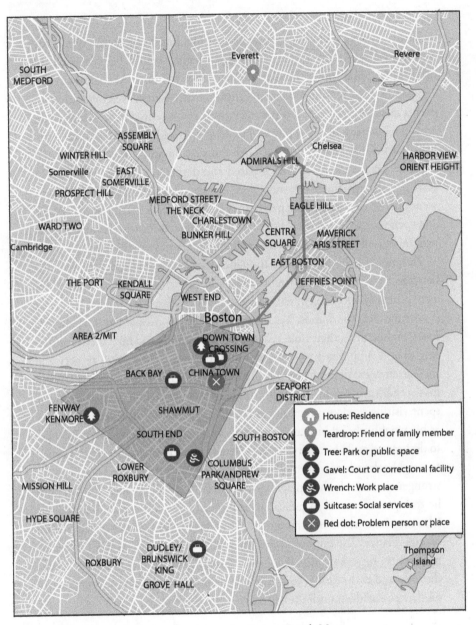

🏠	House: Residence
📍	Teardrop: Friend or family member
🌳	Tree: Park or public space
⚖️	Gavel: Court or correctional facility
🔧	Wrench: Work place
💼	Suitcase: Social services
✕	Red dot: Problem person or place

MAP 2. Affective- or utility-oriented activity space. Source: Google Maps.

enforcing it so whoever they see, they're taking. I was one of the first candidates. . . . It's [the charge] not really that big, but it's big with my record." While José was right in predicting the charges would be dismissed, he missed his appointment that day and had to go to court. As sociologist and legal scholar Issa Kohler-Hausman (2018) demonstrated, even being charged with a misdemeanor that is ultimately dismissed is coercive and burdensome and an expression of penal power. José tried to avoid trouble and undue surveillance. While he was wary of both temptation and surveillance, he also enjoyed social contact and felt isolated and depressed without it. When he stayed in the apartment, he was often depressed and unmotivated; when he went out, he was doing well, participating in programs, getting medical care, and spending time outside. He had lengthy connections with several of these programs, and important social ties to both staff and other service users.

Patterns of behavior and the thought processes behind them were similar between those who lived a neighborhood-anchored life and those whose lives were primarily anchored in services or preferences that took them out of their residential neighborhoods. Yet understanding how people like Donald and José were spending their time, where they were going, and how they were getting there is important to understanding their experiences with reentry and their attempts to desist. José's time in his residential neighborhood was spent in his mother's apartment. While his mother was important to him, the time he spent visiting services, programs, and public spaces were at least as important as his neighborhood in understanding his reentry experiences, his challenges to desistance, and his social networks. The same is true for those that returned to neighborhoods to visit old friends and hangouts or to use drugs. Having stronger ties outside their neighborhood meant spending more time on public transportation and in public spaces, exposing them both to more people who may have useful information and/or who may be sources of temptation or surveillance. The importance of the nonresidential areas is not surprising, particularly for urban populations who often have little control over where they live and reasonable ease of travel. For this group, looking only at place of residence provides a misleadingly narrow glimpse into their daily lives.

THE APPEARANCE OF PROGRESS

A sizable subset of the people we interviewed were extremely unstably housed, which led to unpatterned movements and a very diffuse and irregular activity space. For those who moved three or more times in the follow-up period, these moves occasionally reflected growing stability. For example, Michael, a Black man in his 30s, moved from a shelter to a rented room to a shared apartment, all in different neighborhoods. More commonly, however, the moves represented high levels of instability, often including periods of incarceration, residential program stays, couch surfing, and homelessness.

For some, what looked like increasing stability was also derailed at some point during the year. James, a white man in his 40s, first stayed in a Salvation Army shelter. He was originally from South Boston, and while he would like to live there again, the neighborhood is now "full of yuppies" and he could not afford it. He said "I was supposed to be placed [in a residential program] in South Bay. They just threw me to the street. As a matter of fact, they threw me to the street with a warrant. Right? Which was supposed to be clear." He first went to the Long Island shelter but said, "there's all kinds of drugs there. So something just made me walk down the street here. I walk down the street here [near the Cambridge shelter where he was then staying], and they took me. That's kind of where I am now." The program was one of progressive freedoms, starting with being in a shelter bed, then moving to a restricted housing unit, then earning more freedom. James was caught with a prohibited cell phone, and so was bumped back to a shelter bed. He bristled at the rules, both of the shelter and of Drug Court, "It's just hard. Just trying to take, just hard having somebody telling you what to do all the time. Especially when I just came from that setting. . . . I think I became institutionalized."

James said the shelter "was not a good fit for me. I think you saw that. I think that was blatantly obvious. I didn't even want you to see half of what you seen there." He was asked to leave after being caught again with a cell phone. "They called probation and told them what happened. 'Report in to the judge.' I think it was two days later. A lot of people don't go before the judge because it's a fifty-fifty shot of being incarcerated again because you violated the rules. I took the chance." He stayed at the shelter on Long Island, until he could enroll in a program, which he credited for "saving" him from going back to prison. By the time of our next interview, he was staying at a halfway house in the South End. A man with whom he had been in a recovery home a decade earlier—"he graduated at the same time; he stayed clean, I didn't"—now worked in a shelter and helped him get into a program. The halfway house he went to was similarly structured with graduated freedoms, with a period of restriction to "get acclimated to the rules."

James sought work on craigslist, "I put, '45-year-old skilled mason currently residing in a halfway house with over a year clean and sober, looking for a chance—looking for someone to give me a shot.' I responded to like twenty of those ads and finally someone called me up and said, 'I've got a little work for you.'" James showed me photos on his phone of the work he had done. He also showed photos of his visit with his teenage son, the first time he had seen him in over a year. "I went down there for lunch and came back. I've got to be consistent. They're sick of me going to jail. They're real sick of me living, you know, like I was. . . . They're real sick of me doing that. We're just taking it slow and stuff like that."

After four months, James graduated from the halfway house. "First off, did wonderful. Graduated the program. Life was great. It was real hard living in that. I mean, you came to that area. That's a bad area. That's called Methadone Mile. It's infested with drugs and prostitution and everything. I stayed clean throughout the whole ordeal, OK?" Still, in our final interview he described this time as precarious: "I know all these people. . . . Then I kept fucking hanging around with people. Sooner or later, you get sucked into that thing. If you go to the barbershop so many times, sooner or later it just happens." James then moved to Dorchester, to a "three-quarter house. . . . It's a sober house. . . . I live with three other gentlemen who are sober or semi-sober. One is drunk all the time." He then continued, "To back up a little bit. I stayed sober throughout that ordeal, but at the same time, I didn't change all my behaviors. My behaviors as far as hanging out with the wrong people . . . I was just hanging around with the young girls. By young girls, I mean young 20-somethings. . . . Wrong, wrong, wrong move. Blowing all my money on them. I would have been better off—not to be rude, but I'm going to be frank with you—just buying a prostitute." James gave one of these women some of his prescribed Suboxone, and then bought more on the street. "Yeah, I got arrested for buying that one Suboxone. Now I'm fucked. . . . I have a prescription for Suboxone, I go to get arraigned, I tell the DA that. . . . What I did is still a crime, because I bought some. It's still a crime and I own that. I was in so much trouble from before, Andrea. My fucking probation in four different courts is violated. All my probation. I've been going court to court. BMC [Boston Municipal Court] let me go. Dorchester, my Drug Court, they wanted to detain me."

While James was not detained as a result of this case, and the charges were ultimately dismissed, he did call it "the beginning of the end. I started making some very bad choices. I was involved with a younger girl again who didn't have my best interests at heart. . . . I got high a few times, which gave me a dirty urine. . . . I could have went left and went right. If I just reeled it back in, I could have gone through that little hurdle there. . . . Instead I went the other way." While James said he had been spiraling for a while, he described the specific incident that led to his arrest. "What happened was I was on my way for work and I broke into this guy's garage. For what, I don't know, I had no idea. . . . I was a fucking mess. I don't know why I did that. I had no idea. I was dressed for work, I went downstairs in my clothes and work boots, dungarees, work coat." He attributed this to taking Valium. He had previously left the three-quarter house, because his girlfriend slept over too often and he had several positive drug tests. James said the three-quarter house was also transitioned into a halfway house for women who had been relocated from Long Island. He then rented an apartment in Dorchester. "It wasn't the best situation for me either, because some people get high in there." But he pointed out that the area was not the problem: "The area was fine; it was my state of mind that wasn't. It was nothing to do with the area. The area is nice, but by that time, my state of mind was not nice." James ended up serving additional time, both because of probation violations on earlier charges and new charges for breaking and entering. When he went to court this time, he said, "Just give me the time. . . . Just give me the time; please just end it."

For the first several months of his release, James's housing seemed to suggest increasing stability and positive progress in his reentry, from a shelter to a halfway house to a "three-quarter" house to a private apartment. In reality, it reflected decreasing stability, as he began using drugs again. As he said, he could have righted his path along the way, but did not do so before he was reincarcerated. Each residence along his trajectory masks a complexity of what he was experiencing. In James's case, much of this instability was tied to drug addiction. James had a lengthy criminal history, including 140 distinct charges beginning when he was 13 years old, largely for drug possession, breaking and entering, and related charges. While James had some income from his work as a mason and began a fledgling connection to his son, for many, a history of drug use often leads to extreme social and economic marginalization, including alienation from family members. For those who cannot stay with or rely on family for support, housing is often extremely unstable.

Arturo's experience highlights an even more tenuous reentry experience than James's. Arturo was a Black man of Caribbean descent in his 30s. He and his wife had come to Boston from New York, where he was born and raised, several years earlier. "It was more or less a geographical change. Umm, dealing with gangs and addiction." When I asked if that was a good move for him, he responded, "Well, basically you take you wherever you go. Where you live has no relevance on what change is made." He was most recently incarcerated because of a situation that "all boiled down to being a player. You know, playing on this woman's intelligence for ten months, and she found out I was married, and you know, she wanted . . . some of the money she spent on me back. And I'm not giving you any money. She basically puts some charges on me, saying I took money." He originally was given probation, but he violated his probation because of a "failure to stay alcohol and drug free." He was incarcerated, then paroled. He violated his parole by failing to report a change of address. When he was incarcerated, Arturo's wife and their three children moved in with relatives because she could not afford the rent on their apartment by herself. "Me and the relatives don't see eye to eye," Arturo said, so he could not stay with them. Before his release, he was hoping to rent a room close to his family and the job he hoped to return to.

It took me four months to find Arturo after his release. When we met, he said "I ran into a bump in the road, but I figured it out." Arturo had relapsed; "It was right away. Basically, facing being homeless, not being able to obtain the right funds in order to get a room. So the anthem that addicts normally say, 'F it,' came about, and I was on a run for about three months." Arturo originally had planned to go to a sober house.

My plan was to go to a sober home and I had contacted [an employee from his home AA/NA group] prior to my release, and he assured me that, "OK, all you have to do is bring the one-fifty [$150] and you'll be all set." So apparently, the same week that I got out was the same week where he took his vacation, so I was unable to get in contact with him. I could've contacted the facility, but then I would've had to pay the registration fee, which was another three hundred bucks. I didn't have four-fifty. If I had four-fifty, I probably would've got another fifty bucks and just got a room and worked in a barber shop and stuff like that. Probably wouldn't have had the relapse. I was frustrated.

The day of his release, his wife picked him up, they ran errands, and they spent time with their children. They tried to get the money for the sober house but couldn't. Around midnight,

> I got a bright idea. I can go do one, I'll be all right. It was just a roller coaster ride. I'm up, OK, positive thinking one minute and negative thinking the next. When you're in the streets and you're homeless, your mind is filled with negativity. How I'm going to get more money, and once you have more money, now you want to get high again, because you already feel like you messed up, so . . . I had this whole release plan, getting out, steps that I was going to take as far as my short-term goals was concerned, and there's your plan and then there's God's plan and the Devil has a plan as well, and you can be on either side of the fence with that. We have choices.

During Arturo's drug run, he also developed "a habit for heroin," in addition to his long-standing cocaine use. He said "I was dope sick one day and I was like, 'Oh no, this is not for me. This hurts, this is horrific. I'm going to detox." He got into detox. "Detox is pretty easy, because I went to the bottom of the barrel [detox facility]." Then, "through the grace of God, a halfway house accepted me from detox, because normally you would have to go to holding, and being that the Island [Long Island] closed down, there's really no holdings, frankly, no beds in halfway houses. So, I was just fortunate and God was looking out for me."

At the time of our second interview, Arturo had been staying at a halfway house in Roxbury for three weeks: "The area is not all that great, but it's down the street from where everything else is going on." He got a job with UPS through a temp agency, but it was a seasonal, holiday job with odd hours. The halfway house would not allow it because of the irregular hours. They also wouldn't allow him to work as a barber, as he had been planning, because it was a cash job, without the pay stubs he needed to provide.

By our third interview about three months later, things were going "rough, real rough." He was working at a mall store, for a probationary period. "I guess I wasn't working fast enough for a store that was way behind because of the storm." This was the winter of 2015, when Boston experienced record snowfalls that had closed the mall on multiple occasions. He was then renting a room, along with three other men, in a Mattapan apartment for five hundred dollars per month. At the time I met with him, he was behind on his rent and afraid he would be kicked out. The landlord was the uncle of a friend; "He was more or less like a friend when I come in, basically turned into a business now because he's trying to do things with the renovation. At the end of the day, I'm not just going to walk out into the cold. I'm not from Boston. Just taking all my stuff and going into a shelter. I can't carry it. I can't carry it. It's not happening." Arturo considered it a favor that he was allowed to stay there: "But you got to understand people go through things, go through trials and tribulations, man. And reach rough patches in life to where it doesn't move according to the plan."

In addition to being unemployed and behind on rent, Arturo was fighting with his wife over rumors. "People want to talk. They can't stop it. Seeing what they don't understand. They'll talk. They'll want what you have. Especially females. She gotta come to terms with it though. A lot of her friends are attracted to me. Do I jump on that? No, I never disrespected you in that way, so for me to do something now is preposterous." He also owed child support for three of his older children. He said he was twenty-five thousand dollars in debt, mostly because of back child support.

> It's in arrears. It's just avoiding, avoiding, avoiding, avoiding, avoiding, avoiding because I wanted to be vindictive. I wanted to say, "F you. You'll get it on my terms." Working off-the-books jobs or as soon as child support catches up with me, I would jump to the next job. If I put everything on my resume, my resume would never even get read because it would be about this thick. I'm serious. I've had so many jobs trying to avoid child support. It doesn't build good character. It just shows that you ran from the inevitable. You have to pay that.

Arturo credits his wife with changing his attitude toward child support. "Honestly, it's due to my wife. . . . You can't keep running from your doggone problems, now just get it over with because it's going to be there when we're really trying to establish ourselves." Still, at the time of the interview, there was significant tension in his relationship with his wife, and he seemed to be wavering on his commitment to his marriage. He was contemplating going to Florida to visit a woman he had known since childhood.

He left the room in Mattapan a week or two after our interview. "I was here and there, this is me and my bags when I got arrested. I got bags. I got a bag of clothes over here, and then a bag of clothes over there and a bag of clothes where I'm at right now. I was everywhere." By our next interview, three months later, he "had gotten into a little something with this individual wanting to purchase some crack cocaine." He got into a physical confrontation with the women over the money. "She was trying to beat me for my money, so I tried to grab the money." According to Arturo, this happened at the same time a child was shot in front of a nearby barber shop. A reporter saw their confrontation and threatened to call the police. He said, "OK, well damn, I'm not trying to be here if she's sitting here crying robbery. I didn't rob her. They're not going to believe that, so I took off running and I got arrested." I asked why he ran, and he said, "I thought, I mean, I had some type of warrants. I didn't just want to take the risk of being a robbery charge. Which I got a robbery charge anyway." He was able to get bailed out of jail, with the help of a bail fund. "Basically now, I'm just trying to pick up the pieces." At the time of our interview, he had been staying with a sponsor, until that man's daughter came home and there was no longer room for him. He then spent a night in what he described as "this house, there were a couple of addicts in there and they were active, but I needed a place to stay. So he's [his acquaintance], 'you can have that little sofa section right there.' And this house is like a hoarder house. They really need to throw a lot of crap away and then they got these dogs and these dogs just pooping everywhere."

Arturo's recent experiences exacerbated the tension with his wife. "When she found out that I was still hanging out with the same people, she basically wasn't trying to come around or let the kids come around." Despite this, he no longer planned to go to Florida, "I realized I loved my wife, and Florida was just another woman." He aspired to live with his wife again, "picket fence, the American dream. The American dream, just dog, kids, just enjoying that until I'm called to lay to rest." About a month after this interview, Arturo was arrested again. He was arrested for a "stupid thing. Snatched a pair of headphones, four-hundred-dollar headphones and I get caught." He learned he had a warrant for a home invasion in a neighboring county that he believed was a case of mistaken identity. He said, "Yesterday was my thirteenth anniversary. I know my wife was sitting there like, 'This fucking guy's always locked up' or something." When I asked if he had talked to her, he said no, that "she's not putting the phone on or nothing." He wasn't sure that the phone number he had was one she was still using. I asked if his wife knew where he was. "Oh yeah, I've been sending mail. I've been sending mail. I've written my mom, tell my mom to call her. My mom probably has a number for her. Hopefully when my mom writes me back, she'll give me that phone number."

At the time of his most recent arrest, he had been renting a room in Dorchester. He had been there for about a month, after several months of "I was here and there, friends' house, stuff like that." Arturo was unusual among the people interviewed in that he had access to a car, until it was towed after his arrest.

> My wife had gave me the car because she didn't feel it was a safe car. I just fixed it up. Car got towed. Car's been sitting in the tow yard with all my clothes in it. All my clothes. I'm basically going to come home to nothing because unless my wife finds that title where I can just sign the car over to them instead of having to pay any money. Like, "Look, here take this. Let me just get my clothes." I don't know how long they keep a car there until they consider it abandoned. After they consider it abandoned, what they do with the items that are in there? I don't know.

Arturo had been keeping his belongings in the car rather than his room because "it was like a little trap house. I didn't want to go in there when it was all active, so I waiting for it to calm down. Went over and got my stuff. I just never took it out of the car. Being lazy."

The last time I saw him, Arturo was being held in the Suffolk County House of Correction, with three open cases. For two of them (robbery and larceny, described above), he planned to plead guilty but was trying to delay resolution so that he did not get moved to a different county for the third case. "On those cases, I'm trying to keep those continued in our district court, so I can remain here until I also find out what's going on with this. I'm not trying to go to Billerica." It was the latter case he planned to take to trial. He said a cell phone he had lost was found at the site of a home invasion. He was waiting for a probable cause hearing "to see if they have enough to indict. Whatever. Which my lawyer that seems like he's not even confident about this doggone case. He was being real redundant in the dangerousness hearing. Real redundant. I'm like, 'Dude,' I'm looking at him like. Then he's agitating the judge like he's basically, he's cross-examining these police officers and he's basically just quoting the police report. This is a dangerousness hearing. This is not a trial. What are you doing?"[6] Arturo described what was in the police report and questioned the entire event and denied any involvement with it. He said his court-appointed lawyer

> failed to mention that I was a father with a wife and children and stuff like that. That I was having problems with substance abuse. He didn't do anything for me. This dude's just sitting there reading this, that police report, and babbling. I'm looking at him like I could represent myself better than that. I'm quite swift with advocating for myself. He's not making any valid points as to why the judge should feel that I am not dangerous. Sure I have

a record. Then you letting them bring up stuff that was dismissed. . . . "Oh he has an eight-page rap sheet in Massachusetts." Well, at least four of those pages is dismissed.

Arturo made calculations about the likelihood of conviction and the seriousness of the penalty. For the robbery charge, a reporter witnessed the incident and called the police. He said,

> I mean because the *Boston Globe* [reporter]. I mean she's definitely going to show up to court. She's definitely going to say something. I can get up to 2.5 [years] in the House of Corrections. They're not going to be able to prove that I assaulted a police officer. They're not going to be able to prove that I robbed this girl. She's not going to really show up to court. Her credibility, she had a warrant. She got caught with crack cocaine, she got caught with a crack pipe. The only charge that's really going to stick is the assault and battery. You can get up to 2.5.

While Arturo saw his alleged victim as unreliable and unsympathetic, the witness was more of a threat to him, and the penalty was enough that he did not want to take the risk. Arturo, like most others, had a strong belief that taking a case to trial, and losing, would result in a longer sentence than if he pled guilty. If being sentenced to state prison was a possibility, people were particularly likely to plead out if they thought they could avoid this. In contrast, Arturo thought the home invasion charges were serious enough, but the evidence flimsy, that it was worth the risk.

Arturo's experience highlights not only his own quotidian and legal vulnerability, but also that of his family. When he was incarcerated, his wife and children had to move. Their own limited options exacerbated Arturo's instability after his release. His frustration with his instability, in terms of his housing, employment, finances, and relationship with his wife, all contributed to his own behavior after his release. He felt he had less to lose and had few accomplishments to encourage him.

Both James and Arturo stayed within a fairly contained region. Both lived in multiple neighborhoods, but within a region of the city, and moved every few months. They also both maintained ties, if tenuous, with family members. They spent time in the neighborhoods in which they lived, but they moved frequently. Both had children that they aspired to have stronger relationships with, and Arturo remained married to his wife and (mostly) wanted to continue that relationship. Particularly in Arturo's case, these relationships also kept him tied to an area. Others either lacked these ties or their closest ties were equally unstable. In these cases, they were particularly unanchored.

UNANCHORED ACTIVITY SPACES

For many, even defining a residential neighborhood in an analytically mean-ingful way was impossible. Several people stayed at shelters, which in most cases meant they were on the street during the day. This was further compli-cated when the bridge to Long Island, home to shelters and drug treatment facilities in Boston Harbor, abruptly closed in October 2014. Kevin, a white man in his late 20s, attributed his parole violation in part to the Long Island bridge closing. He was in a drug treatment program "out on Long Island, and it closed down. And they moved us from the safety of Long Island to across from Boston Medical Center, and there's like a war zone over there, like right around Boston, and it just wasn't a good fit. I didn't pay attention to the rules as much, and I left the program before parole could pick me up." Kevin said he had been doing "awesome" when on Long Island, and many of the men he had been there with faced the same struggles when they were moved. "When we left Long Island, we had twenty-eight guys in the program. Within a week, we were down to eleven." They were staying in a shelter with "three hundred guys all getting high at night, and we were sharing bathrooms with them, so we're around it. Wasn't a good situation." Kevin was reincarcerated for a little over two months. After this, he moved at least five times, including short-term moves out of state to try to manage his addiction, stays at sober houses, and temporary accommodations with several friends.

Pablo, a Black man in his early 50s who also had stayed regularly at a Long Island shelter, echoed Kevin's positive sentiments about it and his frustra-tion with it closing.

PABLO: Long Island was so cool. It was like a place to go to rest. Have you heard? They shut it down. When they shut that down, it's like the home-less people just scattered everywhere.

AL: How did you feel when they closed it?

PABLO: I was mad. I was. I was pissed off about that. That shelter was so good. It was good food, it was good living arrangements. The best part, you got a chance to get away from all the chaos and all the trash and all the drama. That's what I think is the most important thing for a recovering addict. He needs to get away.[7]

As I discuss in chapter 4, the closing of the Long Island bridge and the services housed there also frustrated the residents of the South End. As more people spent more time in the South End, using services and staying in shelters, including one newly created, tensions were also heightened between them and residents who felt the neighborhood had crossed a "tipping point" of too much disorder. Some started lobbying the city to move at least some services to the Shattuck Hospital bordering the southwest edge of Franklin Park between Dorchester and Jamaica Plain.

Before the bridge closed, Pablo split his time between the shelter and sleeping in Boston Common. He and Kevin both emphasized their belief in the importance of a geographical change and distance from the "drama" (Laub and Sampson 2003; Kirk 2012). Not everyone was willing to live in a shelter environment to achieve this distance, though some desired it, and the Long Island programs were the only ones in the area that provided this.

While Pablo spoke favorably of Long Island, he generally did not like shelters, leading to a lot of "bouncing around."

PABLO: My addiction was so bad on me mentally that I was in fear of going into the shelters. I don't like shelters. Shelters, some of them, are like jail. A lot of rules, a lot of regulations. I would go hustling. Hustling me up some money. Me and my girl would go to a cheap hotel or we'd find somebody in the neighborhood and rent a room from them for twenty, thirty dollars a night. I was all over the place. Like a bouncing ball. I'm just bouncing.

AL: Like a different place every night?

PABLO: No, like different places every week. I would go here. Then there'd be arguments over drugs or money. We'd go over there until drugs or money argument. Over there, drugs and argument, money. Over there, drugs and argument, money.

AL: Were you in the same sort of area? Or were you all over the city?

PABLO: Yeah, Mattapan, Dorchester, to East Boston and Cambridge. Yeah, we bounced around a lot.

In the time that I knew him, Pablo split his time between shelters and the street, lived with a girlfriend, and was incarcerated several times. His incarceration history reflected his drug addiction and homelessness, with drug possession charges and assault charges resulting from a fight he got into at an area shelter.

Sandy, a white woman in her 30s with a history of addiction and shoplifting, was not willing to live in shelters, programs, or sober houses, because they would require her and her boyfriend Carl to live separately and would therefore also be more expensive. She followed a pattern similar to Pablo's, "bouncing" around the region, and faced significant housing instability throughout the time I knew her. Sandy met Carl through a mutual friend while they were both incarcerated. Her initial plan was to move to Carl's father's house, in an inner-ring suburb north of Boston. She said, "I don't want to be on the street. My family, I don't talk to my family and it's just kind of like the only place I have, can go right now." In our second interview, she described her release.

> SANDY: I told you I was supposed to move in with my boyfriend and his father. Well, that lasted like not even twenty-four hours. He, the father, kicked us out. But so I don't even know. I don't know if my boyfriend's lying to me about what happened, I don't know. So, we've just been bouncing around. . . . He—his father—is a bipolar prick. I said, 'Well, I have a funny feeling. Hey, Carl, are you sure you, like, let him know this plan?' 'Oh yeah, yeah, yeah, don't worry.' But so then why were we kicked out the next day?
>
> AL: So where are you staying now?
>
> SANDY: At this friggin' cheesy motel in Mattapan that I have to pay seventy-five dollars a night for.[8] Which obviously puts me in a position again to do illegal stuff because my family sucks.

Sandy's ties with family were strained because of her long-standing problems with drug use. Carl was similarly isolated. Sandy regularly stole from stores and picked up several new shoplifting charges over the course of our interviews. She and Carl stayed together, moving repeatedly, between motels, the street, and rented rooms.

Before moving to the Mattapan motel, she and Carl stayed with an acquaintance in Charlestown, on the opposite side of Boston. She described this as "a nightmare. Everybody was getting high. I wasn't sleeping. I wasn't eating. So I'm like, [with sarcasm] 'everything is just like awesome.' I'm so stressed with everything. I have not gotten anything accomplished. . . . I haven't been able to do anything positive for myself. I'm just trying to get, surviving and making sure I have somewhere to sleep." After the motel, they spent a few nights on the street. She described this experience, "He

[Carl] was out cold. . . . Some guy fucking started touching me. I woke up to some guy rubbing my boob. . . . After that, I was never going to sleep on the street again. I've never been so scared in my life. He's kneeling down and smiling." After this, they moved into a string of rented rooms. She ran into one woman that she knew from the House of Correction at the bus stop, who offered Sandy and Carl an extra room. However, the woman "was addicted to Klonopins and would abuse them. One day she didn't have any and freaked out and pulled a butcher knife out on me and Carl. I'm outside crying and another girl I know from the [methadone] clinic came over. It happened that her friend was looking for somebody to move in. . . . It just worked out perfect that day."

All these moves happened between our second and third interview (three and a half months apart). By the third interview, Sandy and Carl were staying in a second rented room in a north-shore suburb. They moved to save money, as "Me and Carl were paying $175 a week with no income, so we were putting ourselves in situations. Stealing to go back to jail. Just our living situation. Now where we're at, we only pay $80 a week, but we get high all the time." Around this time, they also both went to detox and started going to a methadone clinic in Chelsea, which was eight or nine miles from their room. This meant daily trips, on two buses, an hour each way, to get to the clinic. By our last interview, she said, "At this point, I just want to get the F out of where we're at. It's been a nightmare. . . . Eight months too long."

Pablo and Sandy's experiences highlight the difficulty of researchers relying on residential neighborhood as an indicator of reentry. Sandy experienced a lot of housing instability in her first year post-release. She and Carl spent time on the street and in rented rooms. While her relationship with Carl lasted the entire year, and seemed strong, they were alienated from family and relied heavily on disposable ties for housing (Desmond 2012b). While she grew up in Cambridge, she did not consider anywhere "home." They moved all over the Boston area, particularly in the first few months, with their residence changing by the day or week, often with sizable geographic jumps. Any neighborhood in which she and Carl were living was based on practical exigencies, not affective ties or access to resources. In her most stable period of housing, she had to spend a significant portion of her day traveling to and from the services that helped her stay drug-free.

Sandy's living conditions also shaped her understanding of success. For her, "doing good" was doing one positive thing a day. In our fourth interview, she said, "I haven't been on the street in a long time. I think right there that's

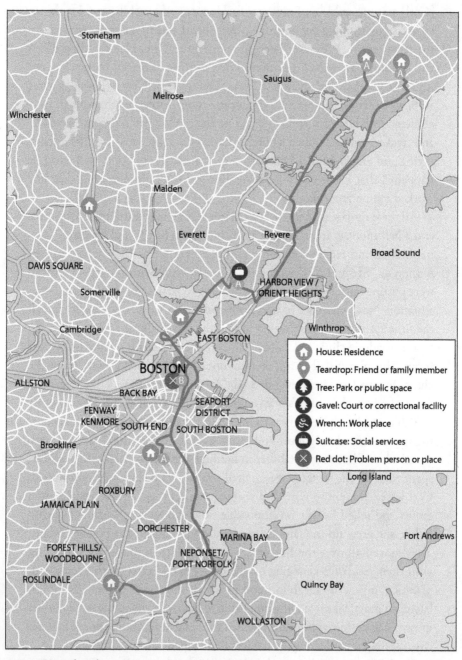

Legend:

🏠 House: Residence

📍 Teardrop: Friend or family member

🌳 Tree: Park or public space

⚖️ Gavel: Court or correctional facility

🔧 Wrench: Work place

🧳 Suitcase: Social services

✕ Red dot: Problem person or place

MAP 3. Unanchored activity space. Source: Google Maps.

change in itself. I've got these stupid shoplifting cases, but I think I've come a long way since I got out. I still have a long way to go, but I'm getting there." While she continued to struggle with addiction, shoplifting, and acquiring new charges, she and Carl slowly gained some stability. She felt encouraged with these small, positive steps. Still, Sandy did not have a "neighborhood" or "community" as we typically understand it. To the extent she returned regularly to any place, it was downtown Boston, where she shoplifted. Similarly, Pablo and Kevin's "neighborhoods" were an ever-revolving series of temporary beds or rooms, though at times, both gravitated to public spaces where they would hang out, get high, and see old friends or acquaintances.

People with unanchored activity spaces lived in all corners of the Boston area and had no lasting social or emotional ties to any of the places. This is not uncommon among returning prisoner populations. Sociologist Jessica Simes's (2018) study of neighborhood attainment after state-level incarceration in Massachusetts similarly found that 25 percent of people returning to the Boston area entered institutional settings, returned to prison, or lived in extreme marginality. In addition to not having a meaningful neighborhood, many in this group similarly lack another anchor, either relationally or spatially, or regular activity space. In Sandy's case, she maintained a relationship with her boyfriend for the entire time I knew her, but they were similarly unanchored. This is a significant caveat to neighborhood effects studies with a returning prisoner population, and, as with those with affective- or utility-anchored activity spaces, highlights the importance of looking beyond residential neighborhoods to how people use and move about space.

CONCLUSION

The housing instability of returning prisoners is not new information. Research has documented the likelihood of moving post-incarceration and the neighborhood attainment of people who have been incarcerated (Harding and Morenoff 2013; Simes 2018; Western 2018). It is less common, however, to address how this impacts their reentry experiences and how they experience place, while having few connections to any particular place. This complicates our understanding of neighborhood and neighborhood context and their importance for people exiting prison. A sizable minority of the people interviewed in this project had no stable residence and no stable connection to any place. They moved frequently because they were staying in shelters, on the street, or renting rooms in motels or apartments. This group tended to have long histories of drug use and often attenuated relationships with family as a result. This also limited their connection to any place. These experiences highlight how their positionality and experiences reinforce their vulnerability and disadvantage.

As the next several chapters illustrate, neighborhood *is* significant for many. My interviewees retained emotional connections to places, whether or not they still lived there, and their social connections were often tied to those places. In an urban area, it was relatively easy to travel to a neighborhood, if they needed or wanted to. This was an important dimension to their day. Traveling meant spending significant amounts of time in public, potentially crossing paths with friends and intimate partners, as well as police or other agents of social control. While many regulated their time spent "hanging out" outside, for fear of surveillance, many also needed to travel, for work, for court visits, and to maintain social ties.

THREE

Dorchester

RETURNING TO A "HIGH-CRIME" NEIGHBORHOOD

> Fiends, junkies, alcoholics. You know what I mean, like, it's the
> capital, it's Dorchester. That area's—there a lot of killings that be
> happening over there. But for the majority, once all the knuckle-
> heads is away, you know what I mean, everybody's behind bars,
> it's kind of nice, you know, 'cause it's quiet.
>
> STEPHEN, Black man in his 20s

> When a crisis happens, everybody comes together. We all pull
> together, get together, mourn together, so to speak. When it
> comes to certain things like that, and when it comes to celebra-
> tions, we're always together. You might not even really know
> anybody, but there's certain times when we all get together and
> have a good time.
>
> KEN, Black man in his 40s

DORCHESTER HAS A REPUTATION for being a high-crime area of Boston, and many residents are acutely aware of the crime and violence that
happen in their neighborhood. Still, many also see many strengths of living
in Dorchester, and particularly emphasize a sense of belonging and community. A major dimension of community in Dorchester is its familiarity,
which many long-term residents draw on to feel safe. They did not need
to be close friends with their neighbors, but they felt they belonged when
they were known by and recognized their neighbors and area business owners. They also emphasized a feeling of responsibility for their neighborhood,
including ownership over "the crime problem" (Leverentz 2012; Leverentz
and Williams 2017). Crime was not something committed by outsiders or
something that would be resolved merely by calling the police. People who
committed crimes might be their neighbors, and residents often felt responsible to respond to crime issues internally, not just rely on the police or the

state. They might call the police (Bell 2016), but they also might intervene directly to stop criminal activity or to redirect someone who was involved in criminal activity.

Returning to a Black, low-income, and/or high-crime or -incarceration neighborhood is typically framed as undesirable for returning prisoners and for those neighborhoods. The perspectives of both people returning from the House of Correction and other residents paints a more complex picture of what it means for the former to return to Dorchester. One factor that drew people back to Dorchester after release from the House of Correction is a sense of familiarity. For them, familiarity included close connections with family, friends who may provide needed services or supports as they adjust to life outside of prison, and associates who may be a connection to a past life they wanted to stay away from. Sometimes members of their social networks served multiple roles simultaneously. Thus, they had complex experiences with and attitudes about Dorchester. Rarely, however, did they express an interest in leaving their neighborhood, and some expressed an intense connection to it. While occasionally having access to criminogenic networks was a part of this connection, more commonly it was the comfort of being in a familiar area where they felt they belonged. For those who were trying to avoid offending, police contact, or reincarceration, this often entailed a careful navigation of relationships and places (Harding et al. 2019).

As an area that had transitioned from white to Black and was more recently experiencing some gentrification, with white residents moving in, race was a common topic among those we interviewed. Black, Latinx, and long-term white residents tended to have similar views on the neighborhood and who "belonged." They were wary of gentrification, because of common fears of displacement, but also welcomed some positive changes. Similarly, they were mildly wary of some of their new neighbors and their perceived aloofness. Newer white residents expressed more fears of their Black neighbors. They did not feel the same sense of belonging that longer-term residents felt, and they rarely engaged with their neighbors. Their lives were oriented outside the neighborhood, for connection, services, and leisure (see also Browning et al. 2017b). These residents felt less connected to the neighborhood and their neighbors, and often felt less safe in it.

In many ways, the perspectives of those we interviewed in Dorchester— both those with ties to the House of Correction and those without—reflect a fairly unified neighborhood. This is consistent with a large body of research that has consistently found close ties and a coherent identity within disadvantaged neighborhoods.

DORCHESTER AND ITS NEIGHBORHOODS: CODMAN SQUARE TO UPHAM'S CORNER

Residents know Dorchester both as Boston's largest neighborhood and as the once historic village clusters and squares—like Four Corners, Uphams Corner, Bowdoin-Geneva, Neponset, Adams Village—within it. In resident interviews, we focused on the sections roughly along Blue Hill Avenue and the Fairmount commuter rail line. Much of the residential development along Blue Hill Avenue followed the construction of a streetcar line down the center of the road in the late nineteenth century (Vale 2002). Blue Hill Avenue was also a linear business, cultural, and religious center to Boston's Jewish community (Vale 2002). Gradually, beginning in the 1920s, the middle-class Jewish population began moving to the suburbs, and the Blue Hill Avenue corridor transitioned into a working-class ethnic neighborhood with declining institutions (Vale 2002). Several public housing developments were also built in the area in the 1950s (Vale 2002).

While there was a dramatic increase in the size of the Black migrant population in Boston between the Civil War and the turn of the twentieth century, Boston never became as popular a destination as other major northern urban areas, such as Chicago and Detroit (Thernstrom 1973; McRoberts 2005). Initially, most of Boston's Black population lived in the West End. They then moved to the "Black Quarter" of the South End and Lower Roxbury, where they experienced a "de facto program of Black containment," even as the size of the Black population grew (McRoberts 2005: 19). It wasn't until the 1960s that large numbers of Black residents began moving into Dorchester from the South End and Roxbury (Vale 2002; McRoberts 2005). Approximately seventeen hundred mostly Black and Puerto Rican families in the South End were displaced as urban renewal expanded from the West End into the South End (Gans 1982; Mollenkopf 1983). A number of them moved into formerly predominantly Jewish, Irish, and Scottish neighborhoods of Dorchester. As the Jewish population along the Blue Hill Avenue corridor rapidly left in the 1950s and 1960s, Black people moved in (Vale 2002). As in other urban neighborhoods during this era, blockbusting by real estate agents and mortgage-lending banks furthered the racial transformation of Dorchester (Vale 2002; Harding 2010). During this period, the city of Boston also lost approximately 20 percent of its population (McRoberts 2005). While the public housing developments were originally built for the "worthy poor," like veterans and the white working class, the composition and institutional standing of the developments changed shortly thereafter and became associated with crime and violence in the city (Vale 2002; Harding 2010). Some Dorchester neighborhoods were better able to capitalize on a system of neighborhood-based politics and resource allocation, while others fell through the cracks (McRoberts 2005).[1]

Today, Dorchester neighborhoods are racially and economically diverse, with whiter areas east and closer to Dorchester Bay, larger Black populations further west, and neighborhoods with large Asian populations in the middle. Dorchester Avenue, or Dot Ave, serves roughly as a dividing line between whiter and Blacker areas, and Blue Hill Avenue is a major thoroughfare farther west. While there is demographic variation in Dorchester, there are sizable Black and poor populations, particularly in the stretch between Codman Square and Upham's Corner and along the Blue Hill Avenue corridor. The area is 63 percent Black, compared to 24 percent for the city as a whole. Twenty-four percent of the families are below the poverty level and the median household income is significantly lower than the city as a whole; only two of the area's seventeen census tracts have a median household income above the city's median. It is a high-crime area—over half of Boston's 2017 homicides were in the two police districts that cover this area—and has a reputation as such. Despite the variation across Dorchester, many still paint it with a broad brush of being Black, poor, and dangerous. It is this stereotype that led me to choose to focus on Dorchester, and in particular the sections for which these descriptors were most true, from Codman Square on the south, roughly along the Blue Hill Avenue corridor, to Upham's Corner in the north.

Omar McRoberts (2005) described the Four Corners area of Dorchester: "In the mid-1980s, Four Corners began to gain a national reputation as a 'rough' neighborhood. A thriving, gang-driven drug market and rising violent and property crime rates kept residents in perpetual fear. A spate of drive-by shootings drew wide media attention to the neighborhood and its problems and put the name 'Four Corners' on the proverbial map, albeit under less than flattering circumstances" (4). This era also spawned the idea of "superpredators." In an article in the conservative magazine the *Weekly Standard*, political scientist John Dilulio Jr. (1995) wrote, "Moral poverty begets juvenile super-predators, whose behavior is driven by two profound developmental defects": namely, they were present-oriented and self-regarding, according to Dilulio. They "perceive no relationship between doing right (or wrong) now and being rewarded (or punished) for it later. . . . They regret getting caught. For themselves, they prefer pleasure and freedom to incarceration and death" (Dilulio 1995). These super-predators were also primarily seen as young Black men. While the predictions of a dramatic rise in violent and remorseless young men proved wrong, policies and approaches were shaped by these ideas (Fagan 2010). In Boston, police initially responded to rising violence with a widespread stop-and-frisk policy aimed at young Black men in Roxbury, Dorchester, and Mattapan (Kennedy, Braga, and Piehl 2001). In 1996, a collaboration between police, clergy, and social scientists, including criminologist David Kennedy, came together to create Operation Ceasefire. Operation Ceasefire sought to intervene with the small number of young, gang-involved men who were most involved in violence in the city, using both carrot and stick approaches (Kennedy et al. 2001). This was credited with contributing to a 63 percent decline in homicides in Boston.

FAMILIARITY AND SOCIAL CONTROL

Long-term residents in Dorchester emphasized relationships with neighbors and social networks as both a defining feature of neighborhood life and a source of safety. Evandro, a Cape Verdean man his 30s, described what he likes about his neighborhood, "I think I just like the, I like their diversity. The cultural diversity, including the yuppies and all that. I like the fact that it's been home for twenty-plus years. I see violence changing, it's not as bad, like I said, bad as it used to be in the '80s and '90s. Plus, I have a lot of friends and families that live around there, so." Deidre, a Black woman in her 50s who was a lifelong resident of Dorchester and lived in the home she grew up in, said she felt safe in her neighborhood "Because I've been here so long, and I think I know a lot of the folks here. Although there's a lot of new businesses, and I don't know these folks, but I try to go in and introduce myself and kind of visit them enough so they're like, 'Oh, she lives in the neighborhood' kind of thing." Johnna, another lifelong Dorchester resident and Black woman in her 30s, echoed Deidre's perspective. She said she felt safe because "I feel like I know a good amount of people. If I don't know them, surprisingly some folks are like, 'Hey how are you doing?' They know me. I feel like I'm a familiar face to people. For the most part, people are familiar faces to me. I feel comfortable with that." While residents often have close friends and family that live nearby, it is equally important for many that they feel "known" as a neighbor in a broader sense.

Similarly, Hector, a Puerto Rican man who had lived in Dorchester for approximately fifty years, talked about racial/ethnic divides in his neighborhood, including an influx of white residents. While most of the groups, including "Vietnamese people, Caribbean people, Hispanics, and of course, they have Black people too," tended to associate with others who were like them, Hector said, "We say hi. Everybody is nice and friendly." He trusts everyone, because "they're my neighbors. I trust you and I don't know you. I trust you, until you do something wrong." In each of these cases, these residents had lived in Dorchester (often the same house or neighborhood) for decades. This alone may bring a sense of belonging, yet they also mentioned changes in neighborhood populations, and becoming familiar with newer residents and newer businesses in the neighborhood. They need not know their neighbors well to gain this sense of familiarity; it was often enough to be among familiar faces and to be recognized as a resident.

Valuing familiarity was also true of the longer-term white residents in Dorchester. Brian, a white man who had lived in his Dorchester neighborhood for twenty years, said, "I feel like I can trust most of our neighbors. I think it's partly based on relationships. How long you've known people." While this trust had been violated occasionally, he generally felt they "watch out for us" and that "there's some shared values. I think there's a shared value around wanting to see a strong, healthy community. I think there's a value of wanting to care for your neighbor or love your neighbor. I think there's a general value around general willingness to help out, to do things to help better the community beyond my own self-interest." When Brian and his wife moved to the neighborhood, "We made an intentional choice and said, 'we want our neighbors to be our friends.'" Millie, a white woman in her 60s, chose to move into her Dorchester neighborhood over thirty years earlier because it was affordable. She had previously lived nearby, and worked in the neighborhood. She was familiar with it after a nearby house was featured on *This Old House*. She said,

I kind of knew this neighborhood. So, there was that piece. We couldn't afford to buy in the suburbs, for example. Then, it was when Bob Villa was doing the original *This Old House*. . . . That house right on the point was the original This Old House. Of course, it was the first show Norm Abrams was doing all the carpentry. We were all glued to it every week. We lived in Quincy, we used to come over and look at it. So, I knew something about this neighborhood. . . . It was definitely affordable, at the time.

When Millie went on to describe problem areas in the neighborhood, she emphasized, "We have to consider, it's not that they're problem areas, it's that there are problem people. Where those problem people are become problem areas." She named some of these problem people, by name. In one house next to her lived one such person, who was "just a problem. . . . The police were there constantly. Her sons were in trouble. Finally, she was evicted, she was gone. It changed the whole area. It's that. It's not the place, it's a couple of individuals who drive it up." This is a common narrative in area community meetings as well, and spans speakers—including residents, community activists, and police officers—and across race (see also Leverentz 2012). When asked to describe her neighbors, Millie said, "For the people that I know, I would describe them, again with these couple of exceptions that I've pointed out, I would describe them as hardworking, I can't emphasize that enough. It's like a lot of people here are working so hard. . . . I think everybody is doing the best they can. . . . They're trying to take care of their families to just live their lives." This attitude extends to the mother of one of the young men she identified as a major problem in the neighborhood: "She loves her son, it's her only son. She doesn't know what to do." She describes one neighbor, who had previously been involved in drug selling and had been incarcerated, as having "gone from being a problem in the neighborhood, to just being our local ne'er do well" who supports himself doing small, odd jobs in the neighborhood. For better and for worse, Millie knows her neighbors as individuals. In Millie's case, she can name many of her neighbors and relay stories of their lives. Some others recognize their neighbors and greet them in passing, but they don't know them intimately. In all cases, however, this familiarity is a key dimension of living in Dorchester.

While residents often talked in favorable and loyal terms about living in Dorchester, they also are aware of crime and violence. They contextualized this crime and violence in several ways. First, they tended not to generalize. A small number of individuals caused intolerable problems and needed to be dealt with. Others engaged in some petty criminal activity or were incarcerated but were generally good people. In these cases, other residents may want the behavior to stop, but the people behind it were otherwise welcome. And most residents were just living their lives peacefully. Millie, along with many of the other longer-term residents in Dorchester, could identify "problem people" by name, while describing the majority of her neighbors as "hard working."

Many of the people we talked to sometimes intervened directly when they saw problematic behavior. For example, Duane, a Black man in his 50s who had lived in Dorchester for several decades, said, "This used to be the hangout spot for—I'm going to say —like three sets of gang members. I call them gang members; I use that word loosely kinda. Put it this way, there were associated adults and—I'm going to say—teenagers that used to congregate here, sell drugs hand to hand blatantly. When I moved in, they would sit on my stairs; they would throw trash in my yard." He called the police, but he also confronted the gang members directly. He said, "I was the guy to go out there and face to face . . . the only way to solve a problem is to confront it face to face. . . . If you don't go outside, you can't identify who the assailants are or who the perpetrators are. And, as you know, intel is the best weapon to deter something from escalating." Duane still avoided some areas if they were too "hot," particularly at night and when he was with his girlfriend. He rhetorically asked, "Why would I? I'm taking too much risk." Duane made judgment calls given the individuals involved, how familiar he was with them, and the seriousness of their behavior, and responded accordingly. That might mean ignoring the behavior, talking directly to the people involved, or calling the police. There are two key characteristics of Duane's response. First, like Millie, he spoke about crime and social disorder in the neighborhood with specificity. He knew the individuals who sold drugs or engaged in violence in the neighborhood; he did not generalize to groups or classes of people or a vague sense of trouble. In addition, he spoke to and sometimes confronted these people directly. He was not naive about crime and did not always engage with possible offenders, but he did engage in direct social control in his own area.

Despite, and sometimes in response to, crime and violence, many residents perceived Dorchester to be close-knit. Ken, a Black man in his 40s, described his Dorchester neighborhood as close-knit, "Because when a crisis happens, everybody comes together. We all pull together, get together, mourn together, so to speak. When it comes to certain things like that, and when it comes to celebrations, we're always together. You might not even really know anybody, but there's certain times when we all get together and have a good time." Importantly, this sense of being "known" and knowing others in the neighborhood did not require close ties (Carr 2003) and at least sometimes crossed racial boundaries. Some of these ties may date back to childhood, though they still were not necessarily close relationships. Deidre and Johnna, two women who emphasized the safety in feeling "known" by others in their neighborhood, could not necessarily identify all their neighbors by name, but recognizing them was enough to generate a comfort level in the neighborhood. As the quote from Deidre illustrates, these were actively constructed relationships and reflected an approach to neighborhood life. When new businesses moved in, for example, Deidre made a point of becoming familiar to them so that she retained a sense of familiarity even as the neighborhood changed. Longtime residents defined their neighborhood in terms of the people in it, and it was these relationships, however limited, that made them feel they belonged and were safe.

GENTRIFICATION AND MOVING TO DORCHESTER

While gentrification was less pronounced in Dorchester than in South Boston or the South End, it was a prevalent theme in resident interviews. A number of residents noted an influx of new development and newer, middle-income, mostly white homeowners. Evandro (Cape Verdean, 30s) described this as both good and bad, "It's good because new property is being constructed and it's being fixed up. Bad because if people can't afford it, like lower-income families can't afford it, then they're forced to move from an area that they're familiar with, comfortable with." He said "yuppies" are moving in, "like Southie. I think just people are able to afford the rent and the new property. Those are the type of people that are moving in." He also described this "newer generation" as less close-knit. Similarly, Hector (Puerto Rican, 60s) said some longtime residents are concerned about the impact of changes, but also "up here the buildings are beautiful. The houses are beautiful. You see a lot of cleaning and everything going on. You call City Hall and they come, clean, take care of it." Duane, a long-term Black homeowner, said, "You know my house in the past month appreciated probably like $15,000. As a homeowner, I want to keep it that way. Let's not kid ourselves, we all have a stake in this community."

Some of the newer white residents who chose to move to Dorchester felt like outsiders, which included a sense of danger. They also tended to look outward to other neighborhoods for socializing and other key aspects of daily life, rather than considering themselves more fully a part of Dorchester social networks. Karen, a white woman in her 20s who had lived in Dorchester for a year, did not feel a sense of community in her neighborhood. She said, "I think I really was an outsider.... They definitely had more of a sense of community with people who also lived there forever and ever." She also was acutely aware of the racial differences between herself and many of her neighbors, which shaped her comfort and fears. When a Black man yelled at her out of his car window, she thought, "Maybe I just looked super-, I don't know, affluent, and like I didn't belong there. Yeah, that's all I could think of, was I know how big of a deal gentrification is. It was like, 'OK, you're in my neighborhood and you're causing it.'" After this incident, she avoided walking the same route. She felt similarly out of place when she went to a grocery store in the local business district. She said, "It was really just the feeling of like, 'I don't belong here.'... I was definitely the only white person in the store, which normally I'm fine with." Karen sensed a stronger sense of unwelcomeness than longtime residents expressed. They saw newer residents practicing self-imposed distancing, rather than longer-term residents being unwelcoming.

In Karen's time in the neighborhood, she "would probably hear sirens, police cars going down Park Street [one street over from the district police station], probably every night.... I definitely heard gunshots. I don't want to say every week, but it was frequently that I could hear them from where I lived. Back in February or March they actually found a dead guy right here." When asked if she took any precautions for her own safety, she said that when she left work after dark she took an Uber for the half-mile trip home from her job. Karen preferred the part of her neighborhood with more single-family homes with yards and fewer pedestrians. She said of this part of her neighborhood, "It definitely, the yards are better kept up, there's not trash in the yards." In contrast, in the other part of her neighborhood, "there's a lot of trash. The houses definitely need paint jobs. The paint is peeling. Going that way, there's also more businesses." Karen reported typically feeling safer when there were fewer people in the streets, and on streets with what she perceived to be more aesthetically pleasing, better-maintained housing.

Candace was another young white woman living in Dorchester. While she felt safe in her building, she complained about her neighbors: "I don't feel like they value quiet and I don't feel like they value cleanliness." Her primary complaint about her neighborhood was the lack of amenities, "that's the one problem. There's no gym close by. There's not a lot of restaurants...."

There's not a lot happening [here] for young folks." As with other newcomers across neighborhoods, she avoided certain parts of the neighborhood, because "there's a lot of sketchy people out on the street, the houses aren't great looking, looks run down, and I've just heard over and over that it's not nice. That's terrible, to let that inform you so much as it has, but I've really heard a lot of not so nice things." Like other newer white residents across the neighborhoods, Karen and Candace highlighted the importance of amenities and aesthetics and they felt Dorchester fell short.

White middle-class newcomers to Dorchester were more likely to view their Black and lower income neighbors as a threat than as a source of safety and familiarity. Newer white residents focused more on the amenities and aesthetics, like restaurants, parks, and housing stock (Mayorga-Gallo 2014), and types of people, rather than social networks of which they were a part. They derived a sense of safety or danger from these aesthetics and signs of social and physical (dis)order. That these racial dynamics contributed to a sense of safety and danger parallels public opinion research on fear of crime (Chiricos et al. 2001; Quillian and Pager 2010) and on the racialized signaling of disorder (Sampson and Raudenbush 2004; Drakulich and Crutchfield 2013). Newer white residents in the South End and South Boston expressed similar experiences and priorities.

Not all recent movers were white and middle class, and not all had the same orientation to their neighborhood. Black residents who had more recently moved into Dorchester tended to focus on ties to neighbors and had a network-oriented sense of community. Greta, a Black woman in her 40s, had lived in her current neighborhood for three years and in Dorchester for just over a decade. Her motivation for moving to Dorchester was distinct from Karen and Candace, who were both looking for convenient and affordable housing. She said,

> I used to do community work way back when, and I used to live on the outskirts of Roslindale, which is near Dedham and West Roxbury. I was doing community work in the heart of Dorchester, Roxbury, and one of the women that we were working with said, "Well, you don't really know what it's like to live here, because you don't really live here." So I moved my girls and I into the heart of Boston, Dorchester. Right in the heart of Dorchester, . . . because she was right. What do I know about this neighborhood if I don't live in it.

She described the initial transition to Dorchester as "traumatic," as her first neighborhood was a "hot area. Really a hot area. Like I said, prostitution, drug deals left and right, shootings, people getting beat up in front of my house. It was one of those streets." While there was crime and violence a few blocks from her current house, she felt safer, "We may hear about it about three streets over or something like that. I don't have a problem with my youngest [teenage daughter] walking home from school. It's fine, not a big deal." When asked to physically describe her neighborhood, she emphasized her neighbors. She said, "A lot of my neighbors take pride in their house, how it looks on the outside, keeping to trash day....Very friendly. Once they get to know you, very friendly, very open, stuff like that. I think it's a good neighborhood. Once they know who you are, it's 'Hey, how you doing? Hey, how you doing?' So it's really nice." While she said that crime did contribute to "trust issues," and so developing relationships took time, people were friendly.

Katherine, a Black woman who had lived in Dorchester for about nine years, similarly described her neighborhood in terms of social ties. She said,

> I have neighbors that I know look out for other people's properties, that, a lot of people say, "Oh, I don't know my neighbors." I pretty much know a lot of the neighbors because when I moved there, they came over, introduced themselves, or they also came to meetings or I see them passing by. You may not always know everybody by name, but you know they're part of the neighborhood. You see them park their car there or go to their house or that kind of thing. You don't know all the names, but you know they're neighbors, not visitors.

She also recognized a sense of commitment to the neighborhood among her neighbors, "It's not like a group of people that you think, 'Oh they're going to be moving shortly,' because you can see that they're actually doing stuff. They plan to stay there and they would help you out if you needed a hand." While Katherine sometimes worried for the safety of her teenage grandson and took basic precautions like alarming her house and car, she generally felt safe in her neighborhood and trusted her neighbors. For these newer residents of color, their weak ties to neighbors reflects a sense of collective efficacy in the neighborhood, and a sense of belonging for them and their neighbors (Sampson 2012). Black newcomers to Dorchester embraced the social networks in the neighborhoods and derived a sense of safety from them. In this sense, their perspective paralleled that of the longer-term residents of all races and in all neighborhoods who relied on social ties to feel safe. It was distinct from most white newcomers who relied on perceptions of social and physical disorder and crime narratives that implicated their Black and Latinx neighbors.

In Dorchester longtime residents expressed some concern about gentrification in their neighborhoods. Newer residents who were perceived as gentrifiers were sometimes looked on with some disdain by more established residents, but they did not generate fear or diminish their sense of safety, even as they were relatively unknown and were perceived as less invested in the neighborhood. They were typically middle or upper-middle class, and often white, and were not perceived to contribute to crime or disorder in serious or dangerous ways. They were seen as less committed to the neighborhood, more likely to call police, and less likely to invest in their community. They were potentially a threat, but in terms of how their presence signaled economic changes in the neighborhood. Even this generated a mixed reaction, as the influx of residents also brought increased home values to homeowners and improved city services. Similarly, those exiting the House of Correction who commented on changes to the neighborhood emphasized increasing quiet and stability. At least so far, the neighborhood remained accessible to them, often because of family connections. While some residents feared displacement, it had not yet become a major issue. In contrast, newer white residents who had moved into Dorchester expressed more trepidation and discomfort with their Black neighbors. While the longer-term white residents had similar narratives about community and social networks as their Black neighbors, newer white residents were wary of their Black neighbors.

THE DUAL-EDGED SWORD OF FAMILIARITY

For those returning from the House of Correction, familiarity is also a key characteristic of Dorchester. They often know people that live nearby, including family, friends, and associates. This includes people who support them, whom they can ask for help if needed, and who might connect them to drug selling or other illegal activity. In some cases, the emotional or instrumental supports and the criminogenic networks are the same person(s). In addition, living in Dorchester is convenient. It is fairly central to where they need to go, and they can easily access public transportation. So, both in terms of people and services, it meets their basic needs.

For Jackson, a Black man in his 30s, "That's just my familiar, especially getting out of jail. I know people I can go say, 'Hey, I need this,' you know.

I can't drive right now. I got friends with cars and stuff like that. It just makes it easier for me to be able to do some things. The T is all over the place right there, so it's easier to get around between there and Fields Corner." As described in chapter 1, Jackson had limited options of what to do or where to stay when he was released. For him, returning to Dorchester was simultaneously returning to a place that he could afford and access support from friends and associates and also that could easily lead to selling drugs again. John, a Black man in his 30s, had similar social networks as Jackson, but with a balance that made it easier for him to avoid engaging in additional illegal activity. He, too, was known in the neighborhood as someone who sold drugs, and it would be easy to return to this. In our final interview, John said his greatest accomplishment since his release was not resorting to selling drugs, "because it was up the point that's all I had left to do. . . . Post up on a block, nine times out of ten you're going to get an up [drugs to sell]. I just stood firm."

Unlike Jackson, however, John returned from the House of Correction to a small apartment he shared with his cousin and roommates. John slept on a futon in the living room and would occasionally stay with his aunt (until she was evicted and moved into a shelter a few blocks away) when his younger roommates got on his nerves. John was trying to redefine his role in the neighborhood, and thus carefully navigated his Dorchester neighborhood. For one, he tried to avoid being seen with young men in the neighborhood. He said,

> Some of the young dudes around here. They like, umm, they into gangs and, you know, being that I'm with them, I don't want to be seen with them, 'cause I don't wanna be labeled. You know what I'm saying? I try to stay away from them. They look up to me, "Hey, what's up? OG." Every kid is not bad, it's just you know, how they was brought up. But still, I know how Boston is. . . . Once I see something that I don't like, I do this, "Alright, man, bro, see you later."

One aspect of "how Boston is" is the harassment he felt from the police. He gave one example: "One time I was walking with my hair out and I had my pants sagging and they pulled me over. Told me I fit the description of something that just happened. And I'm like 'Yeah, alright.'" This was a common story from Black and Latino men across neighborhoods, though it was particularly pronounced in "high-crime" neighborhoods or in downtown areas. John said the neighborhood had "got quieter. It got quiet. This wasn't a quiet neighborhood." He attributed this in part to new surveillance cameras in the neighborhood. This expanded the ability of the police to monitor resident behavior, and it likely shaped the behaviors of men like John, who tried to avoid experiences of harassment.

In addition to a general aversion to the police, John had a restraining order against him from his son's mother, who lived nearby, so he was also wary of running into her.

> My PO says he's been getting calls about me harassing them and I'm looking at him like "I don't even be around them, so how am I harassing them?" I said "First of all, we live in the same neighborhood, so if I walk, we going to bump into them. Yes, I have seen them but they haven't seen me." He said, "Well I think they did." I'm saying to myself, "Even if they did see me and I'm slow walking, I'm still in violation for that?" He's like, "Not really. You just got to watch it. You see she called. From now on, when you see them, you call me just to protect yourself."

The fact that he was on probation heightened the threats that he faced from the police and from his son's mother. John did not need to break the law to be arrested, and he did not need to intentionally harass his son's mother in order to violate his restraining order. This meant that he faced heightened risks just by leaving his house, particularly given that most of the time he walked and so spent a lot of time in public spaces.

John's experience illustrates the potential dangers of returning to an old neighborhood or to a high-crime neighborhood. In John's case, he faced possible threats from criminally involved social networks, his child's mother, and the police. Going about his daily business, often on foot, put him in potential contact with all three of these threats. Still, he had a stable place to live, even while he spent most of that first year looking for a job. While he had connections to get back into drug selling, he faced not only that temptation but also a more general sense of being hypervisible to police. That hypervisibility applied to John, in his old neighborhood, to other Black and Latino men in general (regardless of whether they were living in an old neighborhood), and to people who felt they "stood out" in their neighborhoods. For John and others, this translated into avoiding being in public where possible. John said, "Now I don't even go out and hang out there because I don't want to bump into her [his son's mother] or bump into him [her new boyfriend]. Because if anybody get too nervous, 'Oh I'm going to call the police,' because even if they call the police on me again, I'm breaking the rules and all that." At the same time, however, John spent most of his time in his neighborhood and walked most places he needed to go, including to court to report to his probation office and do community service and to take his dog for a walk in a nearby park. By our final interview, he had recently started working on a demolition crew, and took several buses to get to that job. Before that, he had to learn how to use public transit because he was so unused to leaving the neighborhood.

Netta, a Black woman in her 30s, also stayed in Dorchester when she was released. She initially planned to stay with her "sponsor," a woman she met in prison and had done well upon her release. Instead, she stayed with her mom because her son was also there. This, however, led to a probation violation: "Instead of her giving my probation officer my mother's number saying, 'Hey, listen, she's over here,' she [her sponsor] says 'I don't know where she is.' My probation officer puts a warrant up for my arrest. . . . She said, 'I'm sorry, your friend told me she didn't know where you was.' 'Wow. You knew where I was. I just wasn't in your house, but you knew where I was.'" Both her sponsor and her mom lived in Dorchester. "I think it's gotten better over the years. . . . I don't know, I think every neighborhood is what you make of it. I'm a pretty quiet person so I stay to myself for the most part." Netta stayed with her mother while trying to get her own housing for herself and her two children. Several months later, she stayed in "the cheapest hotel that I can go to" to get out of her mother's house. The hotel was also in Dorchester. She was arrested a few days later because of accusations that she had not paid her bill.

A friend who worked at the hotel suggested that there was a "shady" manager who "messes around with people's stuff. He steals money but they haven't arrested him yet."

> I get bailed out Saturday and I go to the hotel to get my things and I call Tom [a hotel employee] and he says, "Netta, this is not uncommon. It just so happens that you're Black so they arrested you. Plus they found out that you had a record. But they would never do this if you were a white person." He says, "I've been working here for a very long time and they should've said something to you like, 'Hey, there's a dispute Ms. B. You've been here for a little while and we just want to let you know that something's up.' Instead, they called the cops. So I'm like, "Why wouldn't they tell me? I paid my bills." So now I'm dying because I'm on probation, I don't know what's going to happen, I have to go to court. I go and print out my credit card statement. Because they basically said, the detectives said, I remember them saying I never paid the bill and that they didn't have my credit card. Lie.

Netta gave me a long explanation of this incident and what she thought happened. She said she typically paid for her room with a debit card, but when she was low on money, she asked her son to charge the room to his credit card for a few nights. He then disputed the charges for the hotel. She believed he did this without considering her vulnerability as someone with a lengthy history of theft and fraud, who was then on probation.

Netta plausibly looked guilty based on her past behavior, as reflected in her criminal record and because she was on probation. She also felt vulnerable because she was a Black woman, and so inherently more suspicious, and because she was staying in a hotel with a "shady" manager in Dorchester. Her "suspiciousness" was a combination of how she was perceived and where she was. Because she was on probation, she could be sent to prison just for being arrested. Netta showed me her bank records, to provide evidence for her story. Netta said she always admitted guilt whenever she was caught, but this time was different. Still, she had significant mistrust of the criminal legal system. She also told me about faulty records that almost prevented her release from the House of Correction, probation violations because of miscommunication, and lingering open charges because the DA refused to take action.[2] In addition, she was suspicious of her son's behavior, who she feared was following in her footsteps.

After this, I lost touch with Netta for about a year. During this time, she had been living in a neighborhood in North Dorchester with her husband, whom she married about two months after our fourth interview and about ten months after her release from the House of Correction. She described this neighborhood: "It's nice. You can get to everything. Now that I don't have my car anymore, I can take the train because the Red Lines have new stations right up the street and the beach is right down the street too in South Boston. Everything is pretty accessible. Family Dollar's right there, Rite Aid, everything is pretty accessible. Dorchester Ave is right there. It's pretty nice. It's quiet, except you hear a lot of police sirens and stuff around."

Our final interview took place in the state women's prison. Netta posted bail on the hotel charges, but her probation officer (again) filed a warrant for her arrest. She said her probation officer told her, "Well no one told me, so I put a warrant out for your arrest. . . . I thought they were going to hold you. . . . Oh well, you can come in and take care of it." In response, Netta said, "'Well, I don't trust you.' That was the end of that. I never went back to probation. I never checked in again. I never did anything. I never back to the [earlier shoplifting case]. I never did anything. I never got in any more trouble, but I never went back." Then, "I was on my way to work and detectives were waiting for me outside of my job. They knew I had a warrant. When they tried to pull me over, I did not stop. . . . I think my concern is that I know that I'm going to go to jail. If they knew where I worked, they knew where I lived. It's just a matter of time before they get you." As a result, she was also charged with reckless driving. She ended up in state prison, rather than the House of Correction, because she was arrested in another county which houses its county-sentenced women in the state prison. One of her goals while incarcerated was to clear up as many of the open cases as she could, so that when she was released she would be free from all supervision.

Netta's sense of vulnerability was, like John's, shaped by race. She felt more vulnerable as a Black woman and that she was seen as more inherently suspicious. For her, though, her criminal record was an important dimension. Many of the Black and Latino men felt targeted solely because of their race and gender. Just being in public was enough to generate suspicion. Netta felt acutely vulnerable because of her status as someone on probation and her experience with the probation officer. She believed she was more vulnerable to arrest as a result of the hotel incidents because it paralleled her earlier charges. It was a combination of being a Black woman and having an extensive criminal history that made it so difficult for her to move forward.

Cathy, a Black woman in her 20s, highlights a different kind of ambivalence of the familiarity of an old neighborhood. She, like many others, describes growing up in Dorchester as "street life, drugs, city life." She had several friends who had been killed in Dorchester. She complained about the quietness of the suburb to which her mom moved several years before as having "not enough going on for me." Prior to her most recent incarceration, she lived in the suburbs but regularly returned to the neighborhood in which she grew up. In addition to her old neighborhood having more excitement, it also contained reminders of her friends. She said, "I think it's still a piece of them. I think that's why I'm so much drawn there because they're still there, in a sense." Cathy went on, "But it's just . . . just growing up in that neighborhood, you know. You know that people that be standing on the porch, the old people. You know the people that work at the corner store and her [Cathy's murdered friend] kids are still over there and her grandmother still over there. It's a sense of comfort, at the same time, but it also brings pain, too. Because in just remembering, you're walking by a pole that you decorated in remembrance of her." For Cathy, in addition to having the same sort of familiarity in Dorchester that many residents drew a sense of community from, it provided her a connection to her friend who had been killed. This was a bittersweet reminder for her, but it was important.

This may have been particularly important to Cathy while incarcerated. She talked the most about Dorchester and her ties to it in her prerelease interview. Shortly after her release she "just like drove through. I chilled with a couple of people for a little while. It's still the same, I didn't miss nothing, nothing while I was gone. I heard about it all in the news. I heard about it all when I got home. Like, my little brother's best friend, he got killed like two weeks before I got out. It's still the same how I left it when I left." At the same time, she was spending most of her time with her immediate family; "my circle is small, but never alone." For Cathy, her memories of Dorchester and the people she knew there were important, but she managed her life outside it, particularly as she occupied her time with her family and her job.

For many of those with a history of incarceration, their neighborhood remained important to them because of the complexity of their social networks there. The reality of both criminogenic social networks and heightened surveillance was real for many. Even these were complicated, as the same networks that could connect them with drug selling opportunities, for example, may involve the same people who could provide them with a place to stay. People who were connected to violent pasts were also beloved friends and family members. Moving away from the bad meant also moving away from the good. For those who did remain, then, this meant that they needed to learn to manage the dangers and risks and to exist in their neighborhood in new ways.

NAVIGATING DORCHESTER

People returning from the House of Correction defined the neighborhood both in terms of their memory of it and their current engagement with it. This often led to starkly different descriptions, from that of gang activity and violence to peaceful habitation. For example, Charles, a Black man in his 20s who was planning to return to live with his sister, described her neighborhood as "quiet. I'm not so in the neighborhood like that." Charles describes the neighborhood as quiet, but also distinguishes his own plans to do something positive with whatever happens in the neighborhood. This suggests that his own engagement with the neighborhood is "quiet" more so than the neighborhood itself. He goes on to describe how he spends his time: "I'm only there like nighttime when she needs me. Besides all that, I'm either down at the shelter trying do something positive with myself, like get housing, you know what I'm saying. I'm in school, GED classes. That's about it. And then other things I do is Common Purpose [a batterer intervention program]. I have to do, do court. So, I'm not usually home during the day. I'm usually out in the town just chilling, out with my friends or I chill with my cousin. That's about it." For him, it's quiet because he's not in the neighborhood. When he is, he says, "To me, it's quiet. I'm not usually outside. I'm inside the house. We in the house either chilling playing video games or I'm smoking a cigarette chilling. That's about it." He also spent much of his time with his mother in Roxbury. At the time of our third interview, he was dividing his time between his mother's house and a new girlfriend's apartment in a Cambridge public housing building.

Over the course of the year, I met Charles at his mom's one-room apartment in Roxbury, his girlfriend's public housing high-rise apartment in Cambridge, and his sister's apartment in a Dorchester triple decker. He similarly described the Cambridge neighborhood as quiet, "I really don't be out here like that." Despite his efforts to stay out of trouble, he told me about two women who had accused him of rape, allegations he denied and that he suggested were an effort to break up him and his girlfriend. "Everybody's trying to mess up my relationship with her and it's just not working." Shortly after, the relationship did end, with him getting a restraining order against her. "She kept on harassing me. I put a restraining order out on her. I'm getting harassed. This girl's calling my phone, talking about going to get some people to fuck me up. My PO's like, 'You want a restraining order?'" She in turn pressed charges against him. Charles's strategy to staying out of trouble was, "I don't stay in one spot too long, unless I'm over at my people's house. . . . Because one spot, it just gets rowdy. I really don't mess with a lot of people like that. I really cut a lot of people off because they've been acting funny." While he initially hung out downtown, by our last interview, a year after his release, he stopped doing that. Because "just too many funny people down there. That's why I don't go down there." This was also the only area where he felt harassed by the police: "To tell the truth, I really don't get stopped nowhere but downtown." For Charles, it is less about whether a neighborhood is good or bad and more about his engagement with the people in it and how he navigates those relationships.

Stephen, a Black man in his 20s who grew up in Dorchester, returned from the House of Correction to once again live with his grandmother, "because I have nowhere else to go." When Stephen was about to be released, he thought he would go back to street life. Instead, he decided to try to stay out of trouble. In our second interview, he described this.

> Well, you know, I was saying it was different because, well, to be honest with you, I thought I was going to, after I do my time, I was going to get back on the streets, make a lot of quick, fast money, like I usually, like normally, every guy around my age will do. But being incarcerated, giving you time to think, and I ain't trying to go back, so when I got out, I just watched everything, I mean. And it's not really the same for me. I really don't know how to explain it, but it's, look, because I'm an alcoholic, too, and I been clean for a year, about a year and a half from jail time and recently, the month and change I've been out. Everybody drink and it's hard to do it, but I mean, I stay here and take it 'cause I got, I mean, I got strength to do it. I mean the will power. I'm saying, looking at the same thing, looking at everybody doing it, and I'm just sitting there, just coming home, just looking at everybody like, and everybody got money, it's hard. I mean I don't want to jump back at everybody telling me, "Come on, let's go make this money." I ain't trying to jump back in the game 'cause I know where that's going to lead. I mean, especially, I got my kids there, too, and that's what I really think about, too, my kids.

Stephen's narrative of trying to avoid trouble and avoid reincarceration was common among people in the months after their release. He was tempted to return to the street life he had been involved with as a young man and before his most recent incarceration. At the same time, he wanted to build on the accomplishment of not drinking for the past year, and to strengthen his relationship with his children. His primary motivation was to avoid reincarceration, "I mean, I ain't tryin to go back. I mean, that's why I ain't jump into the game, but the more, the more I sit around, the more it keep on approaching me, and that's what I want to do. I mean, I'm just fighting with my demons right now. That's all it is." Stephen's narrative, again common among our respondents, is in line with criminologists Ray Paternoster and Shawn Bushway's (2009) idea of desistance as avoiding a feared self or sociologist Peggy Giordano and colleagues' (Giordano et al. 2002, 2007) interaction-oriented theory of cognitive transformation. In Paternoster and Bushway's formulation, people may initially desist to avoid the outcomes of not doing so. For Giordano and colleagues, being open and exposed to possible hooks for change might make desistance possible. Stephen, and others, had similar narratives of avoiding going back to prison, which shaped their behaviors in public. They wanted to avoid both behaviors and the surveillance that could result in arrest.

I asked Stephen to describe the neighborhood. His account was similar to that of others who grew up there:

> Rough. You know what I mean? Fiends, junkies, alcoholics. You know what I mean, like, it's the capital, it's Dorchester. That area's, there a lot of killings that be happening over there. But for the majority, once all the knuckleheads is away, you know what I mean, everybody's behind bars, it's kind of nice, you know, 'cause it's quiet. It's like from when I was younger to now, it done quieted down, more of like a family place. 'Cause besides the houses getting built now, they done built houses there already. New families, kids, kids riding bicycles up and down the streets, scooters, you know what I mean. It done changed a lot, but if you was to ask about five, six years ago? You mean, you couldn't even go down the street or do nothing at nighttime. You worried about being robbed or you know, I mean, worried about going up a person's street unless you from around that area. I mean, if you from around that area, you can go anywhere around there. But nowadays, it's not the same. I mean, so it's cool.

Stephen is highlighting both changes in the neighborhood and changes in his own engagement with it. He notices changes in who is living in the neighborhood, with an increase in the number of families and new construction. He also is reflecting on his own involvement in the neighborhood. Previous times he has gotten out, he has gone back to street life, but this time he does not want to do this. He attributed this to getting older; "Everybody said with age, I mean, you think more, you know what I mean? You don't want to go through the same stuff you've been going through, so I'm not trying to do that." Stephen also echoes other residents who gain a sense of safety from their familiarity with the neighborhood. His description of the changes to the neighborhood if a few "knuckleheads" are removed parallels longtime residents' distinctions between a small number of bad people who cause serious problems and a much larger group who may get in some trouble, but who are not a serious threat (Leverentz 2012). Even when the crime and violence was more prevalent, according to Stephen, if you are from the area, you could move freely in it because you knew how to do so.

A few months after his release, Stephen began drinking again after his daughter was taken into Department of Children and Family custody. By our fourth interview, he was working in construction and trying to regain custody of his daughter. He described his neighborhood again: "The neighborhood is OK because I don't hang out in the neighborhood anymore. I walk to the store, or whatever, and I'll, say, shout to people, and I keep it moving. Because I try not to lose off of track. I show I ain't changed, say hi, and keep it moving. I'm busy, I've got something to do, this and that. A lot of people still be like, 'You're acting different, you don't chill no more, drinks and that.'... The neighborhood, basically, it'll be the same, but without me in it." Stephen's neighborhood is comprised of the social networks he has there. His daughter, who was staying with a foster family while he tried to regain custody, lived a few blocks away. Still, he was only allowed to see her at their regularly scheduled visits at the DCF office. He said, "They don't want me, I can't. It's like you'll get in trouble if we see you walking down there. I'm like come on, man, I've been on that street before the two of you moved in. I've got somebody I used to talk to right here that lives on the street, across. My cousin's aunt lives right there; you all want me to stay off this street, that's crazy." He spent most of his time alone or with family members. "I really spend most of my time in the house where I am more safe and comfortable. I got my own flat screen, my own DVD player, my own movies, and I can sit and relax and then ain't nobody messing with me and I ain't messing with nobody." Stephen's careful negotiation of his neighborhood is common, particularly among young Black and Latino men who were trying to stay out of trouble (Harding et al. 2019; Fader 2021). Stephen wanted to avoid distractions or temptations as he tried to find a job and avoid drinking or other forms of trouble. In addition to avoiding arrest, he was trying to demonstrate that he was a good father and deserved custody of his daughter. He maintained superficial relationships with others in the neighborhood but limited his involvement with others who were drinking or getting in trouble. As with Charles, the "negative" characteristics of the neighborhood itself were less relevant to Stephen than his ability to engage successfully with the people in it.

THE PERCEIVED STIGMA OF WHITENESS
IN DORCHESTER

Dorchester, particularly the sections I focus on, has a reputation of being a Black neighborhood. Overall, it is diverse, with sizable Black, white, and Asian populations. While there is more gentrification on the eastern (and whiter) east side of Dorchester, pockets of other areas, like Uphams Corner, had experienced a rapid rise of socioeconomic status of residents between 2000 and 2017.[3] The racial and ethnic diversity of Dorchester and demographic changes meant that racial dynamics were a common topic. For those returning from the House of Correction, race was a prominent topic among the white men and women with ties to Dorchester.

Kevin, a white man in his 20s, spent some time in a Dorchester sober house when he was initially released from the House of Correction. He grew up in a small town south of Boston. Prior to his most recent incarceration he had been staying in Harvard Square. He initially started spending time there after he got kicked out of several Boston shelters because of altercations and because "I have a big problem with authority." He described the appeal of Harvard Square in our first interview:

> I eventually gravitated there being homeless because homeless in Harvard Square is not even like being homeless really. Like, it's safe. To me, it's safe.... I remember staying nights on the street in downtown and you can't, you can't sleep. You have to worry about yourself all the time. And Harvard is not that way. That's why I gravitated there. Like, the homeless people there. The homeless kids there ... are like some of my best friends. Like, it's a close-knit society. Whereas, downtown, you fend for yourself. So, staying in Harvard Square and then coming to Boston to do all my stealing and stuff. Get my drugs and then go back to Harvard.

In our second interview, he was happily living in the Dorchester sober house. He said he had been to Harvard Square once, the night he was released, but he hadn't returned "because it's the same old bullshit out there and I don't want to be involved with it." While Kevin was having a good experience at the sober house, he described the neighborhood around it as "bad, real bad." When I asked him to elaborate, he said:

> The only white people in the neighborhood are the white guys in my house. Don't get me wrong, color doesn't mean everything, but it means a whole lot. Gang bangers everywhere, hoes walking up and down Blue Hill Ave all night. My street's a one way. You walk off my street and turn onto another little street that intersections with Blue Hill Ave. Right there at that intersection, there's two or three cop cars any time after dark with their blues going, just sitting in the parking lot waiting for something to happen. It's craziness. Little kids go to sleep with a lullaby; I can't go to sleep unless I'm hearing the sirens. It's crazy. We heard gunshots two nights ago. It's a part of life and I don't think anything of it, because even when I was using, it's part of the game. They're killing each other, so I don't care. If they're going around shooting innocent white people, then I'd have a problem, but they're killing each other. Go right ahead, that's how I look at it. As long as they don't bother me.

Kevin uses explicitly racist narratives, equating Black men with violence and justified victimization, and white people as potentially innocent victims. Even though he had engaged in many of the same behaviors he was criticizing, he aligns himself with the police not the policed. When he was living in Dorchester, Kevin said he was regularly stopped by the police "because I'm a white kid in a drug dealer neighborhood. . . . You pulled me over, I'm the only white kid within a ten-block radius from here, and you think I'm buying drugs." He said once they knew who he was, they stopped harassing him. "They know I'm clean, they know I'm in the sober house, they know I'm trying to do the right thing." This, he feared, drew unwanted attention to him in a neighborhood where being friendly with the police would be viewed with suspicion.

Several other white people exiting the House of Correction with ties to Dorchester similarly lived in shelters or sober homes there. They described their neighborhoods in similar terms as Kevin. For example, Melissa, a white woman in her 30s, spent two years staying at a Dorchester shelter, because "I didn't really have a choice. It was an income thing." She described it, as "terrible; it was dangerous and I shouldn't have been out after 5. . . . Chaotic . . . drug dealers, drug addicts, um, yeah, um pretty crazy. . . . Gang members. It's terrible." She was originally from a suburb and planned to move to another with her fiancé when she was released. She described this new area as "completely different. I mean, there's chaos everywhere you go. I mean, nobody's perfect. But I mean, there's a little bit more people, more functionable there." Melissa highlighted her feeling of physical danger when in Dorchester, which was more common (across place) for women than men. Men feared the police and attracting police attention, women tended to fear victimization, particularly when in public places.

Philip, another white man in his 30s, had lived in Dorchester for over a decade. The neighborhood he had been living in prior to his incarceration was "a good area. Dorchester's weird though, because you can start real nice, and then you can go to the middle of the ghetto like that. . . . People get the conflict of Dorchester, it's a bad area, because you hear the news, all the shootings all the time in Dorchester, but there's real nice parts of Dorchester." Like Kevin, he said he is stopped by the police "once in a while . . . because I'm a Caucasian male in a predominantly Black area. Most Caucasian, they said—I think it's racial profiling. Most kids that come in this area that are white are out here getting high or they're up to no good." Philip described the neighborhood saying, "It sucks over there. People using drugs, getting high. At the end of the day, it's my decision if I go and use." He distinguished between "citizens" who are "healthy, American citizen paying taxes" and "terrorists. . . . Yeah, they're ruining—Dorchester's a beautiful area, man. This used to be all Jewish, believe it or not, back in the sixties, and it was beautiful. They got everybody, just ruined everything." Philip highlights white flight as the start of the "ruin" of Dorchester. Nicholas, a white man in his 20s, grew up in South Boston, but had also been living in Dorchester prior to his incarceration. He described people there as "all different crowd of people. . . . It's just not as familiar [to me] and people think differently."

Kevin distinguished his attitudes about race in and out of prison. He said, "When I'm in jail, OK, I have to live a certain way to make sure people have got my back. Whatever. When I'm on the street, I'm a normal human being, I'm not going to not like you because of the color of your skin. I treat everybody the same." He told stories of doing small kindnesses for neighbors and fellow sober house residents and said, "I don't try to raise havoc where I live. Don't shit where you eat. I've always been told that. Even if I stick out like a red Christmas light in a bunch of white Christmas lights in the neighborhood, I'm still a part of that neighborhood, so I try to act like it." Still, he adopted many of the stereotypical narratives about race and crime. His experience with the police also was starkly different than how Black and Latino men described their experience with police.

Three months later, Kevin used drugs after a friend overdosed and died. "This morning, I took a drug test at my sober house, and I failed that. I knew I was going to. I had all my shit ready to go." Then, "I said I was going to the store, and I jumped on a bus and took off. I'm not bringing any of my stuff with me. They'll hold it there until my family picks it up." Kevin made his way to Harvard Square that day, and when I saw him later that afternoon, he didn't know what he would do or where he would go. He was once again ambivalent, with some friends encouraging him to keep trying to stay sober and others willing to sell drugs to him or use with him. Over the next six months, he went to Florida to stay with relatives and get additional drug treatment. When he returned to Boston, he was supposed to go to a sober house, but did not.

At the time of our fourth interview, he was staying with a friend in Quincy, just south of Boston. "We were homeless together like eight or nine years ago, and he got his shit together. I didn't. I used to live with him and his girlfriend years ago, and I hadn't seen him for like four years. He hit me up on Facebook. We started talking, and a week later, he said I could move in." He described the area: "It's nice, but I have a lot of problems in Quincy with the police and stuff years ago, so I don't go out of the house and walk around Quincy. I either get on the T, or I stay in." He said, "They [police] all know me in Quincy; it sucks. It's always going to be a problem. . . . They go above and beyond the line of duty to make my life a living hell there." Kevin's narrative of navigating Quincy is similar to that of Charles or Stephen's description of their life in Dorchester. For Stephen and Charles, however, being known to police created an extra layer beyond the inherent conspicuousness of being young Black men. Kevin only attracted police attention when he was known as an individual troublemaker. While he thought he attracted attention as a white man in a Black neighborhood in Dorchester, he also quickly came to be known there as someone "trying to do the right thing."

In our final interview, three months after the fourth and about fifteen months after our first, Kevin said he was "on an evil, evil tear right now. . . . Lots and lots of drugs." He had a falling out with the friend he had been staying with. "His place, it was like something [hanging] over my head, and I have no problem hitting the streets and I called his bluff. I said see you later. I have no problem running the streets. I mean it sucks now that I'm older, but it's not that big of a thing." Kevin's relationship to place paralleled others' in a few ways. He clearly reflected racist attitudes of some white respondents, which, for Kevin, were perhaps exacerbated by experiences in prison but not limited to that. He hinted at the ways he had to align himself with other white prisoners in prison.[4] Outside, he also adopted racialized narratives of "criminals." He associated his Dorchester neighborhood with gangs, crime, and violence, and accepted the need for the presence of police. His crime-ridden description of Dorchester was like that of many respondents, and he racialized these descriptions much like other white respondents. Yet Kevin also shared an orientation to his neighborhoods that was like that of many of his peers from the House of Correction, and some other residents of all three target neighborhoods. From Harvard Square to Dorchester to Quincy, he considered himself a part of the neighborhood. For him this meant engaging with others as neighbors. He frequented neighborhood stores and recognized people who worked in the store and who lived in the same area.

William, a white man in his 50s, grew up in South Boston but had been living in a southeastern (and mostly white) Dorchester neighborhood for a little over a decade. He was friendly with his neighbors, "I like being nice to people." He described his neighborhood as being "surrounded by cops and firefighters." A few months later, he said "My neighborhood's absolutely great. I mean that's why it's taken me so long to get out because I'm a little comfortable there and it's nice because it's all cops or firefighters. They call it 'my blue heaven' because it's only firefighters and cops, so there's no real crime. Everyone's 'hi, how are you?' Everyone with dogs on the street." After his release, he started taking classes at Roxbury Community College. He took public transportation to get there, rationalizing this choice, "I actually enjoy taking the T because it shows I'm putting in the effort to get to school. I don't know. I just think I'm getting more than experience out of it. . . . It's nice to interact a little bit with people, too. You know what I mean?" He described his classmates: "It's very diverse. It's crazy and I'm not saying this in a bad way, I'm the only white guy in all my classes. I understand now how they felt back in the sixties. As far as being the minority. All my teachers are minorities." In a later interview, he complained about his classes: "I hate to say it, but like every once in a while, over there I feel like there's racism going on because seriously in all my classes, I'm the only white person there and everything over there is geared to how Black people fit in America. What does it mean to be Black? Do Black lives matter? I get almost sick of hearing it because it's almost like I feel like they're teaching racism."

Both Kevin and William align themselves more closely with the police than most of the Black or Latinx people we talked to, particularly those who had been involved with the criminal legal system. They (sometimes) felt targeted, when they were known as individuals, but this was more tied to their past behavior or looking out of place. Kevin felt conspicuous as an outsider, but that quickly turned in to a "friendly" encounter. While it made him feel conspicuous among his neighbors, he no longer felt targeted for arrest. This was notably different from the Black and Latinx people (especially men) who felt targeted by police, either in general or in particular neighborhoods. Their experiences highlight one way in which people have varying experiences within the same neighborhoods, and how race intersects with place to shape people's experiences within neighborhoods.

LIVING OUTSIDE OF DORCHESTER

Rarely did anyone that we interviewed who had spent time in the House of Correction choose to leave Dorchester. There were, however, several that considered it home, though they did not then live there. A few respondents praised their new location because of the differences from Dorchester. Bruce, a Black man in his 30s, described himself, "I'm from Dorchester. . . . I'm the stereotype. I'm a six-foot-two criminal." [5] His most recent incarceration was a result of a fight with his girlfriend on Dorchester Avenue during the Dorchester Day parade. "The police claimed I shoved her; that was frivolous shit." He believed this arrest was, in part, because his girlfriend was a white woman. He said he prefers Cambridge to Boston. "It gives me peace of mind. I ride my mountain bike there—I'm known for that. I'm surrounded by kids. I don't want to be surrounded by violence. I've already played that role because I was moving like that. I used to be hardheaded. Changing my environment might help. There's a lot of peacefulness in Cambridge. It's cleaner. I ride my bike. I'm impressed with how they do. Everybody is together. They are trying to make something of themselves. They work out, they keep busy." In our second interview, he said, "There's a lot of resources [in Cambridge] if you utilize it properly. You can get a lot of stuff accomplished. But I've seen people get a lot of shit accomplished. But at times, this situation can get pretty stressful. Gets pretty tough."

Despite framing Cambridge as a fresh start in our first interview, he had a history of getting in trouble in Cambridge as well. Prior to his most recent arrest, he was staying in a tent near the Charles River. "I had a nice spot where I could lay my head at until I got my housing. I had a nice tent, set up in the woods. Nice, away from trouble. I get out of jail nine months, seven, nine months, and all my stuff is gone." While he considered the more remote areas peaceful, he routinely hung out in Harvard Square and was known to police in that area. Eight months passed between our second and third interviews, and when I finally reconnected with him (with the ongoing help of the sister he sometimes stayed with), I learned he had been detained in MCI-Concord. He said, "I can't be hanging around who I used to hang with. It's like relapsing. Every time I go to jail, it's because I keep hanging around these guys. The same people at Harvard Square. I am too old for that now. Cops know me very well out here." He described the two incidents, a few days apart, that led to his latest charges. "Again, hanging around the wrong group of people, down here in Harvard Square. Go to the river, these guys are drinking, they are smoking, and they are doing the typical weird stuff. This is all in the course of nighttime. Supposedly somebody got assaulted. Now I don't see anybody get assaulted." A few days later there was another fight. "I actually tried to de-escalate that. Before I could even tell my boy to chill out, don't even involve yourself, it was already too late. They were already across the street, they were already fighting and then I guess there was a weapon involved, a baton. I ended up getting injured because I tried to stop my boy from hitting this kid in his head, messed up my hand. Yeah." Bruce said the first case was dismissed, and he was planning to take charges related to the second case to trial, believing that the Commonwealth did not have sufficient evidence to convict him.

Bruce's relationship with his sister was tense. He initially went to her apartment, but when we met a week after his release, he was staying on the street after getting in a fight with her. He said, "She was treating me like some stranger and I'm telling her, I'm your older brother and I don't like you're saying stuff to me. . . . Like, 'Yeah, my landlord doesn't want anybody here unless they're on a lease. You gotta pay extra money.' I don't have no issue with paying the money, but it's how she went about saying it." Bruce's goal was to get an apartment in an elderly/disabled public housing building, because of his SSI benefits. After his second release, after his detention on the assault charges, he once again stayed with his sister. He stayed with her off and on for the three and a half months until our fourth interview, when he was staying with a girlfriend in Providence, Rhode Island. A few months later, he was back in Cambridge, because "it's just too much. My girl was bothering me, so I had to leave her. She's too much, she was aggravating." While he stayed with his sister off and on again, they were once again "not on talking terms." He stayed with a female friend and at a Cambridge shelter. He complained about people there:

> Then it being Cambridge. People are very judgmental out here. Think I've told you this before. They're judgmental, very ignorant, and they haven't hit rock bottom yet. . . . "Oh look at that Black dude over there, yeah he's scaring me.". . . Everything I own I buy. I don't steal people's bikes, I don't break into people's house. I don't rape people. I don't do none of that shit. But you're scared of me because you're fucking brainwashed from this fucking government. You're brainwashed, you're sick, you're scared because you live this perfect life. You had a farm, you had all these acres. Me, I lived in the ghetto. I lived in Dorchester my whole life. There was bullets. I was ducking and dodging bullets. My mentality level is different from anybody that's probably in here. You know what I mean?

Bruce liked the peacefulness of Cambridge when he found it. But he hung out with associates in Harvard Square, which regularly led to him getting in trouble. He was known to the police. Many of his complaints about

Dorchester—being in contact with gangs and violence and racist policing—he also experienced in Cambridge. He said, "Massachusetts plays the race card; Cambridge is known for that." Still, he maintained an identity of being from Dorchester and considered it home. His initial probation charges were in Dorchester District Court, which he preferred, "I think Dorchester Court is better for me anyways. A whole lot better. . . . Because I'm from Dorchester originally, and I just think it's more me. It's more appropriate for me. That's where the case originated from so." Bruce liked Cambridge precisely for the reasons he perceived it to be different from Dorchester. Yet he still felt like he was from Dorchester and felt a level of comfort in the familiarity of Dorchester similar to those who still lived there.

Cathy (Black, 20s) was more ambivalent about living in Dedham, the southwest suburb where her mom lived, which she found to be boring. She had lived in Dedham for about ten years but said, "It's a little too—it's not enough going on for me. There is only one bus that comes through there every hour. There's really no check-cashing places. One corner store, one gas station. It's not for me." She said Dorchester shaped her experience: "But then, at the same time, it's like, because a lot of people that grew up in Dorchester, we all have the same type of choices. People make different choices than other people because I've seen people that have grew up in Dorchester and made it out. I was just one of them people that what I seen is what I ran after. That's what was convenient at the time, you know. That's what caught my attention, really." One of her brothers had died, and another was sentenced to fifteen to twenty-five years in prison when he was 16. Her father was recently released from prison. After her release, she did go to Dorchester. "It was cool. I just like drove through. I chilled with a couple of people for a little while. It's still the same. I didn't miss nothing, nothing while I was gone. I heard it was a crazy summer. I heard about it all in the news. I heard about it all when I got home. Like my little brother's best friend, he got killed the two weeks before I got out. It's still the same how I left it, when I left." Over the next few interviews, she didn't mention Dorchester, but did talk about spending her time at home and with a smaller circle of friends and family. She was also working, first in a movie theater and then at a supermarket and cared for her son. She did want to participate in programming through College Bound in Dorchester but sounded less anxious to return.

For Bruce, Cathy, and others, living outside of Dorchester was necessary largely because that is where they had family with whom they could stay. Bruce also contrasted Dorchester, where he was known to police, to the more peaceful parts of Cambridge. Even so, he talked about a similar engagement with the police and with racism in both places. Both also highlighted their feelings of ambivalence toward being in Dorchester, with its crime and painful memories, and not being in Dorchester, with its history and familiarity.

CONCLUSION

A concentration of returning prisoners in high crime Black neighborhoods is often framed as a public policy problem. From the perspective of people who have been incarcerated, the assumption is that they are returning to criminogenic social networks and a lack of services and supports. For other residents, a high number of returning prisoners might pose a public safety threat and a drain on resources. The narratives of Dorchester residents, however, paint a more complex picture. Crime and violence are real concerns of all residents, including those who had been incarcerated. However, most recognize that violence is caused by a small number of residents and that many of their neighbors are hardworking and—at worst—neutral forces or minor inconveniences in the neighborhood. This includes people who may have been incarcerated. For the most part, long-term residents and residents of color embraced their neighbors and made efforts to be familiar. For many of those returning from the House of Correction, their connections in their neighborhood were bittersweet. They have long-standing contacts, some of whom may be connected to their offending pasts. These same people also may provide access to services and needed resources, and a comforting familiarity. They felt known and knew how to safely navigate the neighborhood.

While people had a sense of connection to Dorchester, living there is not always easy or trouble free. Residents contend with the possibility of victimization and the presence of social and physical disorder. People talked explicitly about race and racial dynamics. Residents of color identified their neighborhood as a Black neighborhood but were largely tolerant of their white neighbors. Newer white respondents were more likely to speak with trepidation about their Black neighbors. Young white gentrifiers, particularly women, also were conscious of being "outsiders," and largely oriented their lives outside the neighborhood. Those returning from the House of Correction are very conscious of a police presence and the common experience of racial profiling. White men who have been incarcerated feel conspicuous in predominantly Black parts of Dorchester. For them, white men in that area meant drug users. Formerly incarcerated white women, if they did not grow up in Dorchester, felt vulnerable to danger and violence.

For all, the various perceived dangers shape how they move about space and approach their lives in the neighborhood. For those who were trying to avoid surveillance or temptation, this often meant keeping to themselves and staying at home, thereby removing themselves from public spaces and from public life. Those who felt vulnerable to victimization (often young white women) similarly avoided being in public spaces, particularly at night or alone. For others, it was precisely being a familiar public face that made them feel secure in the neighborhood. Despite perceived dangers, many residents also expressed a commitment and loyalty to the neighborhood and to most of their neighbors.

FOUR

_____

The South End

RETURNING TO A "GENTRIFIED" NEIGHBORHOOD

There's always things to do. There's a lot of amenities, restaurants. It's a nice group of people to live around, so it makes me feel pretty safe despite being closer to the city. I like the architecture. The brownstones. It's very appealing. The streets have trees on them, brick sidewalks. There's something very conceptually or physically appealing about that. There's a great doggy day care which is part of the perks of it. Yeah, all those things. Nice perks amongst the living spaces.

JANE, white woman in her 30s

It's hard. They call it Methadone Mile. Because it's true. Everybody that's there . . . they're always out there, you know, me being one of them at one point last year. They're just like, 'I got pills, I got Johnnies, I've got Adderall, I've got Clonidine, I've got Klonopin, I've got Xanax, I have Suboxone.' So, try and stay sober. It's extremely hard unless you've got someone to support you.

AMANDA, white woman in her 30s

NOT SURPRISINGLY for an economically bifurcated and racially and ethnically diverse neighborhood, there is substantial variation in how people view life in the South End. Most value the neighborhood's central location in the city. Beyond this, their experience of the South End as a neighborhood is dramatically different. There are at least two primary groups of residents in the South End: higher-income residents who are largely white, and lower-income residents who are largely people of color. Within these broad groups, members recognize key intragroup distinctions that might be less obvious to outsiders. These groups, and how they engage with their neighborhood and with each other, illustrate some of the social processes through which neighborhoods matter. Individuals interact with their neighborhood in ways that reflect both personal and place identities. In the South End, we can see what "diversity" means from people who are positioned in different social locations in the neighborhood. The groups have cognitive maps that correspond to their framings and engagement with the neighborhood. These varying experiences and neighborhood frames also have led to different groups contesting control and access to the neighborhood.

The South End has a well-established reputation of being diverse and of welcoming diversity. Some of the wealthier residents embrace this identity, and have some tolerance for public housing, shelters, services, and those who use them. They see these residents and clients as part of the fabric of the neighborhood, along with beautiful architecture, restaurants, and parks. They typically do not have close relationships with their less-advantaged neighbors, but they believe they are an important part of the neighborhood, and their existence is part of the South End's appeal. Newer higher-income neighbors often do not share this perspective on diversity with the longer-term residents. Instead, they focus on the style and amenities of the South End. When they do praise diversity, they highlight the early gentrifiers (e.g., gay men) more so than their poorer neighbors. These new wealthier residents view the poorer sections and areas with larger numbers of people of color and neighboring Roxbury, which is described as the "heart of Black culture" in Boston, as places to avoid. Earlier gentrifiers criticize this perspective as placing more importance on financial investments than on the people in the neighborhood. Lower-income residents and residents of color emphasize the importance of social relationships for their sense of place and define the South End in these terms rather than its architecture or entertainment value. Many highlight the negotiated coexistence of law abiding and criminally involved neighbors, while others describe the neighborhood as bad and dangerous. The latter group includes most of those interviewed, because they had served time at the House of Correction. Their main frame of reference was the House of Correction, along with the Pine Street Inn, the Southampton Shelter, or any of the several methadone clinics and halfway houses in the area.

From the perspective of prisoner reentry, the South End holds promise. Many of the services needed by people exiting a correctional facility are nearby. There are several homeless shelters, halfway houses, and residential programs in and adjacent to the South End. There are also several methadone clinics, for those struggling with opiate addiction, and other programs targeting people who are homeless, experiencing addiction, or who were formerly incarcerated, along with the public hospital. All these services are located in a central location that is accessible to public transportation, is not socially or physically isolated, and is not in a neighborhood of concentrated disadvantage. It is not the stereotypical neighborhood disproportionately impacted by incarceration (e.g., poor, Black), and yet it has services needed by many who have been imprisoned. This convenience, however, is tempered by a dystopian description by many of the users of those services. It was often those returning from the House of Correction who described the neighborhood in the most negative terms. With a concentration of methadone clinics, for example, comes people eager to take advantage of clients by selling them drugs. Shelters with behavioral restrictions on residents and limited hours means people hanging out near the shelters and sometimes sleeping nearby. According to their descriptions, there is little that the neighborhood offers beyond those of neighborhoods of concentrated disadvantage, but the joint presence of a concentration of services and high-income residents can give it a heightened level of social control.

HISTORY AND DEVELOPMENT OF THE SOUTH END

The South End was first developed on former marsh land, beginning in the 1850s. Because of building size and material restrictions, this early development consisted of similar-looking single-family rowhouses.[1] A few decades later, after wealthy residents moved to nearby Back Bay, working-class rooming houses were built and many of the rowhouses were turned into lodging houses (Boston Landmarks Commission 1983; Mollenkopf 1983). Boston City Hospital (now Boston Medical Center) was built in 1864.[2] Both small businesses and factories were present before it became a residential area and grew in number as the area declined in social status. Boston's first settlement house, the South End House, was established in 1904 (Boston Landmarks Commission 1983).[3] From its early days, the South End was diverse in both population and land use. The first (and short-lived) attempt to restore the South End began shortly before the Great Depression. Between 1950 and 1960, the South End's population fell by almost half and went from 74 percent white to 60 percent white. Most who left in this period were elderly single white residents, Black families, and working-class white ethnics (Mollenkopf

1983). Still, the location and housing stock meant it was prime for redevelopment (Mollenkopf 1983).

Unlike the wholesale destruction of Boston's West End (Gans 1982), the South End resisted the city's attempts at urban renewal. Several groups, including "activist white ministers influenced by Saul Alinsky, Black social workers employed at United South End Settlements (USES), poverty program employees, Puerto Rican community organizers, and ideologically motivated white young professionals" worked together to oppose the redevelopment plan (Mollenkopf 1983: 184). Together, they had extensive networks among South End residents. Three public housing developments were built during this era, but much of the existing streetscape remained. Preservation and gentrification began in earnest in the 1960s, but public housing and social institutions remained. The Pine Street Inn, the largest provider of services to homeless people in New England and located in the northeast corner of the South End, was founded in 1969. In 1983, the South End was designated as a landmark district (Boston Landmarks Commission 1983). At the same time, this activism might also have deepened conflict between middle-class and lower-income groups (Mollenkopf 1983).

In *Villa Victoria*, Mario Small (2004) imagines how a first-time observer would perceive the South End:

> I reminisced about what I had witnessed over the past few years, picturing the red brick walkways and cobblestoned streets, brownstones, townhouses, and ten-story housing projects, children on bicycles, elders with candles, and the yuppies, blacks, *boricuas*, and b-boys whose lives and daily rhythms I had studied and recorded in my notes. Above all, I remembered the South End as a street, as one particular street: Tremont, the main thoroughfare running the length of the neighborhood. There was hardly any aspect of the neighborhood's culture, landscape and people one could not witness on Tremont; the street epitomized the neighborhood. What first impression, I wondered, might an observer have of Tremont Street, in particular? No doubt it would seem, to many, like the most integrated mile in America (15).

Not surprisingly, a few pages later, Small adds, "But, like many first impressions, this vision of the South End is misleading," because it masks the social segregation and isolation of the Puerto Rican community in the Villa Victoria development (2004: 18). Writing over twenty years earlier about another South End public housing development, the pseudonymous "Dover Square," Sally Merry wrote, "Dover Square is a neighborhood of contrasts," describing

Chinese, Black, white, and Puerto Rican residents, each of whom had their own standards of behavior and their own "distinct attitudes about other groups, about crime and who is responsible for it, and about solutions to the crime problem" (Merry 1981: 24). The diverse population and architecture masks a reality that includes social isolation and segregation among different neighborhood groups (see also Mayorga-Gallo 2014). Still, the impression of the South End as a vibrant, diverse, and accepting neighborhood holds and remains an important part of its neighborhood identity (Tissot 2015). The report calling for the designation of the South End as a historic district based its recommendation not only on the architectural significance as the "largest essentially intact Victorian row house neighborhood in the nation," but also "its social significance as one of the most racially, ethnically, and economically integrated communities of its size in the nation" (Boston Landmarks Commission 1983: 18). Both the social and physical dimensions remain an important part of many South Enders' neighborhood identity.

ARCHITECTURE AND AMENITIES

Many of the South End residents we talked to describe the neighborhood in terms of its architecture and its diversity. Andy is a white man who moved to the South End over twenty years ago because it was, at the time, affordable and he wanted to live in a gay neighborhood. Now, he likes the "community feel," noting a tree lighting that "reminds me of a Victorian Christmas when you walk up the streets and you see the brownstones and so forth." Newer middle- or upper-class residents describe it first in terms of its aesthetics and amenities: red brick rowhouses, with a rich tapestry of architecture, restaurants, and bars. Jane, a white woman in her 30s who has lived in the South End for three years and plans to stay there, described what she likes about the neighborhood:

> There's always things to do. There's a lot of amenities, restaurants. It's a nice group of people to live around, so it makes me feel pretty safe despite being closer to the city. I like the architecture. The brownstones. It's very appealing. The streets have trees on them, brick sidewalks. There's something very conceptually or physically appealing of that. There's a great doggy day care which is part of the perks of it. Yeah, all those things. Nice parks amongst the living spaces. Not as crowded as Back Bay. Yeah, it's nice.

Joe, a white man who has lived in the South End for eight years, similarly emphasized the neighborhood amenities. "It's very walkable. There's a lot of good restaurants, a lot of good things around. There's a lot of attractions. It's close to whatever you want to do. It's relatively close to transportation, but not so close that you get a lot of transient pedestrian traffic. Generally, interactions with everyone have been pretty good. I never really felt like I was—I felt like it was a nice area to be in." For people like Andy, Jane, and Joe, the South End is an attractive place to live. It paints a pretty picture, and includes nearby entertainment and amenities geared toward them. It compares favorably to other high-end neighborhoods in the city. They define "community" largely through the physical appeal of the area. People, to the extent they are mentioned, are part of the neighborhood aesthetic, not people with whom they have relationships. It's just inconvenient enough that not too many outsiders come through the area, but it is still accessible.

Often these residents talk almost interchangeably about people and things as they reflect what the South End has to offer. For example, Sally, a white medical student in her 20s who had lived in the South End for four years, similarly described the "feel" of different parts of the area both in terms of people and what the buildings looked like. In response to a question about this "feel," she said:

> SALLY: Sure. I think that, I mean honestly, it first comes down to just who the people are who are hanging out in the streets. Then also, the houses. Definitely there is, I would say this part of, the south part of the South End, has a lot of really nice brownstones, and also has a wealthy population. Also, primarily white, I would say. Then crossing over into the south of Mass Ave side, is definitely a lower socioeconomic side of people. I'd say primarily Black and Caribbean. Then there's some homeless shelters there. Just the, I think the housing changes immediately.

> INTERVIEWER: What does the housing stock look like over there?
> SALLY: It's kind of hard for me to even tell you. I guess there's more of a nondescript, big apartment buildings and lower income housing.

For Sally, both people and the physical infrastructure shape her sense of place. For her, Black and Caribbean people live in nondescript apartment buildings (and hang out on the street), and wealthy white residents live in pretty brownstones. The latter is the desirable, while the former is to be avoided when possible.

Massachusetts Avenue is a widely recognized boundary between the South End and Roxbury. This was occasionally contested when new developments were proposed or when crimes occurred. A renovation of the Alexandra Hotel on Massachusetts Avenue, for example, was initially designated by the city as a South End project and later amended to be in Roxbury.[4] Roxbury residents, on the other side of Massachusetts Avenue, objected to another hotel for naming itself the Residence Inn/South End, though it was located in Roxbury. These designations become important both in political terms, when residents of one neighborhood do not get notifications about development in another and when development signals neglect or gentrification to residents, as is a common tension between Roxbury and the South End. As one Roxbury resident noted in a news article about the Alexandra Hotel development, "The South End sounds different from Roxbury. . . . Roxbury has probably a bad connotation to it, because Roxbury is considered mostly Black and poor, and the South End sounds much more affluent."[5]

Interviewees also noted physical differences on either side of Massachusetts Avenue. Ronald, a Black man who had lived in the South End for over twenty years, said "I think for homeowners there is a perceived difference in the real estate value. For some people there is a difference in the perception of safety." Sally (white, 20s) described a medical student residence building just south of Massachusetts Avenue: "Kind of like this odd duck of a community of a bunch of medical students. Then, there's the CVS that's right there that attracts a lot of homeless people, and people who are definitely actively using substances and whatnot. Just definitely seeing the group of people who hung out on that block was completely different than people you'd generally see three blocks north." Sally felt less safe in that building, which "didn't have as much of a neighborhood feel. For sure there were times that I didn't feel safe walking around by myself. . . . I think just mainly being concerned for my safety, always having to worry about walking around with a backpack with a laptop in it, for example. It would make me a little bit nervous. I don't necessarily feel that way when I walk around the South End, really at all." Developing a sense of community based on what the area looked like—housing stock, signs of social or physical disorder—was a common response among relatively newer residents. And for Sally and some of her neighbors, the people were a key component of what the neighborhood looked like and how comfortable and safe she felt in it.

Jane (white, 30s) also used Massachusetts Avenue as the boundary between appeal and disorder, based on changing aesthetics and perceptions of social disorder. She said, "We don't really cross Mass Ave to—I guess there's no real attraction down there to walk that way. . . . Actually, going into the city there would be more stuff. It's also a little less safe on that side of Mass Ave. We don't really stroll to that part of town." When asked what made her feel less safe in this area, she said, "Well, there's a lot of people on the street. There's a lot of loitering. There's more open space that's not vacated that you'll see camps of vagrants, homeless people, etcetera, living around there. There's a lot of vacant lots, which has the same population that makes you feel a little bit less like there's going to be other people around you, so maybe it's not quite as safe." For Jane, the kinds of people she saw south of Massachusetts Avenue made her uncomfortable. In contrast, in her part of the South End, there is a "nice group" of people that makes her feel safe, including a "large gay men population, which is a very nice group of people to live with. They're very welcoming. There's a lot of art. It makes me feel safe." Again, Jane equates the physical aspects of the neighborhood (art) and the people (gay men), using both to describe what the neighborhood looks and feels like. In this context, the neighbors are not people with whom they have relationships, even superficially, but rather part of the aesthetics.

The focus on architecture as a characteristic appeal of the South End was highlighted primarily by people who could be classified as gentrifiers, and particularly among newer residents. In contrast, when Lisa, a 26-year-old Black woman who had grown up in Villa Victoria, one of the neighborhood's public housing developments, was asked to describe the physical appearance of her neighborhood, she started by describing it as "friendly and family-friendly." She, too, distinguished between the brownstones and larger apartment buildings, though she characterized the latter in more favorable terms: "Well, Dartmouth side is a lot wealthier. It's more brownstones. Meanwhile, once you pass West Dedham it's more housing complexes and so you'll have more of a mix of financial incomes and family situations. I do see a lot more families on the West Dedham side. Meanwhile, you might have some professionals or bachelors and bachelorettes on the Dartmouth side. I think also just because you have a lot of businesses when you just start going towards the Back Bay area and you're going to attract a different type of community." Lisa's description contrasted with many of her neighbors, highlighting the friendliness of people in the areas many described unfavorably. She emphasizes the presence of families and economic mix. The wealthier areas, for Lisa, sound *less* appealing, at least for her. Places like Villa Victoria house more families and friendlier residents.

Long-term white residents of the South End often emphasize the value of diversity and cross-racial and -class ties. Joan, a white woman in her 70s who has lived in the South End for approximately fifty years, said "one of the real values that our daughters have gotten from living here [is] they have a very sound assessment of what is dangerous and what isn't." She went on to relay a story of her daughter's friend wanting to cross the street when a young Black man approached them. Her daughter responded, "Don't worry about that. That's Eddie. I went to school with him." While many white urban residents rely on racialized stereotypes to assess danger (Quillian and Pager 2001; Sampson and Raudenbush 2004), Joan's daughter could better assess "real" threats. For these residents, knowing a diverse group of neighbors meant they did not rely on stereotypes to make judgments about safety. These relationships are not necessarily close, but they recognize people as individuals and as neighbors.

Jeremy, a white man who has lived in the South End for about twenty years, values the diversity of the South End, though he is also critical of it. He perceives less of a sense of community now than when he first moved there. When he moved in, "It was just different, and better, in the sense that folks would sit out on their stoop and talk to you. It was not always friendly, but it was certainly friendlier than it is now. It's changed as far as diversity. There's a lot less diversity." He thinks this reflects an influx of high-income white residents and perhaps a decline in "issues." "In the South End, there have, over time, been a lot of issues. That acts as a way to get people together, to kind of focus on, either it's crime, drug use, vandalism of cars was a very significant issue." Somewhat paradoxically, Jeremy believes that social problems gave residents a point of connection and a reason to come together. Absent that, they had fewer reasons to work together and so connected less. Beyond this, Jeremy recognizes an ongoing lack of engagement between people of different backgrounds. He said,

> That's the other thing about, even in this diversity, one thing: it's always a challenge, or disappointing, to me, is the folks that live here, even like myself, we don't really get to know some of the African American families. I think, before, maybe it would have been easier because they owned a building next to them. Now it seems like, and a lot of these folks are in subsidized housing where you don't really get that interaction, not because we don't want it, it just doesn't seem to happen. It just doesn't seem to flow, which is really unfortunate.

Again, Jeremy notices a change over time, partly reflecting an increased economic bifurcation of the neighborhood. The Black people he sees that still live in the South End live in subsidized housing, creating a greater social divide with wealthy homeowners, and those who had once owned homes or rented market-rate apartments had been forced out by increased gentrification.

Ronald, a Black man who had lived in the South End for over twenty years, also commented on change in the area since he had moved in.

> I think that there were a lot more people of color. It was much more working class and middle class. The *Globe* had done an article somewhere in the middle 90s about people in the South End talking about a stereotypical profile. The tagline was they get up and do their thing, go to their jobs, work, come home, may have a meal and then they go back out and they work again. It was a very activist neighborhood. People involved in the neighborhood groups and the political party, well the Democratic Party. Just involved in poverty work, anti-poverty work, human services work, all kinds of stuff.

Ronald notices changes similar to those Jeremy pointed out, and both attribute it to an increase in wealthy white residents, a decline in working- and middle-class residents, and a decrease in residents of color. Together, that means less social engagement, particularly across race and class lines. For a while, Ronald said, there was "genuine social interaction" among residents, "but in the past few years there has been a different kind of affluence among the people moving in. It very often feels like they're not really that interested in socializing or being neighbors." While people used to be friendly on the street, now "they just give you the up and down or turn their head. It's like, oh, OK." He still characterized the neighborhood as activist oriented and with a sense of community, although both were less true than in the past. Ronald noted a shift from "investment in the community" to "an investment in the property." Newer gentrifiers were more concerned with their property values than they were in their neighbors, which meant they were less interested in developing relationships with their neighbors, and they were less likely to work against displacement or welcome people who came into the South End to use its services.

Higher-income and professional residents of the South End are acutely aware of the presence of disadvantaged neighbors, including people experiencing homelessness and addiction and living in low-income or subsidized housing. Residents were divided on their views toward people who are perceived to be homeless or addicted to drugs, and their attitudes on these issues also became a touchstone to judge other neighbors. A number of long-term residents criticized some of their newer neighbors for their lack of tolerance for diversity. Sandra, a white woman in her 70s who has lived in the South End for fifty years, said, "I think there are two sets of people, the ones that care about appearances and the ones that care about people, primarily." Sandra puts herself in the latter group, as did many of the long-term South End residents. Like Sandra, Jeremy distinguishes between newer residents who paid "a million-plus dollars," who are less tolerant, and longer-term residents. He attributes this to a more "pioneering" attitude of the early gentrifiers, compared to "today it seems like it's more about money.... 'Did I invest in the wrong place? These drugs and people that are addicted walking down the street doesn't look good for my investment.'"

In talking about the visible presence of people who were using drugs in one section of the South End, Sandra said "What are they going to do? It really doesn't bother me. It bothers me that there's such a problem out there, right? . . . Now these people probably couldn't do anything to you if their life depended on it, right? . . . The only way you might have a problem is if you provoked them. I just don't see what's the—that's not a crime." These residents took pride in their diverse neighborhood and drew a sense of safety from their familiarity with it and the people in it. This familiarity is not only based on the years they have spent in the South End, but also on their orientation to it. Long-term residents continue to place value on diversity, including those who stayed in the shelters and used area social services. They recognize that some in the neighborhood struggled with addiction, but they did not fear them or want them removed from the neighborhood.

Others also recognized clear divides among South End residents. After a police-community meeting in 2013, I spoke informally with three police officers who drew similar lines between groups of South End residents. They attributed many of the resident complaints to tension between wealthy residents and homeless people and the people who came into the area to go to the methadone clinics. One resident association near the Pine Street Inn "gets it," they said, and have learned what is and is not an issue. Those who don't get it, according to the officers, are primarily newer wealthy residents who complain about the timing of delivery trucks and people loitering outside of the Pine Street Inn, and things "people should have been more aware and accepting of before moving into the area." They emphasized the few people that stress how much they paid for their condo and who therefore feel they should not be inconvenienced. More broadly, the officers noted that residents in these expensive condos and those in the housing developments often do not feel comfortable around each other and rarely interact. These divides were reflected in the meetings themselves, which often were tailored to subgroups. The meetings were typically defined by area (e.g., neighborhood associations), but even geographically contiguous areas or meetings that were neighborhood wide tended to draw a homogenous group of residents. Meeting attendance similarly shaped the agenda, issues of concern, and how they were discussed.

For residents who do "get it" and "invest in the community," tolerance included situations of negotiated coexistence, in which criminally involved residents and law-abiding residents knew each other and respected each other's space and place in the neighborhood (Pattillo-McCoy 1999; Browning 2009). This is like the perspectives of many of the residents in Dorchester, who valued a familiarity with their neighbors, even absent close relationships with them. Lisa, a Black college-educated woman in her 20s who had always lived in Villa Victoria, a housing development in the South End, believed that even the casual relationships she had with her neighbors would keep her safe.

> Luckily for me, hopefully I'm not deceiving myself, but I feel like those people who hang out on the corner—because I acknowledge their presence and I respect that. We're both humans. We both went to school together, so we came from the same place but we might have been given different opportunities. I feel protected. I'm not worried about something happening to me because they're around me and they know me and I acknowledge their presence and I'm not trying to be better than or not around, not scared of them, but it's just a matter of knowing where my boundaries are.

Lisa was not involved in illegal activity, but expected to be protected, or at least left alone, by those who were engaged in criminal activity, because of their shared history and relationships. This perspective on safety is paralleled by several of the long-time white residents like Joan and Sandra.

Timothy, a Black man in his 40s who also lived in the South End and had a history of selling drugs, reinforced Lisa's impression from his own perspective. He described his interactions with "people with careers," saying "I interacted with a few. I always kept my distance, because, like, what I did, I don't do it to hurt you. If I liked you, if I was doing something [illegal] at that time and I see you walking by I'd be like, 'Hey how are you doing? I'll talk to you later.'" He described the neighborhood as "college, hustlers, and you have business-like people that go to work every day." According to Timothy, these groups interacted, but did not have close relationships (unless they were in the same family). For both Timothy and Lisa, people who were criminally involved and people who were not could coexist peacefully and respectfully, and they need not fear each other (Pattillo-McCoy 1999; Browning 2009). Because they knew each other as individuals, at least superficially, and had a shared sense of the negotiated coexistence dynamics of the neighborhood, they knew who to engage when, and politely kept their distance when needed. Timothy avoided "people with careers" when he was involved in illegal activity, and Lisa trusted those who were criminally involved to do the same to her. The "people with careers" who were not as familiar or as comfortable with this negotiated coexistence, like Sally and Jane, may fear people like Timothy, but he did not see them as targets or as people to engage when involved with illegal activity.

Some residents were unaware of the smaller halfway houses in the area, as they blended in physically with the rest of the neighborhood and maintained a low profile. Those who were aware of them had few complaints, and several long-term residents spoke positively of them. Derek, a white man who had lived in the South End for twenty years, described one halfway house as "awesome neighbors. . . . In thirteen years, I've been here [on that street], there has not been a single negative incident and there's been numerous positive incidents." Derek cited the halfway house residents' willingness to help with snow shoveling, and the fact that they were often outside smoking and thus served as eyes on the street (Jacobs 1961; St Jean 2007). "They're always out [smoking]. We have never been a victim of burglary, although there's a lot of people around the neighborhood who have been a victim of burglary. Again, it's pretty hard to measure scientifically, but if I was going to commit a burglary and I knew there were people always there, maybe I'd go somewhere else. That's pretty unscientific, and it could be a coincidence, but you know, maybe it isn't." Aaron, another white man in his 40s who had lived in the South End for over twenty years, similarly described a women's halfway house as a welcome neighbor: "It's actually no problem at all. . . . They're perfectly fine and nice." A nearby men's halfway house is "a little sketchier because men are not as polite. So, if I were a woman, that would make me nervous." Aaron generally was not afraid of the men, outside of a few that looked both angry and fit. For both

Derek and Aaron, at worst the halfway houses occasionally had a disruptive resident, but this was balanced by others serving as friendly neighbors and as sources of social control.

While the larger shelters in the area tended to generate more complaints, at least the Pine Street Inn was also characterized as a neutral or welcome neighborhood institution by many residents. Joe, an eight-year white resident of the South End, described living near shelters: "The most public version of that is the Pine Street Inn. I feel like there are times where you see people around the Pine Street Inn that you're concerned about, but by and large I know in the house is quite a few people and I rarely see any people that I'm worried about from that area." Jeremy described area shelters: "For me, I think of the Pine Street Inn, which is pretty far from us, where we are now. I don't think there's ever been an issue. They do some great stuff. I think Rosie's Place, which is awesome. I don't really see a lot of negative things from that. I think that they're well run. I don't think we really have an issue." Sally (white, 20s), who noted her wariness of being south of Massachusetts Avenue, described the area further north as "it's not that bad, but sometimes walking by Pine Street Inn is a little sketchy." The descriptions of Sally, Joe, and Aaron are similar—generally finding the Pine Street Inn a fine neighbor, with an occasional unruly or impolite resident.

The criticisms that longtime residents had of neighborhood divides reflect common criticisms of gentrification—residents more interested in making a profit off their property than in developing a sense of community. Earlier gentrifiers were invested in the neighborhood's diversity and there was some engagement across race and class lines. The observations of Jeremy and Ronald parallel other critiques of multiethnic neighborhoods, in which white residents may express an appreciation for diversity, while maintaining their own power and privilege in the neighborhood (Mayorga-Gallo 2014). This is consistent with their tolerance of halfway houses and shelters—as long as residents of those institutions maintain a low profile, they are welcomed. If they grow too large in number or draw too much negative attention to themselves, that tolerance disappears. While this level of tolerance can be critiqued too (Mayorga-Gallo 2014; Tissot 2015), even that had declined in recent years. Newer residents mentioned diversity less often as a neighborhood virtue. Relatedly, Christopher Browning and colleagues (Browning et al. 2017b) found that residents of higher socioeconomic status were less likely to share activity spaces with neighbors of any SES, and that this pattern is particularly pronounced in neighborhoods of high income inequality. This is consistent with the patterns Jeremy and Ronald noted in neighborhoods like the South End. As the neighborhood became increasingly economically bifurcated, the higher-income neighbors spent less time engaging in the neighborhood. Together, these dynamics meant that newer wealthy residents appreciated what the South End offered in terms of aesthetics and amenities but were not invested in developing social ties among their neighbors or in maintaining diversity.

SOUTH END AS A SITE OF REENTRY

People we talked to who lived in the South End after serving time in the House of Correction usually stayed at one of the area shelters, sober houses, halfway houses, or public housing buildings. Not surprisingly, their descriptions of the South End were less romantic than wealthier residents' descriptions of brownstones, restaurants, and dog parks. Amanda, a white woman in her 40s, had begun using drugs about a decade earlier, and shortly after that started "catching cases." Most recently, she had been incarcerated on drug distribution charges; she had been homeless and using and selling drugs when she was arrested. Upon her release, she had planned to go to a program on Long Island before the bridge closed. She said, "They actually had a bed for me, and then they didn't because the bridge to the Island went out. And so the sister house to them had to fill the beds up. That went out the window for me. I was counting on going there too." Amanda learned that her plan had fallen through four days before her release.

Shortly before her incarceration, Amanda had been romantically involved with a woman who also had a drug addiction, and who "put me through hell." She then was "talking to" a man who had recently been paroled. She described their relationship:

> I'm not in love with him. He actually had put a restraining order on me, I guess in order to keep his housing. Because I received a restraining order in the Bay [House of Correction]. I spoke to him. I'm like, "You put a restraining order on me?" I'm like, "I've never touched you or threatened you or anything." He's like, "No, the building didn't want you here, so in order for them not to evict me, I had to." I was like, "Oh, OK." By the time I got out, it was off. It was only a ninety-day one or something, and when I got out, I had called Larry [another old boyfriend], and he was like, "Honey, I have my own place. Come home."

When Amanda was first released, she went to a drug treatment program in the South End and called her friend Darryl, telling him, "Listen, I have nowhere to go. Is there any way I can come and stay with you for a few days?" A few days after that, she got Larry's phone number from her sister. He told her, "Come home. You need to come home." This is how she came to live in a public housing development in the South End. Amanda's housing instability, and her dependence on friends and romantic partners for housing was common for both men and women. Sometimes, like with Amanda, this meant the rapid development of a relationship and cohabitation. In Amanda's case, she and Larry continued to live together for the seventeen months I followed her. For others, the rapid development and dissolution of these relationships also often led to the need to find a new place to stay (Desmond 2012a).

Amanda had begun using drugs again upon her release, and between our third and fourth interviews, she was charged with stealing a pair of sneakers. The combination of a new criminal charge and a "whereabouts unknown" probation violation led to her being reincarcerated for five months. Still, her boyfriend Larry "really stuck by me, you know; he was there faithfully every weekend. Always made sure I had money on my books." After her release this second time, she was nervous, "being born and raised in Boston, just knowing everybody is hard." Still, "you know what, no matter where you go in life, you bring yourself with you, so like, when I made a move at one point in my life, it was years back. I went all the way to Florida. . . . I felt like I had never been out of Massachusetts, so being in Florida to me, at that point, I felt alienated from the whole world." Amanda was nervous about being in a familiar environment, which for her was the entirety of Boston, but she had also experienced the strain of being in an entirely new area. Amanda returned to Larry's apartment in the South End and started going to a nearby methadone clinic. She described her own challenges navigating the area, amid the drug selling, and said, "So try and stay sober, it's extremely hard unless you have someone to support you."

The methadone clinic was about a mile from their apartment. She often walked when she did not want to wait for Larry but got a ride from him when she could, because "I don't like really being in the area too much." In our final interview, she described her biggest challenge: "Honestly, it's always to make it from the clinic to my house without anybody harassing me with, 'Do you have Benz? Do you got Beans? Do you got Phenergan? Do you have any Johnnies?' I'm so sick of that. . . . Some kid today kept asking me and I just freaked out and called him [Larry] and I'm like, 'I really need you to come and get me.' It's crazy nonsense." While she used to spend more time "hanging outside with people," this time, she said, "I don't hang out. I don't give the cops no worries. I don't give them no reasons to bother me at all. . . . It's crazy. That's why they call it Methadone Mile, because it's true. Every person—not every, but a really good amount of people that are not only on the clinic, but they're homeless, so like, I don't know. I just know I'm doing OK. I'm betting on me and that's what matters the most right now." Even though Amanda lived about a mile from "Methadone Mile," this was her primary reference for the South End. Much of her experience with the neighborhood was centered on either the drug dealing or the drug treatment in the area around the Boston Medical Center and the methadone clinics. In her descriptions of the neighborhood, this is what, and who, she noted. She never brought up gentrification, the aesthetic appeal, or the diversity of the South End. For her, it was her apartment, a series of temptations and hassles, drugs, and drug treatment. In this final quote, she also referenced her knowledge of police surveillance near Methadone Mile. She was regularly harassed by people looking to buy or sell drugs, but also, she could easily be arrested.

Pablo, a Black man in his 50s, was unstably housed in the year and a half I followed him, though he was both directly and indirectly connected to the South End through much of it. After his release, he divided his time between the Boston Common and a Long Island shelter. While he didn't mention it, this likely would have had him passing through the South End, as the bus to and from Long Island dropped people off in the South End, and Boston Common was a mile and a half up Tremont Street. He described the appeal of the Common, "Sometimes I stay out all night, panhandle, hang out with the college kids. Have fun. 'Cause they're, I mean, they're pretty friendly. But they just like to get drunk and have fun all the time. It's like school doesn't exist for some of them."

After this first post-release interview, it took me a year to find him again, once again in the House of Correction. "I was scared too, you know, how addicts hide. That's what I was doing. Hiding from the world." He described the past year, "I got out. Instantly relapsed. Picked up two or three new charges—shoplifting, credit card scams, jumping over turnstiles in the T stations. I had a confrontation with my PO [probation officer]. I wasn't even under the impression I was under probation." He went into a twenty-eight-day drug treatment program, and then, "I hooked up with my girlfriend. Old associates. I'm thinking I can save her now. . . . Within seven days, I'm using. I'm drinking. I'm putting needles in my arms and smoking crack. Soon after that I stopped reporting to probation. I picked up two new charges. Shoplifting and disorderly out of Macy's. Now I'm on the run again. I'm doing all these shoplifting trying to make the outside look good. Like an apple, you see a shiny apple but it got a worm in it. On the inside, I was no good." During this time, he and his girlfriend were "bouncing," staying in cheap motels and renting rooms and avoiding shelters.

When Pablo was released for the second time during this study, he stayed briefly in a halfway house on the edge of the South End. He left there to stay with his girlfriend, who then had an apartment in a public housing building in the South End. "I hate to say it, but women have that effect on men sometimes. Nothing else matters but her." While he described the halfway house as "cool," it also had restrictions: "You know how we find stuff wrong with stuff that is good for us? I just made a rash decision and didn't think about it and I wish I did now." He described his relationship with his girlfriend as "rocky," and they drank and used drugs together. He said, "I know for a fact I can't be with her because too much of my past is involved." While he was conflicted about these choices, he was ashamed to ask for help or to admit he needed it. The director of the halfway house had tried to talk to him to make sure he was making the right decision, but Pablo avoided talking to him "'cause right now, the guilt, the shame."

For our fourth interview, Pablo and I met in a coffee shop in the South End, a few blocks away from his girlfriend's apartment. He originally suggested meeting near Boston Common, where we had met earlier, but said he was trying to avoid his old associates. He then told me, "The reason I was kind of funny about this area, did you see the homeless? This is a bad area for the homeless." When I asked Pablo to describe the South End, he asked me if I'd read the Metro section of the paper. He went on to describe it:

South End is exploding in the city over the violence. It starts from the projects I live in and comes down. Young people showing off, don't know how to deal with nothing, so they try and show off. When I was young, we played basketball, football. That's the way we took all our anger out was sports. I know that ain't even cool, but to be honest, it's exciting. You ever play PlayStation or Xbox? It's like watching an action movie. Sometimes that controls the little part of us. I don't understand it, but that's how it makes me feel sometimes.

Pablo suggested that young people are violent in the streets, rather than taking their aggression out through sports or video games. He went on to describe the area as "very scary. If young kids don't know you, they'll disrespect you or test you. I tell her [his girlfriend] all the time, after ten, eleven o'clock, we ain't going out if we necessarily have to. You stay off the streets after hours." He admitted that some of his information was coming from recent news coverage of area shootings. Still, this was a starkly different description of the South End as presented by most of the other residents we talked to.

Others who had been in the House of Correction and had formerly lived in the South End described it in similar terms. Sharon, a Black woman in her 40s, had been living in a suburb for a number of years, but grew up in the South End and lived there into her 20s. She described the South End as "busy, loud, and you always have to be careful. You know? Umm, you know, usually there's you know, little gangs, all the shooting. You know what I mean? There's a lot of, a lot of bad stuff that happens, you know. And it happen to anybody." Contrast Sharon's description with those of Timothy and Lisa in the last section. Sharon had not been perceived as a "person with a career" and so lacked the protection that Lisa felt. In Timothy's characterization of the neighborhood as "college, hustlers, and people with careers," the House of Correction population overwhelmingly fell into the "hustler" category, regardless of their current behavior or goals. This shaped their perception of and experience in the neighborhood.

While few of those leaving the House of Correction uniformly praised the South End, some did highlight benefits of being there. James, a white man in his 40s, who lived for a few months in the same halfway house referenced by Derek above, described the area similarly, "The area here is flooded with, I don't know if you've seen the people out there by BMC and McDonald's, it's a drug zone." Still, he said,

> I love being in this area. I couldn't ask for, this is where I'd rather be out of any other place. Convenience, everything is all brick around here. It's the perfect time of year that I plan on looking for a job [as a mason]. See job sites going around here going on. . . . It's easier than being out—I've been in many programs. I was in North Cottage before, which is in Norton, Mass [about forty miles from Boston]. I asked to be transferred . . . because it wasn't—It's nice out there and stuff, but there's nothing. I have no [driver's] license. I have no license. If I drive, I'm fucked. I have a T pass and I get around that way. In this area, it helps in a lot of ways. It can hinder you if you make the wrong decisions, quite easy. If you do the right thing, it's going to help.

James also had a history of addiction. He relapsed and was reincarcerated later, after he left the South End. (See chapter 2 for more on James's trajectory.) He recognized the temptations of the South End, but these were outweighed by the benefits of being centrally located and in an area where he could find work.

Similarly, Adam, a 40-year-old Black man who was planning to live in a South End shelter when he was released, described the area as "an alright neighborhood to me." He said, "It's not the neighborhood, it's the people in the neighborhood, you know?" For Daniel, a Black man in his 20s, the people were also the appeal of the South End. In his case, he knew the area through an ex-girlfriend. He described it, "It's cool, chill. There's nothing too big because my ex-girl, she's living in the South End. She still does. It's a nice little area. Everything's close. Everything's around there. It's going to be hard living there because you've got to save a lot of money living there." Even these more neutral descriptions differed from most of the other residents' descriptions. James and Adam both emphasized their own agency in getting into trouble, or avoiding it, rather than the influence of the neighborhood itself (Leverentz 2010). For James, convenience trumped any negative aspects. Daniel referenced the cost of living in the South End, which was as close as any of them came to acknowledging the wealth around them. Their frame of reference was still primarily the "hustlers," drugs, and their ability to navigate them.

A history of drug use and addiction was extremely common among the formerly incarcerated men and women interviewed. Many were familiar with the South End and the area around it, even if they had not previously lived there, because of the methadone clinics, shelters, and the public hospital. Several people talked about the value of distance and quiet that Long Island afforded them, but this was also temporary, where they could go for treatment and not be expected to work or meet other needs independently while they were there. For those staying at the shelter on Long Island, they needed to take a shuttle bus there each morning and night (which ran from the South End). As will be elaborated on in chapter 6, permanently living in a quiet area was sometimes seen as beneficial, but also isolating and cumbersome. Few had cars or driver's licenses, and their work opportunities were limited outside the city. Rarely did anyone talk about a relocation to a distant town or suburb in wholly positive terms. For those who moved after release, they typically believed the distance from old networks was useful for them, but it also led them to feel lonely and isolated, and added to the challenge of meeting their needs. Neighborhoods like the South End were much more convenient, for better and for worse.

Notably, the broader group of residents of the South End were all aware of the neighborhood's economic bifurcation and mentioned both lower- and higher-income residents and people who came into the area to go to the clinics or to buy or use drugs. Their attitudes ranged from tolerance to fear, but all mentioned the range of residents, while also describing the South End in terms of the architecture, restaurants, and amenities. The lower-income people were part of the cognitive maps of the wealthy residents of the South End, and vice versa. In contrast, the people who had recently left the House of Correction focused their descriptions on the lower-income parts of the South End—the public housing, the shelters, and the halfway houses. They described the South End in dangerous and negative terms (e.g., drug zone, war zone). Rarely did they mention the higher-income residents, or the housing stock or other amenities—in positive, negative, or neutral terms. They rarely mentioned the value of the neighborhood in the same terms as their wealthier neighbors, but they also did not mention feeling stigmatized or judged by those neighbors. This contrasts with those with ties to South Boston (see chapter 5), who felt like the old neighborhood had changed too much for them to be welcome. In this sense, they benefitted indirectly from the diversity of the South End. For the most part, however, in many ways the presence of their wealthy neighbors was irrelevant to them.

CONTESTED TERRAIN: POLICING THE SOUTH END

Recent changes in the South End challenged the tolerance of even those most invested in a "diverse" South End. The growing class differences between Black and white residents created a barrier to interaction. In addition, many noticed an increase in the population of people they perceived to be homeless and/or addicted to drugs. Many attributed this to the closing of Long Island in 2014, and the creation of a new shelter on Southampton Street, adjacent to the House of Correction, in early 2015. Even those who praise the diversity of the South End complained about these changes and the effects they have had on the neighborhood.

There has long been some tension between residents and homeless populations in the area. The buses that took people back and forth to Long Island picked up and dropped off people in the South End, ensuring the presence of homeless people in the area during the day. In addition, while many residents respected the Pine Street Inn, the area around it was a common site of resident complaints about loitering. Sometimes, there were also ripple effects of controlling the homeless population in Boston Common, about a mile and a half up Tremont Street. This issue came up in a police-community meeting from 2007. In field notes, I wrote:

> One of the other officers mentioned the effect that clearing the Common has had on the homeless population around there [South End]. For the past two months, police have been clearing all homeless out of the Common, and so some have come to the South End, and are panhandling. He said they have to go somewhere, and many are being pushed to the Back Bay, so "We push back." He said there is no solution to the homeless. A resident asked why exactly they were being pushed out of the Common. He said there was bad publicity, particularly over their drug use and drinking.

The same issue came up at another meeting a few months later, when residents asked about a "clean up" effort in police district A1 (downtown, including Boston Common) focusing on people who used drugs or were homeless. A resident described this as a "whack-a-mole game." The closeness of the House of Correction was also a concern. An officer at a 2009 police-community meeting, as I recorded in my notes, said "that it's hard to keep up with everything because people are constantly being released from South Bay [a common name for the House of Correction]. He said that South Bay acts as a meeting and training ground for people who then return to society with new tricks and ideas. He laughed, though, saying that they are getting advice from people who were caught and locked up, so they can't be too bright to begin with or expect to get away with anything for too long." The presence of addiction, homeless services, and the House of Correction ensured the presence of those who used the services or who were incarcerated in the House of Correction. In addition, there is an interdependency between the South End, downtown Boston, and Long Island.

Some of the boundary maintenance that residents engage in reflects a physical segregation of services and higher-end housing, restaurants, and retail. This wasn't exclusively so, however, with some halfway and sober houses interspersed along a residential stretch of Massachusetts Avenue and the Pine Street Inn in the northeast section. At the same time, while some of the halfway houses were welcome neighbors, many considered Massachusetts Avenue the boundary of the South End. Derek (white, 50s), for example, described the area on the other side [referencing the southeast section on a map]: "This area should be my neighborhood, but I never go there unless I go to a meeting or something because it's unpleasant and dangerous." He went on to describe the people there:

> There are a lot of people who look like . . . this may be subjective and pejorative but look like they don't belong here. Or they look like I don't want to deal with them. It isn't because they're homeless. There used to be homeless people. . . . When I moved here twenty years ago, there were some homeless and it was getting better but there were the same people there every day. You got to know them, you said "Hi" to them; they said "Hi" to you. It wasn't an issue. It isn't that they're homeless, these people just look like they're disoriented zombies, if you will. I'm not going to use political correctness, so you can understand what I'm saying. They look like they're zombies, in some cases they look like maybe they want to attack you or mug you or harass you for money even if they don't mug you, just make it uncomfortable for you to just walk down the sidewalk.

Much like the users of those services, residents of the South End also recognize the changes that resulted from the closing of the Long Island bridge. Kathy, a white woman in her 50s who has lived in the South End for two and a half years, said, "It's becoming a huge problem since they closed the Island. The amount concentrated down on the lower South End is massive." Derek emphasized that the users of the methadone clinics and other services were not all residents of the neighborhood, and that those that were there now were "messing up the fabric of the neighborhood." Sally (white, 20s) similarly described "people who definitely don't look like they fit in. They're disheveled looking, they look like they used to use or are still using substances, I guess. Just profiling." A number of residents noted recent changes during the interviews, with an influx of more homeless people and an increase in people who looked high. Some of them were careful to distinguish this new trend, both in volume and kind, from the previous homeless population, whom they welcomed.

The connections of people with a history of offending and incarceration to Pine Street Inn, Long Island, and public housing developments was a common reference in the police-community and resident association meetings, mostly attended by higher-income residents. These earlier field notes demonstrate that the House of Correction, shelters, and services have long been a source of tension in the neighborhood. This grew after the closing of the Long Island bridge and the opening of the Southampton Shelter. After this, there was a noticeable increase in the visible presence of drug users and seemingly homeless people in the southeast corner of the South End. An area convenience store closed in 2017, described in the *Boston Globe*, under the headline "Store at epicenter of Boston's addiction problem closes." The article explains "the store struggled under a persistent throng of people loitering outside—some seeking treatment, but others deep in the throes of addiction or dealing drugs to a captive market."[6] Others noted the presence of people loitering in front of a hotel in the same area and frequenting a nearby McDonalds. Much of this was concentrated in the southeast corner of the neighborhood, but residents also complained about it filtering throughout the neighborhood.

Aaron (white, 40s) talked about some of the changes he perceived. When he first moved to the South End, he described his area: "My experience in the early '90s of this part of Mass Ave were boarded up places. Our building was kind of burned out. . . . And it was really shitty. The sidewalks were trashed. The buildings were still kind of somewhat boarded up, but more people were living there; particularly on Harrison [it] was really decrepit. But the liquor store was there." Black men frequented the liquor store near his house. Even now, he described his own part of the South End relative to the "fancy" part farther north. He criticized the "good ol' boys' club" that determined the location of the new shelter, "the fact that they put the homeless shelter, closed Long Island and put it right there without asking anybody who lived right here." He suggested locating new services in City Hall Plaza instead, where politicians would see the effect. Now, the homeless people in the neighborhood are drug addicts, not the alcoholics of the 1990s: "Well, so back in the day when, and I say, I wish Liquor Land was there because I miss the nice little drunk Roxbury men, who were harmless and it was the same people. Now, it's—they're basically all white. It's all white. It's like, to generalize, it's the Southie trash. There's a look. I can tell the drug addicts now from the drunks. There aren't drunks anymore." Aaron also believes that these addicts came from outside the neighborhood—South Boston, but also Lynn and other nearby working-class towns. He notes three changes: the people who came to Liquor Land tended to be Black men who were there regularly. In contrast, now, there is an apparently transient group of white people who are addicted to drugs (most notably heroin and other opiates).

Tensions came to a head in the summer of 2019.[7] On August 1, an out-of-uniform deputy sheriff (CO) was assaulted through the window of his parked car while he was on his way to work.[8] He then exited his car and fought with several people on the street. A Correction Officers Union representative was quoted saying, "The Local is outraged that the mecca of crime within the city of Boston has been brought to our front door with disregard for anyone else's safety." A few hours later, the police executed a sweep of the area. They did the same the following night, arresting a total of thirty-four people. A *Boston Globe* article categorized the tension as a reflection of "the contrasts of urban life."[9] Residents complained about the heightened numbers and wider reach of homeless and drug-using people in their neighborhood. While they had been concentrated nearer Boston Medical Center, residents said they had spread farther into the South End. The president of an area neighborhood association said, "From our perspective, this is new. The intensity of what we're talking about is new."

While the mayor and the police claimed the targets of the sweeps were those engaged in drug selling and violence, most were arrested on charges related to drug possession or old warrants.[10] Nine were arrested for drug dealing, eight for drug possession, and eighteen for outstanding warrants. Nearly half of those were for prior drug possession charges. One was charged with assault. The police commissioner claimed the arrests targeted those who were "preying" on people struggling with addiction and homelessness, and many were from outside Boston.[11] In contrast, the district attorney criticized the sweeps, tweeting that "People who suffer from homelessness, substance use disorder, or mental illness are not debris; they cannot be 'swept' away."[12] Advocates and service providers similarly criticized the sweeps. A worker with a harm reduction advocacy group stressed, "It is criminalizing people who have a substance use disorder, as well as people experiencing homelessness or [those who] are poor."[13] Others warned that service users were afraid to go to the South End to access services and were now either going without or traveling much farther to find them.

The heightened tension in the South End since 2014 reflects the same contested boundaries and contested acceptance of diversity that has long existed in the South End. Many middle-class and wealthier residents appreciate racial/ethnic and class diversity as part of the South End, but there are limits to what they will tolerate (Mayorga-Gallo 2014; Tissot 2015). Language around who belongs in the neighborhood and who does not has long existed, made easier with the long-standing connections between Long Island and the South End, which brought nonresidents into the South End, and the presence of the House of Correction, which released prisoners a few blocks away. Newer residents are often less invested in this narrative as part of "their" South End, and so resist all signs of social disorder. Changes in service provision, and how these have affected the South End, have united these groups to largely criticize the current state of the South End and to demand an increased police presence and a shifting of service away from the South End (Pittman 2020). Their justifications vary, from concern for themselves and their property values to a stated concern for the service users, who they believe would be happier and more successful farther south near Franklin Park or back on Long Island. The latter group is careful to reiterate that they still welcome diversity and *some* services but think the current level of services and the social disorder of addicted populations in the neighborhood has gotten out of hand.

CONCLUSION

By looking at the perspectives of people who are positioned differently within a neighborhood, we can begin to see more about how neighborhood context shapes the experiences of people returning from prison. The people who were returning from the House of Correction defined their neighborhood narrowly, in a way that only included the parts of the neighborhood they were more intimately familiar with. For them, their higher income neighbors did not warrant a mention, nor did the amenities that reflect the heavily gentrified parts of the neighborhood. Their descriptions focus on the drug use, homelessness, and violence. Positive aspects of the neighborhood are its central location and the ease of public transportation. In contrast, other residents highlighted both aspects of the South End—the gentrified South End and its amenities as well as the presence of drug users, people staying at shelters, and public housing. Their descriptions of the latter ranged from neutral tolerance or appreciation of the diversity of the neighborhood to fear, particularly of the poorer residents of color.

The two group of residents expressed different cognitive maps and activities spaces. From the perspective of the wealthier residents, the people they associate with the House of Correction, shelters, or methadone clinics also are often those most closely related to narratives around crime and violence. They are not invisible. They may be seen as groups to avoid or to benevolently tolerate, but they are visible and notable. In contrast, the wealthier residents of the neighborhood are generally not perceived as a danger or threat in the same ways that more disadvantaged residents are. Given that most of these wealthier residents are intentionally avoiding the areas where the more disadvantaged residents live, including those recently released from incarceration, those residents may largely avoid contact with their less advantaged neighbors. The people who have been recently released from the House of Correction mostly want to avoid trouble, and have little reason, or financial ability, to frequent the same stores or restaurants as their wealthier neighbors. While these residents may be more likely to call the police, they are not a physical threat and they are not stereotypically dangerous or scary. Other people at the methadone clinics or shelters pose a more immediate threat, and the social distance between them and their neighbors means that the wealthier neighbors do not register as an important part of their neighborhood. More limited mobility, because of reliance on walking and public transportation, also shapes their cognitive maps of the neighborhood, and their daily world, in narrower terms (Browning et al. 2017b). As Browning and colleagues (2017b) found, increasing socioeconomic status decreases the likelihood of sharing activity spaces with neighbors, and this is most pronounced in neighborhoods with high socioeconomic inequality. This dynamic is largely shaped by distrust.

Higher-income residents in the South End keep their distance from their lower-income neighbors and neighbors of color. This leaves those neighbors in a position where they can largely ignore their wealthier neighbors as being inconsequential to their lives and daily patterns. While this may be preferable to overt hostility, it also fails to provide opportunities to benefit from the resources of a higher-income neighborhood. There is little evidence that people returning from the House of Correction are benefitting either from the presence of a higher-income population, or from the concentration of services in the area. The former is largely invisible in terms of their narratives and experiences, and the latter is often described negatively. There is an element of convenience, as services are near each other, and they are located within an easy walking and public transit distance for many. At the same time, it puts them in close proximity with people who could also cause harm or stress. In addition, both the mixed-income context and the presence of social services bring the risk of increased targeting by law enforcement. Even using services is risky now, because of the sweeps, policing, and control efforts around the southeast corner, but also throughout the South End. As is common in "diverse" areas, this benefits the higher-income residents (largely through their sense of neighborhood identity), and not the lower-income service users, or those recently released from the House of Correction.

FIVE

South Boston

RETURNING TO A "WHITE" NEIGHBORHOOD

I think when we moved in, it was kind of like the Wild West. There were remnants of just old bar rooms and a lot of alcoholics and blue-collar workers. And, uh, salt-of-the-Earth kind of people, but it was just when busing started, so that kind of put another picture, another color on it. . . . And if you ever crossed over by the high school, you got the full taste of what it was like, and the hatred, and the vitriol.

CRYSTAL, white woman in her 70s

The '90s, drugs, cocaine was coming in big, heroin was coming in a little big. Also there was more drinking, there was more drinking with me. It was starting to change; it got a little bit more yuppie. A lot of people couldn't afford to live there anymore. A lot of people were selling to get out, and you know, I hate to call it white flight, but that's what it was. Everybody was moving to the suburbs. . . . South Boston is now all condos. I don't know how you can afford to live in South Boston anymore.

WILLIAM, white man in his 50s

DEPENDING ON ONE'S PERSPECTIVE, South Boston has a reputation for being proud and family oriented or racist and exclusionary. While South Boston was historically a largely white working-class neighborhood, with some pockets of wealthier residents, years of gentrification have maintained its whiteness while increasing the average family income. Except for several public housing developments on the western edge of South Boston, which house the majority of the people of color (mostly Black, Latinx, and Asian) and low-income residents of the neighborhood, the rest of the neighborhood is predominantly white and with a median income well above the city median. Today, among the more common complaints of life in South Boston are parking and ongoing development. Long-term residents lament the loss of family connections and an influx of wealthy and disengaged neighbors. Newcomers praise the local amenities, including beaches and new bars and restaurants, and a less exclusionary present.

Still, South Boston has recent ties to organized crime, drugs, and racial conflict. Particularly among those who had lived there for decades, these were acutely felt and a concrete part of their experience in the neighborhood. People continue to reference Whitey Bulger, a well-known gangster and FBI informant who grew up in the Mary Ellen McCormack public housing development in South Boston, his Winter Hill Gang, and area Bulger landmarks.[1] In addition, court-ordered busing of students between (white) South Boston and (Black) Roxbury, and the subsequent riots protesting this busing, were frequently mentioned touchstones of those who were in the area in the 1980s. Many had personal connections to addiction, making them somewhat more sympathetic to addiction as a social problem. While crime was not a major focus of residents, several high-profile homicides shaped residents' perceptions of safety.

Among the target neighborhoods of this project, South Boston had the lowest number of people who were being released from the House of Correction (Forman et al. 2016). Among those we interviewed, several grew up in South Boston but were living in Dorchester or Roxbury before their most recent arrest and similarly were returning to other neighborhoods. In most cases, their lack of a current connection was a result of its unaffordability, not because they did not want to live there. All but one of those we interviewed with ties to South Boston were white; the one person of color stayed with a cousin in one of the public housing developments. Those who did grow up there were part of the white working class that had largely been pushed out as the neighborhood gentrified. They retained their love of the neighborhood, but also saw it as "not for them" anymore.

For these reasons, South Boston may seem like an unusual choice for inclusion in this project. Yet the absence of a clear "reentry" population highlights the ways in which swaths of the city are largely inaccessible to people exiting prisons and jails. The people who do live there are not oblivious to drug use or violence, though for most these are not daily concerns, and issues related to incarceration are abstract concerns. The way crime narratives play out in South Boston provides a useful counterpoint to those in Dorchester and the South End.

To the extent there were "competing" groups in South Boston, they were the longtime residents and newcomers. This reflected class differences in some cases and also differences in neighborhood orientation. While some newcomers planned to stay in South Boston, many others planned to stay for a short period before moving on. These tensions were relatively minor in that they did not generate fear. If residents identified problem areas in the neighborhood, these tended to be associated with the public housing developments and in the direction of Newmarket Square, home to methadone clinics and the House of Correction. Returning prisoner, homeless, or dangerous populations were not on the radar of most South Boston residents as an issue in their neighborhood or as something to cause concern. And those who had spent time in the House of Correction mostly felt pushed out of the neighborhood, along with other working-class residents.

HISTORY AND DEVELOPMENT OF SOUTH BOSTON

South Boston is a peninsula that juts between Dorchester Bay and the Boston Harbor. Dorchester Heights, the top of Telegraph Hill on the western edge of this peninsula, was a key site of George Washington's fortification of Boston. This area was then used as a reservoir to provide water to South Boston.[2] South Boston was annexed to Boston at the turn of the nineteenth century, with wealthy developers purchasing land on what was then known as Dorchester Neck (Vale 2002). Wealthy residents developed parts of the City Point area, near the beach on the eastern edge of the peninsula, and Dorchester Heights. During this early development, the eastern end of South Boston was also the site of several charitable and correctional institutions, "a whole village of reformatories and treatment centers for institutionalized individuals" (Vale 2002: 41). These included a House of Industry (and almshouse), a House of Correction, a House of Reformation (for juveniles), the City Lunatic Asylum, School for the Feeble-Minded, a Small-Pox Hospital, and the Perkins Institute for the Blind (Vale 2002). Once the population, and their political voice, grew enough by the mid-1800s, they protested the placement of these services in South Boston. Both because of resident protests and the desirability of the land and its possible development, many of these services and institutions were relocated to Deer Island in Boston Harbor (Vale 2002). The almshouse on Deer Island became the Deer Island House of Correction, until the current House of Correction opened in 1991. Still, resentment continued among South Boston residents toward city leadership. This resentment of the wealthy residents was exacerbated by the growing industrial area in the northern and western sections of the peninsula, and the corresponding housing for largely immigrant laborers (Vale 2002).

In the mid-nineteenth century, South Boston started seeing an influx of the Irish working class, particularly in the Lower End district on the western edge. Following World War I, South Boston began losing people, ultimately losing about half of its population in the next fifty years (Vale 2002). Both the declining population and the state of the housing conditions in the Lower End made it a target of slum clearance and public housing development. Three developments were built in South Boston in the 1930s and 1940s: Old Harbor, Old Colony, and the West Broadway development (also known as D Street Projects). In this period, much of the area was razed, displacing large numbers of Irish, Lithuanian, and Polish residents (Vale 2002). The Boston Housing Authority used a superblock street pattern, with mid-rise buildings, in an intentional attempt to physically distinguish them from the surrounding "slum" conditions. As in other Boston neighborhoods at this time, wealthier residents and veterans also began moving to the suburbs. As in the South and North Ends of Boston, South Boston resisted the wholesale urban renewal that destroyed the West End (Gans 1982; Vale 2002). South Boston politicians and residents maintained an already developed emphasis on local control and resistance to outside interference.

The 1960s in South Boston was a period of significant racial tension and violence resulting from attempts to integrate both public housing and public schools. Reactions to the attempts at integration, combined with South Boston's history of self-determination, led to a strong and lasting reputation of South Boston as racist and exclusionary. The Boston Housing Authority began integrating South Boston public housing in 1963, after complaints from the NAACP and the Congress of Racial Equality (CORE) to the Massachusetts Commission against Discrimination (MCAD) (Vale 2002). Physical and economic decline was occurring at the same time as attempts at racial integration, further exacerbating tensions among public housing residents and between them and other residents of South Boston (Vale 2002). For some white residents, increasing numbers of Black public housing residents in South Boston was another signal of the "disreputability" of the public housing developments, leading to violent incidents of harassment against Black tenants and other residents of color (Vale 2002).

South Boston also was central to both school busing and anti-busing and anti-desegregation protests in the 1970s. South Boston High School was a central player in school desegregation, and resistance, efforts. The judge responsible for desegregating Massachusetts schools developed a plan to bus half the students from South Boston High School, a mostly working-class white school, to Roxbury High School, a primarily working-class Black school, and vice versa.[3] A "Restore Our Alienated Rights" group formed to protest the busing program. South Boston High School was the site of a number of incidents, including a stabbing of a white student by a Black student that resulted in violent protests by residents and the school being closed for a month in early 1975.[4] The school also became one of the first schools to install metal detectors, and, for a period, it was guarded by hundreds of police officers a day. In October 1975, six thousand people marched against busing in South Boston. This era in Boston history remains salient for those who lived through it, and several of our respondents referenced it. Much like the Charles Stuart case, and its connection to stop-and-frisk policing in Black neighborhoods, it is a touchstone moment in Boston history and in South Boston history.[5]

At the same time that busing was roiling South Boston, so was organized crime and drugs. James "Whitey" Bulger was a central player in gang activity, drug dealing, and other illegal activity in the area in the 1970s and 1980s, until he became a fugitive in 1995.[6] He was the leader of the Winter Hill Gang, was implicated in multiple murders, and continued to be a point of reference for those who lived in South Boston during his era. Bulger grew up in the Old Harbor/McCormack Housing Development, and a number of the key sites of "Whitey's Boston" are in the neighborhood.[7] At the time, for many, there was a negotiated coexistence between Whitey Bulger, his gang, and other residents of the neighborhood (Pattillo-McCoy 1999; Browning 2009). The resentment of residents toward outsiders also continued. For some, Bulger protected them from outside influences—including Black or other people of color who might move in and the judges or politicians who facilitated such moves—that threatened their existence.

Tensions related to the racial integration of South Boston public housing continued at least into the 1990s, and poverty levels continued to be high (Vale 2002). In the 1990s, South Boston was characterized by the portrayal of white working-class masculinity in the movie *Good Will Hunting* (1997) and by gentrification that brought with it dramatically rising home prices. Michael Patrick MacDonald described two prominent narratives of "Southie": the white racist oppressor that had responded violently to the court-ordered busing and a working- and middle-class community trying to maintain its minimal social problems by "not letting blacks in with all their problems" (MacDonald 2000: 4). In the 1990s, redevelopment also began in the Boston Seaport neighborhood, the former industrial area in the northern part of South Boston, into what is currently one of the whitest and wealthiest neighborhoods in the city.[8]

Today, South Boston remains overwhelmingly white, except for the three housing developments. It also maintains a reputation of a white, closed, and often racist neighborhood. Sociologist David Harding found that Black parents in his Boston study distrusted working-class white residents, "particularly the working-class whites associated with South Boston and past racial conflicts over school integration" (Harding 2010: 16). This is consistent with sociologist Monica McDermott's (2006) research, which found that working-class white residents had a strong class and ethnic identity that fostered a sense of entitlement to "their" neighborhoods and schools.

LIVING IN SOUTH BOSTON

Despite South Boston's recent history of ties to gangs and drugs, longtime residents primarily focus on their perceptions of neighborhood strengths, like their close-knit and family-oriented history in the neighborhood. Some see the presence of longtime residents as a primary asset of their neighborhood. Joanne, a white woman in her 70s, grew up in South Boston and moved back after she and her husband divorced. She described her street, "I've been told by a number of people that it has the reputation of being the nicest walk in South Boston. Maybe because there are a number of original families. One, two, three, four. When I'm talking about original, from at least fifty years ago." She added that she had not lived anywhere else for close to the same amount of time, "so I really have nothing to compare it to." Her block is a one-way street, "people don't know why, but maybe that's due to a politician that lived on this street a number of years ago."

While many of the long-term residents were loyal to South Boston, they recognized some of its problems, particularly in terms of its history. Elsa, a white woman who grew up in South Boston, moved away for about a decade in her young adulthood and then returned when she was ready to buy a house; "because it was busing, housing was cheap and affordable." She said her City Point neighborhood was the more desirable part of the neighborhood; "all the time I was growing up in here, this would have been considered the better section of South Boston. More educated." She contrasted City Point with the public housing on the west side of South Boston. Leslie, a white woman who also lived in the City Point area with her husband and two adult sons, owned a three-family building. Initially, they planned to move as her kids grew up. "You know, we weren't going to stay in the city. Although I love the city, but it was like the pros and cons of bringing up kids in the city. And especially at that time [in the 1990s], South Boston was very rough. You know, it was those [Whitey] Bulger days, that gangster, so it was—not that it affected us that much, but the schools that were available were Catholic parochial schools and I wasn't really opting to look at the public schools because of the reputation." Early on, she joined a mothers group, and met other women who helped her navigate the school system for her children. When they considered moving again, she said "I love these women. Let's see if we can do it." Nearly thirty years later, most of that group of women remained in South Boston and they remained friends. In some cases, long-term [white] residents had capitalized on the problems, through its impact on real estate prices, but also had to work around them to feel comfortable staying in the area.

Gentrification began in South Boston in the 1970s and 1980s. Residents who moved in then and remained had a long history with the neighborhood, but a different perspective than those who also grew up there. For outsiders, South Boston was rough and undesirable, though perhaps on the verge of improvement. For example, Crystal, a white woman in her 70s, moved to South Boston as a young adult, approximately fifty years earlier. She and her husband made an offer on a house in the South End, then a "hot spot" [for real estate], which fell through. When her husband suggested looking in South Boston, she said, "Oh, gee, I don't know much about that." The realtor, "was very snobby, and she said, 'Oh, we don't do South Boston.'" This convinced Crystal to consider it, and they ended up buying directly from the owner instead. She said, "It wasn't planned, but it was fabulous, because we found, when we moved in, a whole lot of people. We were the millennials. . . . There's still four or five of us who moved onto this block who are still here. . . . But it was kind of pioneering." Crystal and her husband lived in a row house in the City Point area of South Boston. She described the neighborhood when they moved in:

> I think when we moved in, it was kind of like the Wild West. There were remnants of just old bar rooms and a lot of alcoholics and blue-collar workers.

And, uh, salt-of-the-earth kind of people, but it was just when busing started, so that kind of put another picture, another color on it. Not having children, I had my own business. My husband, of course, because he worked for the *Globe*, which was much hated because they were a liberal paper. But it didn't impact us directly, but certainly as you drove through town. And if you ever crossed over by the high school, you got the full taste of what it was like, and the hatred, and the vitriol that the people—and in some ways, I am a great supporter of neighborhood schools. I think there's a big advantage to it versus busing. But I also see the other side of it that things never change if that's the *status quo* and, and kids of color and other ethnicities are cut out, that doesn't further any society, at all.

Crystal does not romanticize the South Boston that she first moved into. She cited both the racism of South Boston residents and the stereotypes of other area residents, like her Cambridge coworkers, "sort of a righteous group, some of them. And they used to say, 'Are you safe living in South [Boston]?' . . . I mean, you would have thought we were in Lebanon. The perceptions were really very interesting and incorrect."

Crystal and her husband were "pioneers" in that they were middle-class white liberal residents moving into a working-class white conservative neighborhood. She sees this era as the beginning of the development in the neighborhood, when many residents began moving to the suburbs—a shift she attributed to the conflict over busing: "It was unpleasant to a lot of people, because they felt the whole nature of this family-centered community was being ripped to shreds." Busing brought into focus the exclusionary and racist nature of many residents. These residents felt threatened by the idea of their kids being sent to Roxbury schools or Black Roxbury students being brought into South Boston High. For many white residents, they felt their only options were to move out of South Boston or to send their children to parochial or private schools. This contributed to residential turnover, particularly for those with school-aged children.

It wasn't until the past decade, however, that the "real big change" came, with developers coming into the neighborhood. She said that then "nobody cared whether they kept their house or not for the family, because the kids didn't want to stay here any longer. There was nothing, really, for them." Now, Crystal is widowed and says she's approached multiple times a month by people offering to buy her house. "They buy it for cash, and then gut it, and sell condos." New neighbors "either rent, or maybe their parents bought them a condo. They're roommates. . . . They seem to have a lot of disposable income. They love to go out to eat and to the bars and have a nice time." Few of these new residents had school-aged children and most assumed they would move out when they did have children because of the overall perceived quality of Boston public schools.[9] This continued to make the neighborhood feel less "family friendly," as young people had a short-term commitment to the neighborhood and there was a relative lack of children in the neighborhood. While Crystal laments that some of her new neighbors lack a sense of investment in the neighborhood compared to older residents, she also recognizes that "there was a lot that was wrong with it before" as well.

Long-term residents lament the perceived loss of community, following an influx of newer residents who focus on the amenities—like the proximity to the beach, the architecture, and the restaurants—rather than a sense of community. A number of the longtime residents we talked to lived in their childhood homes. They may have moved away temporarily but returned either to care for aging parents or after the death of their parents. For example, Sheila, a white woman in her 70s, grew up in the City Point neighborhood of South Boston and lived there her entire life, save ten years when her son was growing up (when she lived in Dorchester, "but in the Polish neighborhood, which is just over the bridge," distinguishing her former neighborhood from the stereotyped largely Black sections of Dorchester). Once her mother died, when Sheila was in her mid-40s, she moved back to her childhood home. She said it was "nice to be living there because I sure as hell couldn't buy in this day and age." While she was grateful to be living in South Boston, she did not currently consider the neighborhood close-knit. She described the transition: "Oh, now I would say no. But, growing up absolutely. Until, let me see, mom died in when? 1995. I would say things didn't start going crazy till we hit the millennial, 2000, and then properties started going up, up, up. I mean, across the street from me—we won't say my address—across the street from me, there's a shithole that's getting $3,200 a month for rent, no utilities included. So, what does that do? Breeds instability in the neighborhood. You get four undergraduates that party their ass off."

The owners of the building Sheila referred to live just outside of Boston, in Milton, and therefore "they don't give a shit what's happening there. They don't care if those kids are bothering anyone. They're making great money." These shifts have undermined neighborhood stability, according to Sheila and other long-term residents, both because the new residents were transient and because they had different lifestyles than long-term residents. Rising property values and annoying and uninvested young neighbors were two of the biggest complaints of long-term white residents and homeowners.

Garrett, a white man in his 60s, claimed that "70 percent of South Boston is five years or less. . . . That's what I was told and I believe it."[10] Garrett moved away for twenty years, until he moved back to care for his elderly mother when she developed Alzheimer's. He had been back since 1996; a few of his neighbors moved in at about the same time he returned, and the others were all newer. Garrett was one of several people who commented on the lack of children among the newer residents. He said many of them were childless when they moved in, then "all the children grow up to four or five, and then they're subject to busing. So they might have the kid go to a school down in Mattapan or Dorchester. And so they just sell the condo with a high price and buy a place in the suburbs. They move out. I taught school during the busing crisis." Now, he said, "it's a transient community to say the least. And very few, and the residential areas, there's very few children. There's the children that are only in the housing projects." Mary, who had also lived in South Boston for decades, agreed that parents moved out of the neighborhood: "There's no kids, so everything has changed. As soon as people get pregnant, they stay maybe a year or two and they leave. Nobody stays." Elsa similarly said that now there are "Single-family DINKS [Double Income No Kids], or no families. More people with dogs." The result was a less family-oriented neighborhood.[11] Mary also highlighted a perceived tension between long-term residents and newcomers. She said, "People are generally, especially the young people, they just go about their own business. They don't look up. They don't care to be friendly. This is the view I get of them. If they look up, I'll say hello to them, but I think they feel that long-time homeowners don't like them because this is the reputation. . . . I don't know if you have heard that the people of South Boston who have been here forever, they don't want the uppitiest. We don't want outsiders. We want it the way it used to be when everybody knew everybody." Mary mostly perceived this image of South Boston residents lamenting its working-class insular past to be a false impression, but one that she believed colored others' responses to her and other longer-term residents.

While many long-term residents complained about young newcomers, these complaints were mild. Sheila, for example, also called "those kids" generally respectful, "and I haven't had any trouble. I go out and start shoveling [snow], and there's a couple guys—Rod and Rob—I've never met before, and they come down and they help me too." She also relied on area teens and young adults to help her with her technological needs. So while she did not know her neighbors by name, and complained about gentrification and its effect on neighborhood stability, she also remained fairly integrated and comfortable in her neighborhood. She also named several friends that lived in the neighborhood. Susan, also a white woman in her 60s, described the current mix of residents in favorable terms. Susan grew up in South Boston and now lived in the house she grew up in. She and her husband renovated the house after her mother died, and they moved back several years earlier from an inner-ring suburb. She moved away for thirty-five years, but "some people I grew up with still live in the neighborhood, some relatives live in the neighborhood." Her daughter and her family live on the first floor of Susan's house, and Susan describes the neighborhood as "multigenerational." She describes it as "a real mix and it's a very collegial atmosphere." She also mentions helping each other shovel snow as a sign of the friendliness of the neighborhood. Some of the houses "have transferred hands" and been turned into condos or rental apartments, and Susan is less familiar with those neighbors than with longer-term homeowners. But people generally got along, even while they were less close and some perhaps less invested in the neighborhood.

SOUTH BOSTON AS A DESTINATION

A number of the newer residents we spoke with fit some of the stereotypes that longer-term residents had of newcomers. Joshua, a white man in his 30s, moved to South Boston four years before because of "proximity to work, a good nightlife, a social scene." He expected to move in a year or so to buy a house, probably outside of Boston. He described his neighbors as "Approximately 25- to 35-year-olds. Young professionals. Working. College-educated … white." Mark, a multiracial man in his 40s, was born in South Boston but grew up in an area suburb. Mark lived alone and had no children. He had lived in South Boston for three years and defined his neighborhood boundaries according to "most of the bars and restaurants and places that I'll socialize for brunch or, you know, drinks and stuff like that." He described his area, near Dorchester Heights, as a "pretty diverse mix": "It's a mix of families, there's a mix of older folks who've been in that house for fifty years. And there there's like a lot of young professionals." He considers his neighborhood close-knit "ish," because a lot of his neighbors are fairly new to the area.

Ted, a white man in his 30s, had lived in South Boston for about three and a half years and his current house for six months. Like Mark, he described his City Point neighborhood as "Pretty family oriented, especially relative to the rest of South Boston. It's a bit more stable. . . . So yeah, families, stable, largely culturally Irish. People who've been in South Boston for a while, I think. A little more resistant to the influx of new people. And pretty safe and quiet." He perceived his neighborhood to still be primarily longtime residents, though also sees a "huge influx of 20-somethings" on his bus to work. He estimated that he and his wife would live there for another five years or so, depending on her career. While he thinks the neighborhood is close-knit, but "I'm just not a part of that fabric yet." A majority of both longtime residents and newcomers were white; to the extent there was diversity it was class diversity and that was diminishing. While the public housing remained (and is now racially/ethnically diverse), the private housing was becoming decreasingly working class and increasingly upper class. In both Dorchester Heights and City Point, newer residents recognized a strong presence of longtime residents, alongside a young, newer demographic. Mark also recognized that South Boston is "becoming less economically diverse. I think there's less working-class people there, whereas I think for years and years, you know South Boston had a lot of economically diverse people. Blue collar peoples, affluent people. That's what I think made it a really cool place. There's still that, but I think it's trending the wrong way."

Matthew, a white man in his 30s who moved to South Boston a few months earlier, contrasted it with his previous experience living in the South End. He said:

> People in South Boston, I would say upper-middle class, white, majority white. Seems like, I don't know, more like white collar jobs. I'm trying to think how else to describe. I definitely think, well it's hard to tell because based on just my experience living in a building compared to just walking around the streets, if I were talking about just my experience living in this building in South Boston versus South End, like people here, because this building I'm living in is higher rent. It seems like people keep to themselves more. They don't like to talk to other people as much. Whereas I noticed— not that I think this has anything to do with income or anything—but it just seems like other places I've lived in in South End people were more friendly and had more relationships with people like my neighbors and stuff that I don't really have here.

Matthew first concluded that this was evidence that his neighborhood was not close-knit, but he later changed his mind and said it was close-knit, because "I think from my experience just going to restaurants or bars in the area or even with my neighbors, we have a roof deck up here, people seem to really be friendly and when I'm meeting people, but it's not like your doors are open and you're seeing people every day. When I have gone to restaurants and stuff, people, when they find out that I'm living in South Boston, they're like, 'Oh, welcome to the neighborhood. It seems like it's a very friendly place." While Matthew's experience may be colored by his newness to the neighborhood, this perspective was shared by other newer residents, and was consistent with longer-term residents' descriptions of newer residents. They socialized together, particularly in bars and restaurants, but otherwise seemed less invested in developing community among their neighbors. Many did not have shared involvement in neighborhood institutions, like schools or churches.

Newer residents expressed a similar level of wariness to some of their longer-term neighbors as the longtime residents had for newcomers. Those who were aware of South Boston's history saw many of the changes as positive, as the neighborhood was less intolerant than it had been. Mark (multiracial, 40s), for example, recognized

> South Boston has a very bad name, bad reputation, and it's well deserved. It has a very complex history over the last fifty years. So I think there's still some of that. . . . There's a racial component too, I think. There's this Irish ethnic pride that everybody else is outsiders. . . . Having said that, when you get to know people, it's not as bad as you think. I think those people, the real knuckleheads are, a lot of them are gone and they're knuckleheads regardless. But the people you kind of, I came in with a stereotype of everyone is going to be this way. Everybody's going to be kind of a racist and very close minded and that's not the case. People who have been here a long time are great people. And I've been fortunate to meet some of those people and kind of pleasantly surprised that—even I went in with this bias and it's proven to be, in some cases, proven to be untrue.

Mark recognized the truth in the reputation, but also had developed positive relationships with some of his older neighbors.

South Boston is comprised of several smaller neighborhoods that range in architectural styles and reputations. The Fort Point and Seaport areas have a feel that is distinct from the City Point and Dorchester Heights sections. Dorchester Heights and City Point are comprised of single-family homes, triple-deckers, and smaller apartment buildings. The Fort Point area has warehouses converted into lofts and condominiums and similar-looking newer construction. In contrast, the Seaport is home to a lot of large, new, and upscale buildings along with retail, restaurants, and bars. Like Matthew, Keith, a white man in his 50s, moved from the South End to South Boston's Seaport neighborhood. He moved to his current apartment after hearing it was "an up-and-coming nice area to live. . . . Every time I look out my window, I see construction cranes building new structures. More and more people moving in every day." He enjoys the area amenities and plans to live there "indefinitely."

Linda, a white woman in her 60s, had lived in the nearby Fort Port area for about twenty years. She emphatically drew a line between the new development in the Seaport from her neighborhood. "My neighborhood, in my opinion, does not include all this new construction crap that's going up, which is on the other side of Seaport Boulevard. . . . I don't consider that part of my neighborhood. That is the new Seaport Boulevard and former parking lot, massive development. I don't consider the Convention Center part of my neighborhood. I don't even consider the folks who live in the new construction on D Street part of my neighborhood. I consider the historical district, the Fort Point Channel area, my neighborhood." Linda was attracted to the history of the neighborhood, "And then of course the brick and beam because I'm a history buff and as simplistic as the architecture is, it's, to me, it's gorgeous. All of these details are really nice." Her building was a former warehouse. She described it:

> The first former wool warehouses that were converted to condominiums in 1982. And the artists originally squatted here in the early to mid-1970s. And they illegally occupied buildings.[12] Some paid very low rent. Some didn't have bathroom facilities, and they used them as studios. So, it was the artists, as it is with so many areas, that actually helped create what this is today. And the artists, just the fact that it was an artists' colony, if you will, was attractive. But as time went on and . . . the developers started buying and converting . . . then they started moving out.

Linda said she could no longer afford to buy in her neighborhood, as it has "gone from lower socioeconomic level to either high-middle class or into the upper class. . . . So, it's a lot of entitlement." Jennifer, a white woman in her 40s similarly lived in Fort Point, in one of the newer buildings a few blocks over from Linda. She had moved in a few years earlier after winning a housing lottery, and now planned to stay "forever." She too described it as

> a former industrial area. There's lots of artists. I think it was the state or the country's original artist colony, or something. I know it has a history as an artist colony. There's lots of cute little galleries, nice restaurants, and coffee places. My impression is that there's a lot of young tech people in the neighborhood. . . . Definitely lots of young people. It seems racially diverse. When I walk to South Station some mornings, it seems racially diverse. Lots of 20-something-, 30-something-year-olds. It feels very safe. I always feel safe here.

While Jennifer and Linda appreciated similar aspects of the neighborhood, Linda made stronger claims to her more "authentic" connections to the neighborhood and its history. Still, she was outside of the family-oriented "old" South Boston of Dorchester Heights and City Point. Jennifer was less resistant to the newer "tech" residents, who she saw as part of the fabric of the neighborhood, rather than the upper-class interlopers that had recently began moving in.

In addition to valuing the neighborhood for its architecture and amenities, another commonality among newer residents was a general orientation outside of the neighborhood. For example, while Dylan, an Asian man in his 40s, did go to dinner or brunch on West Broadway in South Boston, much of his time was spent in Cambridge, Somerville, or the South End. Mark shopped at the South End Whole Foods. He said, "There are some supermarkets in South Boston that I consciously don't go to. . . . I like Whole Foods and I think there's just a better quality there. It's more expensive, but it's a little better quality of a supermarket." Jennifer spent much of her time outside of home in other neighborhoods, usually going north into downtown Boston and Cambridge. She said, "The only reason I ever have to go to what I consider Southie [i.e., the City Point and Dorchester Heights sections] is some of the stuff is over there, like a fifteen-minute walk, and then the library is over here. The shootings were more like in the neighborhoods, I think. I just have no reason to go to the residential areas, the dense residential areas." Jennifer, like many of the newer residents, maintained an orientation outside of the neighborhood. They spent some time in newer bars and restaurants, but generally shopped and often socialized outside of South Boston and what they perceived as the "old" South Boston.

Like Mark, Dylan had recently moved to Andrew Square, on the border between South Boston and Dorchester, because it was much more affordable than his previous neighborhood downtown. Andrew Square was one of the areas that was cited by several residents as being a less desirable part of the neighborhood. It was on the western edge of the South Boston peninsula, near the McCormack Public Housing development and in the direction of Newmarket Square, the House of Correction, shelters, and methadone clinics. Dylan chose the neighborhood, in part, for its potential for gentrification. He talked about the "duality of the neighborhood. You've got panhandlers and bums, but then you have very, you can tell, yuppies, ourselves being within that group, right? I was looking for a neighborhood that wasn't quite gentrified yet but had the potential and the likelihood that it was going to become much more developed." While he didn't consider the area close-knit, "I get a sense that at one time it was. . . . This whole area was called the Polish Triangle and you can tell that the Polish community is fairly close knit." Many of the Polish residents, according to Dylan, had been pushed out of the area because of gentrification. Still, there was an "ethnic feel" to the neighborhood, along with increasing development, and "I kind of embrace both worlds." Dylan was comfortable in his neighborhood but recognized that not everyone was. A female coworker, whom he described as "younger, 30s, white, fairly privileged," thought the neighborhood was a "problem neighborhood" and "sketchy," because Black people lived in the neighborhood and there are "homeless people, drug addicts. You wouldn't want to leave your door open, but they're not breaking and entering and they're not shooting people." Dylan, however, was counting on these perceptions changing over time.

The newer residents brought a less insular attitude than that of South Boston's reputation, but also in many cases less commitment to the neighborhood. The neighborhood was becoming more class homogenous, with many of the longer-term residents also middle and upper middle-class homeowners. Rents and home prices were out of reach for many who may otherwise want to live there. Newcomers could afford high rents or expensive condos, and many saw South Boston as a temporary place to live while young and childless. They tended to not mingle, at least beyond superficial levels, with long-term residents. The neighborhood was not devoid of its old problems, including racism and addiction, but the culture had shifted substantially from that of an insular working-class white ethnic neighborhood with strong ties to organized crime to a more "worldly" and wealthy white neighborhood.

Drugs, addiction, and gangs were recent problems in South Boston, but there was relatively little current concern with crime. Drug use and addiction were issues, with overdoses in public areas a not-uncommon occurrence. Occasionally, a high-profile violent incident occurs, but this is typically newsworthy because it is unusual. Residents' biggest concerns tended to be development and the effects on the neighborhood, including parking.

Kelsey, a white woman in her late 20s, was a member of South Boston's dwindling working class. She had spent her childhood in South Boston before moving to the suburbs as a teenager. Now she had returned and had been living there for three years. Kelsey was unusual among the people we talked to; she had been motivated to return in part because she had a child. Fewer of the newer residents had children, and at least some of the longer-term residents had considered leaving when their children were in school. She described her reasoning for returning: "I mean I've always gone from the suburbs where you have to drive and everything else, and it's just more distant. The people are different. I grew up here. I wanted my son to grow up here. . . . But obviously a lot of people from the suburbs are moving in, so it's changing a lot, but fortunately my family has not had to move, so they're still here." While she initially wanted her son to be exposed to the city, after being here for a few years, she was thinking about returning to the suburbs: "I want my son out of the city." She described her neighborhood: "There's the more upscale polite and then there's just the other half that comes around and just groups out where it's just homeless, alcoholics, the drugs."

Kelsey was bothered by the visible presence of drug use and the regular harassment she faced on the street. She said that even when she was out with her son, she was regularly propositioned and offered drugs. "This city, it's nice, but all you have to do is go a mile out and you're hitting drugs. It doesn't matter if I'm pushing my [baby] carriage or anything else, it's 'do you want heroin? Do you want Johnnies? Do you want heroin?' They just shout it out, you know?" Her house was broken into. "Clearly I'm sensing a drug addict. . . . And it was just such an awful feeling going back into that house, that someone is getting away with this. And chances are I probably know the person." Kelsey assumed she might know the person who broke into her house because of her childhood ties to the neighborhood, and to people who used drugs in the neighborhood. She added "I definitely wouldn't walk in some areas during nights. Old Colony has changed a lot, but there's also the part that hasn't changed and that's in and out of drugs. D Street, in and out of drugs. . . .[13] There has been people, girls, that have been literally attacked at night and got their purses taken. And people robbing cars. It was just never this out there like that. It was never like that before. Like evening, someone goes and attacks two girls. It's crazy." At least in this sense, and unlike most people we talked to in South Boston, Kelsey perceives the crime and disorder in the neighborhood to be getting worse. Whether that reflects changes in the neighborhood or changes in her role in the neighborhood (from child to young adult) is unclear.

People who had lived in South Boston for a long time remembered the Whitey Bulger days, but this was the past. Mark (multiracial, 40s), for example, said that he sometimes sees people who were associated with Bulger's gang. He said,

> There's people that I know of that, you know, from 'Hey, that guy used to be associated with the Winter Hill gang,' and stuff like that. But they're in their 70s and 80s, older people. . . . Like the building three doors down from me is on the market and it was being sold. The guy who owned it was the owner of the former Triple O's bar, which was on West Broadway, which is where Whitey Bulger's hang out. And this guy was funneling money through him and stuff. So I've seen this guy and I—but, you know, he's 80.

In addition to organized crime, drugs were a longstanding problem in South Boston. Kelsey and her son's father both had histories of addiction and recovery; she estimated that "there's been at least twenty people that I grew up with [that have been involved in illegal activity]. Drugs, prostitution, been stealing. Most have been to jail. Probably six of them have died in the past two years. Yeah, and they're like 27." Kelsey talked about the effect on her peers. She said, "Mostly grandparents are raising children now. A lot of overdoses, kids I knew growing up. . . . There's been kids found in cars, the halfway house. A lot of restrooms. That's why they try to do an injection site because they're trying to keep people out of the private restrooms that, all of a sudden, a mother or person walks in, and they see some dad trying traumatic stuff in the businesses. So that's why they're trying to do safe injection sites in that area to try to prevent trauma from the other citizens." Kelsey is describing harm reduction strategies that can make drug use safer for the user and, in doing so, can also keep drug use out of other public spaces. In Boston, several such harm reduction programs, like AHOPE (Access, Harm Reduction, Overdose Prevention, and Education) and an engagement center run by the Boston Public Health Commission, are located not far from South Boston in the Newmarket area near the House of Correction. Mark mentioned that down the hill from him is a liquor store: "People hang out there and they clearly draw the addicts," and he says that needles and other drug paraphernalia are found behind the high school.

Aside from (and often related to) drug use, the biggest issues in South Boston were social disorder and petty crimes. Community meetings were often dominated by discussion over ongoing new construction and what it would mean for the neighborhood, and sometimes concern over drug use, drug paraphernalia, and related disorder. While crime was not a major focus or common fear of the residents we talked to or at community meetings, several high-profile homicides did draw substantial media and public attention. For example, Linda, asked if she would let her neighbors look after her loft if she went away said, "No. I would not ask my neighbors, I would ask my building manager. He's been there just about as long as I have. He has a key to my unit. I think he has a key to all the units, for obvious reasons. But I trust him with my life. He has access, he can come and go, and he would not give my key to anyone. As with this situation that occurred in the Macallen Building—you must have read about it." The situation that Linda referred to was the murder of doctors Lina Bolaños and Richard Field in their penthouse condo.[14] The murders occurred the week before our interview with Linda. Jennifer also mentioned "the terrible things that happened last week. Before that I've heard about shootings here and there. . . . A double murder happened." Both Jennifer and Linda lived about a mile away from the Macallen Building.

Several years earlier, in July 2013, Amy Lord, a 24-year-old white woman, was abducted in the early morning outside of her apartment building.[15] She was then driven to five ATMs and forced to withdraw money before she was stabbed and strangled; her body was discovered in the Stony Brook Reservation in Hyde Park, on Boston's southwest side. Two other women were also attacked in South Boston within twenty-four hours of Lord's murder. Within a week of this murder, there was a community meeting to address it. The crowd was so large that attendees spilled out into the street of the elementary school where the meeting was held. The meeting lasted well over two hours and included discussions of the Lord case, and other issues residents had. There was news coverage from area TV stations. Speakers at the meeting included local political officials and the police chief.[16] One of the speakers said that "evil touched down on our community." The police commissioner at the time, Ed Davis, said they were working around the clock to close the case. By then, they had a suspect (who was eventually convicted and sentenced to life without parole). The police commissioner was in daily communication with the mayor, and "they will put the community back together." Davis announced that—even though they did not think the case had anything to do with drugs—he had assigned an additional drug unit to the area. This led to applause among those in the audience. They assured the attendees that South Boston was still a safe neighborhood. The city councilor for the area also recognized that "it is not a secret that there's a drug problem in South Boston and Dorchester" (field notes). Amy Lord's murder is the kind of case that often garners media attention—an innocent, young, white woman in a "safe" neighborhood randomly attacked by a stranger (Madriz 1997; Lundman 2003).

Several speakers at this meeting also referenced Barbara Coyne's murder fifteen months earlier. Coyne, a 67-year-old lifelong resident of South Boston, was attacked and killed in her first-floor apartment.[17] The man convicted of her murder, also a lifelong resident of South Boston, allegedly robbed her to get money to buy heroin. A meeting attendee also referenced the death of Melissa Hardy, who was found beaten to death in her former boyfriend's room in a South Boston sober home, a few weeks before Amy Lord's death.[18] The speaker called for greater regulation of sober houses. Other residents raised other issues, often related to the fears over drugs and addiction. Several women spoke about their fears as women, with one calling Lord's kidnapping "most disturbing," because "if we're not safe at Dorchester Street by the businesses, where are we safe? . . . She said that's why the women are so freaked out—it could be any of us" (field notes; see also Madriz 1997).

Precisely because these events were seen as extreme, they drew extensive media attention and public outrage. That the victims were mostly women also corresponded to narratives around innocent victims. From my field notes from the meeting addressing Amy Lord's murder, I wrote, "At the same time the Amy Lord case was framed as an aberration (with a little bit of 'how could this happen here' by residents and a lot of 'this is rare' by police and DA), there was more common framing of the drug problem as a community problem, with little 'get rid of them all' and more calls for balance, prevention, and the need for intervention." Residents had a certain level of understanding, perhaps coming from more widespread personal connection to addiction, of drug use that made them more sympathetic. Of the cases described above, the Coyne and Hardy cases were tied to drug use of the offender, while the others were seemingly random attacks.

The tone of this meeting and the dynamic between speakers and attendees stands in stark contrast to a large community meeting held a few months later in a Roxbury church, for city officials to respond to concerns about police-involved shootings as part of the Black Lives Matter movement, several months after the shooting death of Michael Brown Jr. in Ferguson, Missouri, by police officer Darren Wilson (Cobbina 2019). That meeting involved law enforcement and the district attorney explaining to residents the process that the DA undergoes when there is an officer-involved shooting. While the mostly Black audience members listened politely to a formal presentation, adding occasional side comments, when it was their turn to speak, they told multiple stories of their own experiences with police violence. One speaker said, "If you can't talk your pain in church, where can you." Another "man brought up the 'elephant in the room,' and said the root cause of the issue is racism, and he hasn't heard one person talk about how we can eliminate racism" (Field notes). Residents were frustrated, not only at the problems, but at the police as the source of problems. People regularly complained in community meetings about attention to crime and violence in Black neighborhoods, compared to white neighborhoods or towns. This contrasted with the frustrations in South Boston, of violent incidents by perceived outsiders that would be solved by the police. The mostly white residents of South Boston believed that the police could address their concerns, while the mostly Black residents of Roxbury saw the police as a sometime threat to their safety.

Most respondents who named areas to avoid in South Boston focused on areas near the public housing developments and areas associated with drug selling or use or gangs. While South Boston is about a mile from Newmarket Square, occasionally residents marked the Andrew Square area as a place to avoid because of its proximity to the House of Correction, shelters, and methadone clinics in that area. Janine, a white woman in her 50s who had always lived in South Boston said that she avoids Andrew Square and "the projects," because those were areas where there was "a lot of drugs. Andrew Square is very close to the methadone clinics. They come across the bridge down by the City Hospital [Boston Medical Center]. Um, and just never been one to go to the Projects." Keith (white, 50s) avoids a "little strip" of a nearby street in City Point, because of a "sketchy" house. This wasn't so much a problem area, according to Keith, but a few problem people. Beyond that, he said, "So this is going to sound bad, but there's a pretty sizable housing project right here that's a little—I go there, I've been there, I've biked around, but it's not the best. And let's see, yeah, I guess this area's a little rough too. Just west of Andrew Square. I hopped off my bike to adjust something, and there was a hypodermic needle right on the ground next to my tire. I'm like, OK. So anyway, those are probably the only areas." Kelsey (white, 20s) similarly identified the area closer to Andrew Square as a problematic part of the neighborhood and where there was more drug activity. These areas are also nearer where most of the people of color and where most of the lower-income people in South Boston live.

RETURNING TO SOUTH BOSTON

People returning from the House of Correction have a distinct relationship with South Boston. Most of those we talked to who have a connection to South Boston were members of its dwindling white working class. This also meant that few of those who grew up in the area returned after their incarcerations. Several grew up in South Boston but had not been living there either before or after their recent incarcerations. Several, including James, a white man in his late 40s, wished they could. When I asked James in our first post-release interview if he would prefer to be in South Boston rather than the Cambridge shelter he was staying, he laughed, "Absolutely. That was a stupid question." The proportion of House of Correction commitments relative to South Boston's population is at about the city average, but well below Dorchester and the South End (Forman et al. 2016). Not surprisingly then, few of our interview participants returned to South Boston. It was too expensive for most to afford, and there were relatively few halfway houses or programs in the neighborhood. Several did visit South Boston, often to go to the South Boston District Court for drug court or to see their probation officer. James spent some time there when he was in the area: "I was there yesterday and in court but I just go over there and hang out, stuff like that. Castle Island [the far eastern edge of the peninsula] and just walk the streets. I know a couple people there. Sometimes I go over there and chill with them." William, a white man in his early 50s who had been involved with organized crime in South Boston, tried to stay out of the area because of that history. He did go to South Boston District Court for probation and hoped to do a college internship at the Gavin House, a South Boston recovery home for men.

Those who grew up in South Boston and had spent time in the House of Correction described it in similar terms as other longtime residents—family-oriented and tight knit. They also talked about organized crime, drugs, busing, and later, gentrification. James grew up in South Boston. He described it as "Irish" when he was growing up, though today, he laughed, it was "full of yuppies." Prior to his incarceration, he had been living in Neponset, a primarily white area of Dorchester near the mouth of the Neponset River. He described it as a "nice neighborhood" but would prefer to move back to South Boston "if I could afford it. All those yuppies are driving up the prices." When James was released, he first stayed at a shelter in Cambridge. He said "Cambridge is Cambridge. They're a different breed of people up here, to say the least. There's all types of people. Like when I take the bus by MIT, those people are, those people are, fly rockets to the moon. You know. Smart." In a later interview, I asked James about growing up in South Boston.

AL: You grew up in Southie. What was it like there when you grew up?

JAMES: Black was Black and white was white.

AL: What does that mean?

JAMES: Busing. You [as a white man] hung out with the white guys and there was racial conflict.

AL: How did you experience that?

JAMES: I just stayed away from them. We fought them [Black residents], they fought us, and that was it. Not with guns, with baseball bats and stuff. Street fights.

William, another white man in his early 50s, grew up in South Boston at roughly the same time as James. He described it as: "I'd say it was a nice family, it was a nice family place. All the neighbors knew their neighbors, this and that. You could walk in and out of people's houses. The kids actually played out in the street. They weren't playing Nintendo, all that stuff. I remember we all had street hockey, basketball, everything. I actually, I think it's a lot better than what it is now, because people were more social, you know what I mean?" He went on to describe a divided South Boston of the 1990's:

The '90s, drugs, cocaine was coming in big, heroin was coming in a little big. Also there was more drinking, there was more drinking with me. It was starting to change, it got a little bit more yuppie. A lot of people couldn't afford to live there anymore. A lot of people were selling to get out and you know, I hate to call it white flight, but that's what it was. Everybody was moving to the suburbs. . . . South Boston now is all condos. I don't know who can afford to live in South Boston anymore.

While drugs and related problems were prominent in the South Boston of the 1990's, gentrification was also beginning. William attributed this, in part, to the tensions over busing that led some white residents to move to the suburbs. White residents moved out and were replaced by new, often wealthier, white residents. This made it inaccessible to James and William, both financially and socially. They appreciated some aspects, like the beaches and waterfront and their remaining friends or family, but also did not feel like it was "their" neighborhood anymore.

Kayla, a white woman in her 30s, grew up in South Boston and described it as "a small city inside of Boston. They have good schools. It's an Irish-Italian community. That's it probably." In contrast, she described Roxbury, where she was living before her most recent incarceration, as "it's just a lot of drugs, gang activity, violence." Jackie, also a white woman in her 30s, described the South Boston of her youth in similar terms.

South Boston was a very good community. Everybody looked out for each other. It was tight knit. I don't know what to say. It was a solid good place to grow up. I enjoyed it, I didn't fear for nothing. I believed everybody was there looking out for each other. It was a good community, convenient, access to buses, access to the stores. I enjoyed it. There's drugs everywhere, so that's just, it is what it is. No matter if I'm in the middle of nowhere, if I'm on a desert, I want to get high I'm finding the drug, bottom line. It might have been a little more accessible to me because I grew up in the projects but that really didn't matter; that really doesn't matter because my cousin who grew up in their own home in Weymouth [a town about twelve miles south of South Boston] right down the street, there was the drug dealer also. I think it was a tight knit, good community.

Jackie also commented on gentrification as a key change, though she presented it with a more positive spin than most people who lived there before gentrification. "Now they're building condos all around the projects so it's more upper-class people, middle-class people who are surrounding them, so I guess it gives them a bit more hope and incentive that they don't have to stay stuck in the projects if they don't want to." Jackie portrays the wealthy condo and homeowners as positive role models for their lower-income neighbors. While this dynamic is often at least implicitly a part of the logic of mixed-income housing developments, the reality is that there are often significant social divides that inhibit relationships forming (Small 2004; Tach 2009). The ways other residents of South Boston (and the other target neighborhoods) talk about cross-class divides also suggests that this probably does not occur much.

Only one of the people that we interviewed—Adam, a Black man in his 40s—lived in South Boston after his release from the House of Correction. He divided his time between a cousin's apartment in one of South Boston's public housing developments and a girlfriend's apartment in Mattapan. Adam described Mattapan as "kind of crazy. Well, it all, it all depends on like if you into that life. . . . I don't hang out in the streets." In contrast, he preferred South Boston, because "it's laid back. I like South Boston better because like if I get stressed out or whatever, I can walk around the beach, you know, walk up and down that little stretch just to clear my mind or whatever." He knew few people in either neighborhood, beyond a neighbor that his cousin helped out in his building. Generally, he said, "I just try to stay around, like, people that's, that I consider my, either my family or people I consider family." In this sense, Adam took a similar approach to many of the people we interviewed, across neighborhoods. They limited their contact to a narrow, trusted social circle. Many appreciated spending time away from people, in parks and along rivers and area beaches, and avoiding drama.

When record snowfalls in February of 2015 disrupted train service, Adam spent more time in Mattapan so he could take a bus to his job in Dorchester. From South Boston, "it's crazy. You got these kids that's going to school, then the buses be overpacked. I could leave the house around 6:40, I still don't get to work until 8, 9 a.m. It's crazy." Still, his employer was sympathetic and told him "'You're the only person that's not driving. Get here whenever you can. We know you're still coming to work.'" Adam was fortunate that his employer, in a warehouse, was supportive. He found the job in November through a temp agency that he went to with his cousin; "I had tried other temp agencies, but like with the temp agencies, it's about they're going to give the work to the people that's been there the longest." Six months later, during our final interview, he was still working there and said, "I wouldn't leave them because they gave me a chance." By then, he made fifteen dollars an hour and had health insurance. When he first started working, both his cousin and his girlfriend let him stay with them free of rent to "get on my feet," though he helped out with food. Six months later, he also helped with rent. So, while Adam stayed part time in South Boston, and liked it, he had relatively few ties to the neighborhood. Occasionally, someone else went to South Boston to go to court or to go to programs in the area but had few ties to the neighborhood. Given the relatively limited numbers of programs and services in South Boston, however, there also were relatively few people coming in for these reasons.

To the extent that people we talked to who had spent time in the House of Correction had ties to South Boston, it was as members of the working class, and most often the white working class. They appreciated the same things about it as other long-term residents, but it had become inaccessible to them. In contrast to both the South End and Dorchester, there were fewer options for people with low incomes. In addition, the public housing buildings—once predominantly white—now predominantly housed people of color, making it less likely that the white people who had grown up there still had ties there.

CONCLUSION

Crime and talk about crime were less pronounced in South Boston compared to Dorchester and the South End. Residents named few current "problem areas" and were primarily aware of extreme violent crimes that were well publicized by the media. There are several key periods of South Boston history, particularly its ties to Whitey Bulger and his Winter Hill Gang and racial tensions over busing as an attempt to desegregate public schools, that remained relevant to a number of residents. Particularly for those who lived in South Boston at that time, they continued to shadow life in South Boston today. Whitey Bulger is part of neighborhood lore, and people referenced key people and places connected to him. One of the men we interviewed was incarcerated because of his involvement with South Boston gangs. For newer residents, it was an interesting anecdote that had less relevance to contemporary life in the neighborhood, perhaps beyond the lingering problems of addiction. Busing and the attempted desegregation of public schools played a larger role, as this, and the racism underlying the responses, continues to shape South Boston's reputation.

Gentrification was a key theme in most people's descriptions of South Boston. Few of the people we talked to who were being released from the House of Correction had ties to South Boston. Those who had grown up in South Boston had been pushed out in earlier waves of gentrification, and they no longer felt the neighborhood was "for" people like them. Several people connected busing to the "family-oriented" residents moving out, allowing for gentrification to happen. Newer residents were wealthier and had a reputation for being more interested in South Boston as a short-term playground, until they too left rather than send their children to Boston public schools. The desegregation of the public housing developments was talked about less among our participants than that of South Boston High, though the effects of this may have shaped how people talked about public housing as "problem" areas in the neighborhood. Many of the residents perceived both the history of racist exclusion and ties to organized crime to be moving in positive directions as resident changes had brought a more "worldly" and less provincial feel. Still, the area remained predominantly white and increasingly wealthy.

Crime in South Boston today was a combination of minor disorder (often tied to drug use) and isolated incidents of violent crime, often against "innocent" victims. Residents were typically more concerned with the issues that came with ongoing development than they were with crime. Resident meetings spent little time talking about crime, outside of those singular incidents, and they mentioned few "problem areas" in their neighborhoods. Rather than figuring out how to negotiate life in South Boston, people being released from the House of Correction were largely blocked out of the neighborhood altogether because of the cost and the relatively few services that targeted people with their needs. Some visited, either to go to court or to go to the beaches and park facilities, but they did not live there. While they had similarly favorable narratives of other long-term residents, they now felt that South Boston was both financially and socially inaccessible. South Boston is a counterpoint to the experiences of people returning from incarceration to Dorchester, where people generally felt welcome and able to stay there if they chose to (if not without some tensions), and the South End, with its needed services and related dangers. South Boston was, at most, a pleasant memory for those who had grown up there.

SIX

Small Towns, Poverty, and Addiction

My family has lived there their whole life. Like, my cousin has
been arrested 110 times, my mother has been arrested 110 times.
So it's either the cops can't stand me, looking for a reason—you
know what I'm saying, excuse my language—bust my balls, or
they get along with me.

GEORGE, white man in his 30s

It's different. It's quiet. It's boring, but it keeps me out of trouble,
I guess you could say.

SARAH, white woman in her 30s

MOST OF THE PEOPLE we interviewed who were being released from the
House of Correction were going to the city of Boston or inner-ring suburbs
like Cambridge, Chelsea, or Quincy. This follows the pattern of the institution in which most people are serving sentences based on charges in Suffolk
County and many were living within a few miles of the facility (mostly in
neighborhoods in Roxbury and Dorchester) (Forman et al. 2016). Those
in urban areas had varying levels of stability and mobility, but they all had
relatively accessible public transportation and many had discounted transit
passes. Mobility in more distant suburbs or small towns was quite different.

The towns that I include here as "small towns" range in size from under
ten thousand to sixty thousand residents, with a population density of
between three hundred and twenty-five hundred people per square mile and
at least 75 percent white. In contrast, the city of Boston has a population
of approximately six hundred fifty thousand, with density of about thirteen
thousand five hundred people per square mile, and is just under 50 percent
white. The delineations are somewhat arbitrary, but generally the smaller
towns reflected here are outside of the Route 128 corridor "inner beltway"
circling the city and outside of the Massachusetts Bay Transit Authority's

(MBTA, or T) train routes, though they may be on a commuter rail line. This means that public transportation was limited, at best, and it was expensive to get to Boston. Because of this, small-town residents often led lives anchored in their residential neighborhood. None had their own car, and most relied primarily on walking or getting rides from sponsors, romantic partners, or friends (see also Bohmert 2016). What fell into easy walking radiuses was much more limited in less densely populated areas. Those who did have access to a car often did not have a driver's license, which meant they put themselves at risk of arrest and possibly a probation violation and reincarceration if they drove. The lack of access to transportation made working, accessing services, and maintaining contact with loved ones all more complicated.

The people we interviewed who lived in smaller towns further from the city did so for several reasons. In a few cases, they had connections in these towns and went there to give themselves some distance from their past. Others were from these towns but gravitated to Boston when they were using drugs. When they were released, and they were trying to "go straight," they went back home. In a few cases, people were also transferred to the Suffolk County House of Correction from facilities in more distant counties and so returned home when they were released. Those who were returning to a familiar town faced many of the same challenges as those returning to an old neighborhood. Those who moved to a new town felt particularly isolated, even if they also felt this was beneficial to them.

Most of the people we interviewed who were living in rural or suburban areas were white. This is not atypical for Massachusetts, where most of the people of color live in Boston and a few former mill towns like Brockton, Lowell, and Springfield. This also shaped their experiences in significant ways. Many were known to the police in their towns because of their prior arrests, usually related to drug or alcohol use. They were not targeted because they fit a generic description, as were many of the people of color in cities. Outside of their social circles, the small-town white participants' criminal record was not assumed. These realities were not limited to white people returning to small towns or suburbs, but it was a significant part of their experience in those settings. A few of the Black or Latinx people who spent at least part of their time farther outside of Boston tended to be in mill towns such as Brockton or in nearby cities such as Providence, Rhode Island.

As with most of the people we interviewed in the Boston area, participants rarely had cars. At best, there might be a car in their immediate social circle that they could borrow or a person with a car who could sometimes give them rides. This reflected their economic standing, the expense of a car, and licenses revoked after Operating Under the Influence charges. While some hoped to regain their license after paying fees and attending trainings, others were doubtful because of the extensiveness of their record. The lack of a driver's license or car is particularly challenging in smaller towns and less dense areas, because fewer businesses and services were within walking distance and public transportation was limited.

George, a white man in his 30s, returned to the suburb in which he grew up when he was released. He initially planned to stay with friends. While he did not stay where he had planned, he did spend several weeks bouncing between a few friends' houses. He said he could have stayed at each house longer, but "they have their own stuff going on too; know what I'm saying? I don't like to intrude on anyone, be a burden. I would rather bounce back and forth, just to make it easier." Here, George had an attitude that was shared with many others who were bouncing and couch surfing with friends. They wanted to minimize the burden on any one person or household and not overstay their welcome. A few months after his release, he moved into an apartment that he shared with roommates. These were casual friends or acquaintances, many of whom did not stay long, functioning as disposable ties, with accelerated but short-lived, intimacy (Desmond 2012b). From this time on, he stayed at that apartment with a revolving group of roommates.

George did masonry work as well as odd jobs like snow shoveling. While he was incarcerated, an ex-girlfriend was supposed to monitor his phone. Shortly before his release, he said, "They checked the messages for me and got back to the people, so I have, actually, my ex-girlfriend that's doing that for me. She works on that, so she calls people back and just tells them, 'Oh yeah, he's busy,' you know, da da da, has it all lined up." The day he was released, he walked from the House of Correction to sign up for food stamps and Mass Health (insurance). He also visited a former client for whom he had done work in the past.

GEORGE: One of the first stops I actually made—I don't remember if I told you, but I do snow removal in the wintertime, and I went and

I saw one of my customers that I do snow removal for. My ex was supposed to find someone to go do her driveway. She never did. So, I went there and I apologized to the lady, because I've also done masonry work for her. . . . I didn't know where to go to get money. I said, "Who best to go to? One of my customers that have always taken care of me. At least apologize to them and let them know I'm out, if they need anything, that I'm back around, I'll have the phone back on in the next few days. . . . It was in the afternoon by the time I made it there.

I asked her, I said, "listen I have to know if I can ask you a huge favor. Can I borrow a few dollars, just until next weekend?" And I said, "I'll pay you back." She goes, "Yeah, come back in a few hours. I got to go to the store anyway, so I'm going to grab some money." I went back a few hours later. I ended up talking to her and her husband; they threw me a few hundred bucks. They told me they didn't want it back. They were like, "Here's a hundred bucks. You've always been fair with us, you've always been honest. Just take it." I'm like, "No, I'll be back next weekend to give you the money. And they're like, "No, we don't want it back. It would be an insult." I was like, "OK, I'm not complaining." So, I've been by there a couple times, they haven't had no work for me, but I can stay in contact with them.

AL: Did you tell them where you'd been, why you hadn't been in contact?

GEORGE: Yeah, I told them what happened. I told them the truth and everything.

George lost his driver's license after an Operating Under the Influence charge and owed several hundred dollars in fees. While serving probation for the OUI and related charges, he got in a fight with his girlfriend at his grandfather's house and was charged with breaking and entering. These latter charges led to his incarceration. As a result of losing his license, he had to rely on friends or coworkers for rides and to deliver materials and tools to work sites, which restricted his ability to work. His major goals were to get his license back and buy a truck, so he could more easily work on his own. Both the nature of his work and where he lived made this particularly important for him. George could sometimes ride his bike to work, but some worksites were at a distance, and he could not transport tools. Despite the OUI charge, George said he did not have a drinking problem. He did have a history of getting in trouble, and was known to the police in his town, "because my family has lived there their whole life. Like, my cousin has been arrested 110 times, my mother has been arrested 110 times. So it's either the cops can't stand me, looking for a reason [to]—you know what I'm saying, excuse my language—bust my balls, or they get along with me."

Even without a license, George started working a few days after his release. He got work through a temp agency and reconnected with friends in manual labor jobs. He did clean outs of businesses and houses, demolition work, plastering, and trash pickup. The latter paid thirty dollars an hour, "that was great because I was making five hundred dollars in two days." He was saving money, but "once I save up enough money I can either get a place or I can get my license. I want my license first because that will make it easier for when I have a place, because I'll make more money." George said "that's the only thing that's killing me right now, is that I make good money. Most of my jobs, I make between thirteen and twenty dollars an hour, depending on what it is, but I could be making twenty-five to thirty dollars if I had my license." While George temporarily had access to his grandmother's car until it got towed and he couldn't afford to get it back, he did not have a driver's license. Still, he enjoyed having a car, "because then I didn't have to rely on the woman that I was just seeing to ask her for a ride all the time."

Relative to many of the people I talked to, George had a smooth transition from the House of Correction. He drank casually but did not consider it a problem. Beginning a few months after his release, he had a stable and consistent place to live. Before that, he had several friends with whom he could stay. He was willing and able to do manual labor and was able to tap into his existing work networks and connections to do so. While he was known to the police, he did not have much contact with them over the course of the year. Still, a year after his release, he did not have a driver's license. He said, "I still owe. I paid a few hundred. I still owe almost like fifteen hundred dollars. Work got a little slow. Things got a little hectic here. I took some time off. Now I'm just trying to put everything back together." He was fighting with one of his roommates, because of her behavior, and his landlord, because of repairs that needed to be done on the building. Over the year, he had several sets of roommates. In our final interview, George said his biggest challenges were "probably getting back on my feet and turning this into a home and being able to see my daughter." He had not seen his teenage daughter since before his most recent incarceration. "When I got locked up, I didn't call them. I didn't write them [his daughter and her mother], which was my fault. I should have, but it was embarrassing." He eventually got in touch with his daughter's mother, and sent her money when he could, but he did not talk to his daughter. Each time we talked, he said he was waiting until he had a driver's license to make the trip to their home in Rhode Island to visit.

While George did not consider himself an addict, because of his charges (and related fines), he faced challenges similar to those who self-identified as a problem drinker or drug user in terms of being able to get a driver's license. For George, getting back on his feet meant "financially, and making better decisions." When asked what decisions he meant, he said, "Everything and anything. I don't drink all the time, but there's time when I'm aggravated that I definitely know I don't need a beer, but to me it calms me down." He still didn't think that drinking was a problem for him, though his mother did have a history of alcoholism. He said, "I just think that I should want to drink because I want to drink, not because I'm stressed out." He still felt like he was trying to "put my life back together." He did feel like he had grown up in the past year, and had "learned to communicate a little better." Still, he did not feel particularly accomplished and felt he had a long way to go to achieve his goals. He was also particularly dependent on having a vehicle because of the nature of his work, needing to transport tools, and travel longer distances to work sites.

Others were similarly dependent on getting rides, walking, or finding particularly limited public transportation. Even without a need to transport tools, not having a car severely limited their movements. For example, Donna moved back to a small town in Central Massachusetts. She was a white woman in her 50s with a long history of alcoholism, who had lost her driver's license. She also had a bad knee and so was limited in how far she could walk. Thus, her range of movement was largely limited to a mile radius of her apartment. In addition to Alcoholics Anonymous meetings, she wanted to go to church but didn't because "it was a walking situation." Donna described a typical day: "I get up, get ready, go to the groups. . . . I get up, get dressed, and I walk. When I get back, I'm tired. My knee's killing me, so I just watch TV, play with the baby [her grandchild]. I walk to the park often." Because of her record, which included multiple OUI charges, she did not expect to ever get a driver's license again. Her boyfriend sometimes gave her a ride, but "He works 2 to 11 [p.m.]. He works through 11 so he don't get up in the morning so I don't rely on him. I just have to get to my meetings. I walk there." She was not working, both because she was on disability and because of the "not good" buses in her town. Angie, also a white woman in her 50s who had a similar history to Donna and lived in a nearby town, relied on a paratransit van. She said, "If I didn't have that, I'd be stuck, because there's no buses here." Still, she said, "Sometimes that van, you got to wait an hour and a half because they don't have enough drivers. I'm thankful for it, believe me. At least I can get to where I got to go." She also met the "nicest people" on the van. By the final interview, two years after her release, she had bought a bike, though she also still used the van service and walked. Like Donna, she did not expect to get her driver's license back, after multiple OUI and other charges related to alcohol and drug use.

George's biggest challenges were earning enough money to meet his needs and developing strong relationships. He was hindered by not having a vehicle, particularly given the nature of his work. For those who needed social service support or medical care, transportation became even more of an issue. For multiple and common reasons, people were particularly constrained in their movements when they did not have ready access to public transportation and when they were living in less walkable areas.

ADDICTION AND SUPPORT SERVICES
IN NONURBAN AREAS

Addiction was a common issue among our respondents, including those in small towns. Most of those living in small towns were returning to places where they had a history of drug or alcohol use, and so they were returning to familiar environments with limited formal supports and limited accessibility of available supports.

Donna (white, 50s) was transferred to the Suffolk County House of Correction, but "had never been in this neck of the woods [Boston]," and returned to the town she had been living in prior to her arrest. Donna had a long-standing problem with alcohol. Her parents both died in close succession after she had cared for them. She fought with her two brothers over the care of their parents and hadn't spoken to either since the parents' deaths. She then began drinking heavily. "I used to drink. I am an alcoholic. I used to drink, but I never drank like I drank this bout. It was every single day. I would wake up in the morning, have a half gallon of vodka and I never—I was like a weekend warrior, you know, before. But this was the worst relapse I ever had." She went through withdrawal while in jail; "I went through withdrawals when I first got caught when I went to Pittsfield. Oh my god, it was horrible. It was the most horrible thing in my life. . . . I was hallucinating, talking to the floors, talking inside the toilet. I was seeing my daughter; she died in front of me. It was horrible. The withdrawals were fucking horrible." She had been incarcerated several times before, though usually for a few weeks at a time, and nearer her home. Most of these charges were related to her alcohol use, most recently for operating under the influence and getting in a car accident.

One of the reasons Donna planned to move to this town was because the rents were more affordable than in her nearby hometown. Still, most of her disability payment went to rent. Donna found her current apartment through a friend.

> I didn't think I'd be able to get the apartment. I tried to get an apartment over there, and I told them, "Look, I just got out of jail for drunk driving." They didn't let me have the apartment. This one I lied, I tried to go with my maiden name, but he found out. Then I was straight with him. I said, "Look, I'm on probation, I don't plan on drinking. I plan on this being the happy fifty years of my life. I don't plan on using. I don't want to." He's got a close eye; he watches everything that goes on.

She described her street as a "drug street," but "I just tell them I don't want to do it." Her daughter's boyfriend's family gave her some furniture because she lost everything while incarcerated. Her landlord at the time would not let her back in to retrieve her belongings. She also no longer considered her hometown to be "home," because of the bad memories she associated with it. She described her current town as, "It's just a little hick town. Everybody knows everybody. It's nice. I like it. There's only two [Alcoholics Anonymous] meetings [per week] so I am going to get—I know one girl there. Like when she goes to meetings, I am going to ask her to bring me because I lost my license." Donna felt the meetings were important for her, saying, "I know the tools because, like I said, I lived and breathed AA. I did. I loved it. I always felt so good, but I always end up trying to think I can do it on my own, you know. I can't do it on my own, because I always end up in jail." She appreciated the supportive community she found at AA, and the fact that everyone knows everyone. Still, in our first post-release interview, she said "I get bored and I know I should [go to a meeting], but sometimes I don't go." To stay straight, she said she had to "get a routine and a straight life." A few months later, she said, "I used to love AA. It's just I don't have the oomph to do it this round."

In our fourth interview, while she said she was generally "clean as a bean," she said she relapsed one weekend. She said:

> I told them [probation] I relapsed for a weekend when I got my check. I did everything: coke, heroin, everything. . . . I did everything. For two days,

I was on a bender, then I stopped. I knew I was fucking up. Then my probation officer came for a urine [test]. It was five days after. Then I didn't want to give her a urine. Then I told her, started crying, "Oh, no, I relapsed." I didn't have to tell her, because I did a urine [and] it was all clean. I ratted myself out for nothing.

Donna attributed the relapse to fighting with her daughter and having extra money. Someone she knew sent her a picture of Adderall—"my favorite drug"—and "I started with that and was off and running." She stopped after a few days; "I knew I was fucking up. I don't want to go back to that lifestyle, chasing the drugs. I'm like, 'Fuck that.' I don't want to go back to jail." Donna's probation officer did not violate her probation as a result of the relapse. After this, she started going to a battered women's group and intensive outpatient therapy.

In addition to AA, Donna returned to seeing a psychiatrist and a counselor. She said, "I've been medicating myself for over forty years; now I'm just going to let the doctors do it." Both mental health and substance use issues were prevalent in Donna's family. Donna's father "had breakdowns. . . . He didn't know who we were for—I was 13. . . . One time he had a breakdown and he thought he was God." When Donna was in high school, she was raped by an acquaintance, which led her to drop out of school. Her husband and another romantic partner had been abusive toward her. She also began drinking when she was a teenager. "When I drink, I make bad decisions, really bad decisions." Alcohol use was prevalent in her family. "My father was a mean alcoholic. My brother was an alcoholic. My other brother is a dry drunk." Donna did not explicitly equate her alcohol use to a response to trauma, but she did stop drinking for several years in her late 20s: "First time, I left my husband. I moved in with my cousin and she didn't drink. I started going to AA and I loved it." She then relapsed for about ten years after she returned to her husband, and then "I got straight again when I took care of my parents. Those were good years too." Donna left her husband for good when her youngest daughter was a baby. She decided, "I am not doing another twenty years like this."

Donna's two older daughters both had problems with drug use. "All my kids are addicts," she said. One of her daughters started going to a methadone clinic and the other was taking Suboxone. One of her daughters struggled throughout the year with addiction. Shortly before our final interview, Donna's daughter overdosed. She had been staying with her daughter's father's mother, who "got up for something. It was like two in the morning and she was blue on her kitchen floor. Her uncle gave her mouth-to-mouth and CPR. The ambulance came. They gave her Narcan and she threw up right away and [it] saved her life."[1] Donna was then trying to get a Section 35, a civil commitment for those with substance use disorders. After she got the court order, she had five days to find her daughter. She had to go back to court to get a new order and spent about a week trying to find her. Donna was then using all of her limited cell phone minutes to sort out her daughter's social security and food stamps while she was in treatment. She was saving her last few minutes in case her daughter called from the treatment facility.

When I asked Donna if her daughter had been in treatment before, she in turn asked her youngest daughter, who was in the apartment with us. Her daughter said she "went to jail." Donna added that she "went to jail once for drugs. That's not really treatment." Donna was right, of course, and yet for many of our interviewees, jail (including jail- or prison-based treatment) was as much treatment as they could access, and it was not uncommon for people to frame this as a break from drug use. Donna went on to say that her daughter was also self-medicating, including with Adderall and Klonopin. Donna was in intensive therapy, at the time, and "I'm doing what they tell me. If [my daughter] had OD'd, I wouldn't have gone back. I couldn't take the pain. It hurt so bad. It was really bad."

Donna's main support systems were her boyfriend and a friend who lived nearby. While she saw her boyfriend every day, she did not live with him; "I kind of like the way it is because I don't want to live with no man." By our final interview, she described this relationship as more distant, but he did help her financially. She also kept in touch with one woman she knew from the House of Correction who lived in Boston and thought she might keep in touch with some of the women she met through a women's group. She suspected that her friend had relapsed, so by our final interview, she said, "I don't see her that often anymore." She suspected her boyfriend might also be using. By then, her youngest daughter, her boyfriend, and their baby were also living with Donna. In our final interview, she continued to talk about how scared she was in "real jail" [the House of Correction]. In some ways, Donna's life was not dramatically different from that of others who were struggling with addictions in a city. A key difference, however, was her lack of mobility, and a correspondingly narrow range of service and treatment options. Within her social networks and her neighborhood, she had ready access to drugs or alcohol if she wanted them, but she had relatively less access to supports to help her not use.

Everyone in this project had been incarcerated in Suffolk County. While a few were transferred from other counties, most were convicted of charges in Suffolk County and most had ties to Boston. These ties reflected varied connections to their drug use and their support networks. Some lived in Boston when they were actively using drugs and went to their hometown when they were not. As Lillian, a Black woman in her 20s who was from a mill town, said, "I don't get high in [hometown] for fear of everyone knowing what I try to hide from them. I get high in Boston." Others had a history of drug use in their hometown and lived in halfway houses and other supportive environments in Boston. Regardless of their preferences, they moved to their current towns upon their release because they had a place to live there.

Kristina, a white woman in her 20s, was released after her first commitment in the House of Correction and returned to her hometown. She lived in an apartment in a building owned by her child's father and where she helped with the building management. Aside from helping him, she did not work. She said, "I want to work, but my daughter's father wants me to be available for her. In order for him to pay my bills, I have to just do what he says." She described the area as "probably like not one of the nicer areas" of town. She later said, "I don't even go out after its dark out. I really don't. This area is like a high prostitution, drug area, I guess. I just personally don't go out after dark at all. One time I got jumped by a transvestite, some guy dressed like a girl, and for no reason at all. I was just walking home. That's why when I'm walking, I don't have headphones anymore." Since she did not go outside on her own after dark, her movements were even more constrained. Like most, she did not have a car. "If I'm going somewhere, I walk there. My friend, she drives, so I'll go with her. My daughter's father pick me up and bring me home and stuff. He brings me home at night." In contrast to men, who talked about regulating their movements to avoid police surveillance or peers who could tempt them into illegal behavior, Kristina (and other women) were more concerned with potential victimization, and regulated her movements to protect herself from that.

Like Donna, Kristina had a history of addiction that she continued to struggle with over the course of the year. When she was being released, she said "I don't plan on doing drugs. . . . Like, the only time I break the law is when I'm doing drugs. Do you know what I mean? So if I don't do drugs, I won't break the law basically." She wanted to do more "recovery stuff." She did not go to meetings often but did talk to friends in Boston who were in recovery. With friends who were using, she would talk to them on the phone, but did not hang out with them. One friend overdosed and died the day after her release. In our third interview, about five months after her release, I asked her what had been going on. She responded, "Not much. I did relapse, and I was using, and now I'm on the methadone clinic." She went on to say, "I started using, I don't know, it was probably a couple of months ago, and I just got on the clinic, and besides that, I've been seeing my daughter. You know, I overdosed a couple of times, so my daughter's father is only letting me see her supervised for now, which is understandable." I clarified that this was several overdoses just in the past few months and tried to get her to elaborate.[2] She matter-of-factly said:

> I was with other people. Every time that it happened, I was with other people, and they called 911, and they came and had to give me Narcan. I think one time, I think it was the second time I overdosed, the detectives had come to my house and told me to go to—he asked if he wanted to get me into a program. I just thought it was kind of shady, like a cop coming here, but I guess it was my daughter's father's friend. He knows the cops and stuff, so he was just trying to get me help without letting me know that he knew. Do you know what I mean?

This officer told her, "We do this all the time." She added, "They don't ever do that. They don't try to get you into programs, but then eventually I talked to my daughter's father, and he told me what happened." She contrasted her experiences of overdoses. "As far as the overdoses go, I can't even say they scared me or anything, and I don't know why that is. I don't know. Maybe it's because I don't know what happened. I think it's more traumatic for the people that were there because they saw it. One of our friends overdosed the other day, and I saw it, and it was very traumatic to watch from my end, to see her." She explained this calmly, and with a sense of distance. The person who is overdosing is unaware of what is happening, while those who witness it are. Kristina said the friend who overdosed "was like me. I didn't remember anything. She didn't remember anything." A friend, who was listening in on this part of our conversation, added, "as I was having a nervous breakdown." News of her overdoses spread quickly through her social networks, which included police officers and firefighters.

Kristina said, "I guess it's just hard being back here, as opposed to living in Boston where all my friends were clean. I live here, and it's like everyone in this building gets high or uses drugs, and then I have a lot of friends that are still using, that are coming by because they know I'm home now, and it's hard to—." For a while, her friends came over and used in front of her, while she abstained. Eventually she said, "'You know, I'm going to get high too. If everyone else is going to get high, I'm getting high too.' I think when I said that I was hoping they were going to say that they weren't going to get high, but it didn't work out that way, and I ended up getting high." For a while, this "wasn't an everyday thing," but it began affecting her ability to see her daughter and to keep up with her college classes. She began trying to isolate herself from these friends. I asked if she went to twelve-step meetings, and she said, "No, I'd like to, but I don't know. When I know people, I'm really talkative and a social person, but when I don't know people, I'm really guarded, and I don't like to—I get nervous in groups, like I break out in hives. I don't want to go by myself." In our next interview, she also said "I've never really been into meetings and stuff like that. I feel like I already have enough going on in my life. I know this is rude, but I don't really want to listen to other people's problems." By our last interview, she said she had been depressed for several months, and seemed particularly listless. She was still seeing her daughter but did not register for more college classes. Her days consisted of going to the methadone clinic, and then spending time in the afternoon with her daughter and her daughter's father. She said "I don't really talk to anybody. I pretty much just stay home and see my daughter and that's it."

Kristina had more connections to people who were actively using drugs in her current town, and more friends who were in recovery in Boston, forty miles away. In contrast, Richard, a white man in his 50s, was most actively involved in drugs in Boston. He said he had been "using and abusing myself for heroin"[3] since the late 1970s and "I am doing a life bid on the installment plan." Richard was originally from the West End and his mother was from the North End. He described growing up in downtown Boston. "In the late '60s and '70s, there were gangsters. There was a lot going on. Everyone was making money. It could be violent, it depends on where. Blacks and Spanish weren't allowed back then. It was prejudiced." He moved to the suburbs as a child, "but I just slept there." When he was released, he continued the pattern of just sleeping in his mother's house and traveling to Boston each day. In our third interview, he said he had started using heroin again. Then started going to the methadone clinic, though he stopped going about six months later. He was still staying with his mother, but "I keep it moving.

I leave." At that time (when he was not using drugs), he spent a lot of time walking in her town. When he was using drugs, he would take the bus to Boston, about ten miles from his home, every day. He would go to different parts of Boston: "Depends on who I call. Who's got the best stuff. What a waste of a life." Richard was unusual in his commitment to traveling to Boston most days despite the cost and distance.

In our final interview, about sixteen months after the first, Richard was in a residential drug treatment program. He had just beaten another case, which he took to trial, "because I wasn't just laying down for them no more, and I didn't want to go back to jail." Another older open case, for public urination, had been dismissed. He said, "I've been trying to get this detox, I've been trying to get further treatment for the past seven months. I don't know if I told you that before. I'm coming really clean now in the end. . . . I was messing up." He said he had been to detox multiple times in the past year but was then going on for further treatment. He also had overdosed three times since he'd been out of the House of Correction. Once, he was in Boston Common and once he was in a parking garage; passersby called 911 and he was given Narcan. For Richard, he considered himself a "city" person, even after over forty years of living in a suburb. Given that his life and his social networks were still rooted in Boston, he gravitated there while he was using drugs. With the exception of our final interview, which took place at a suburban drug treatment facility, we also met in Boston or Cambridge at his suggestion.

Commuting to Boston was cumbersome, time consuming, and expensive for those living farther out. For those who equated Boston with getting into trouble and using drugs, being expensive and time consuming was beneficial, as it was a barrier to giving in to temptation. Some, though, had affective ties to Boston, and they maintained some level of connection to it. The problem was not the city itself, but the person's relationship to it.

STARTING OVER IN A SMALL TOWN

Most of our respondents had limited choice in where they lived. They lived with family when they could, which often kept them in familiar areas. Occasionally, a family member who lived farther away provided an opportunity to start over. Sarah, a white woman in her 30s, moved to the same small town where Kristina lived, to "chill out" and "get sober." She was from Charlestown, a neighborhood in Boston between the Mystic and Charles Rivers that has a history and reputation like South Boston, with a large working-class Irish American population, Irish gangs, and more recent gentrification. Sarah described the Charlestown of her childhood: "A lot of drugs, a lot of crime. A lot of people's dads and stuff, a lot of my friends, their dads were in jail, robbing banks and stuff like that. I thought that was really cool. I thought they're doing that for their families because they want to give their families a better life. I justified it. . . . People either are in jail, you're dead, or you're actively using. That was around me my whole life. It was hard not to fall into it." Sarah was raised by her grandparents, her teenaged mother, and her father. Her father spent much of her childhood in prison. "They told me he was at work or whatever. I think it took a couple of days for them to tell me that he was in jail, he wasn't coming back for a little while." At this point, she started to drink more. Still, she described her childhood as good, with some bad memories. Sarah described how she ended up incarcerated, highlighting another dimension of Charlestown's reputation.

> I was addicted to drugs, so a lot of that had to do with the money. I needed the money. A lot of people, like in the area where I live, rob banks. I kind of grew up with that. I am from Charlestown, and I don't want to use that as an excuse but, like, my whole life like I have been around a lot of bank robbers, I guess. It wasn't a really hard decision to make. I needed money and I wanted it really fast. I wanted it now and that popped into my mind instantly, so that is what I did.

Those charges resulted in incarceration at MCI-Framingham and county-level probation sentences. When we met, Sarah was being released after serving out a probation violation for not reporting to court. Despite a relatively short record of charges, "the judge told me I was no longer probation material, which is fine. I'm kind of done with being on probation and being in jail. It's been a long time, you know. It's going to be a new start for me." She planned to stay with her aunt, "which is somewhere that I don't really ever go and I don't really know much about it up there. I don't really leave Boston much, so I think it will be nice just to be with family. . . . I didn't want to go back right into the city." Sarah initially planned to stay with her aunt for a few months before returning to Charlestown, where, she said, "everybody knows everybody. Everyone knows everyone's business. A lot of drugs there, a lot of crime. It's where I have lived my whole life though, and it's a really good sense of community there. There is a lot of like Irish Catholic hardworking people. I am just really familiar with up there. I feel safe there." She saw staying with her aunt as a "vacation" and a chance for "peace and quiet" after being in the House of Correction and before returning home. "I am proud to be from Charlestown. It ruined my life but I am proud to be from there."

When I first visited Sarah at her aunt's house a few weeks after her release, she said that she liked it there; "I do like it. It's different, it's quiet, it's boring, but it keeps me out of trouble I guess I could say." After this interview, I lost touch with her for about twenty months. When I finally got in touch, she described what had happened in the meantime,

> I went back again. I violated probation. I hadn't picked up any case or even gotten arrested for anything since the initial bank robberies back in 2008. It was just a probation violation because I was using and I stipulated to do urines and stuff. I didn't want to go in and pee dirty and then have them send me off to jail, so I just skipped out on probation, stopped going. Then I got pulled over with a friend of mine for a broken tail light and they ran both of our names and, of course, I had a warrant. So I went back [to prison]. I just wrapped up the rest of my probation basically.

She was again staying in the same town, but now with her parents. This time, she said "It's just boring. I don't have any friends. I like going to [twelve-step] meetings and stuff, but I don't even really know where to go to meetings up here. I really don't want to go in places like that on my own, alone. I don't really do much up here. It's just really, really boring." She went back to Charlestown once or twice a month and went to meetings then. A few months after her initial release (when we met), she said,

> I just eventually started using and just stayed down there [Charlestown], because I knew if I came back up here, it's probably not good for me. I had a habit at that point, so I didn't want to leave the area where I could score drugs every day. . . . For a few months, I think it was four months, I'd smoke pot and stuff, but I wasn't using heroin or anything. I think I went down to Charlestown maybe March or April and then I stayed down there pretty much until I got picked up [in October]. . . . Just moved out of my aunt's and moved into my friend's house. She had a drug dealer living upstairs and it was just bound to happen. It's people, places, and things. They're not lying about that, it's true. It is.

Now, when she visited Charlestown, she stayed with sober friends, went to meetings, and stayed away from the public housing developments where she used to use. She also saw a doctor in Charlestown. She took the commuter rail to get to Boston, "But that's expensive—$10.50 each way." In our final interview, she said she was avoiding Charlestown: "Well, not even so much Charlestown, like the projects. Only because I, that's, I didn't really do much up there besides get high. . . . That part of Charlestown. A lot of it is the people, too. That's a trigger for me. Like if I see somebody high."

Sarah's daughter, who lived with her father's family, stayed with her every other weekend, and they "go to the park, we make meals, stuff like that. Watch TV together. If I have a little money, we'll go out and eat ice cream. She likes to go for ice cream. We went apple picking a couple of weeks ago. Stuff like that." She maintained contact with some friends on Facebook, but "a lot of them are dying [of overdoses]. . . . You see it on Facebook. Every time I log on it's an obituary. A lot of people dying. A lot. It's really scary actually. It's not a good thing they're dying, but it's good for me. All the more I don't want to get back into that." For her, Facebook was important in keeping in touch with some of her friends. "I mean a lot of my friends I've known since kindergarten. It's important for me to keep in touch with them. . . . Some people it's important to keep in touch with no matter how bad they're doing. I want to keep in touch with them. I think a lot of people are dying. That's why I feel it is important. They're friends that I've known forever, to keep in touch with them because you never know. They could die."

Facebook helped her maintain contact when she was physically far way, but it also helped her manage those interactions as she tried to avoid being in the same physical spaces with people who were actively using. "I don't have the urge up here to use drugs at all. But when I get down in certain areas and stuff and certain places that I used to get high, absolutely it makes me feel like I want to get high. I just remove myself from that situation." Sarah maintained that balance by talking to people on the phone or Facebook but limiting where she went. Since she was living far way and in a relatively inaccessible area, this was easy for her to do. Those who were living in towns or cities where they had larger social networks had to navigate these relationships in person. Some still relied on Facebook and other social media to keep some connection, while managing these relationships and maintaining some distance.[4]

Between our third and fourth interviews, Sarah relapsed again. She said, "Nothing set it off. I was just having to meet with a couple of people that day that were getting married. And I said I'd only do just one time, you know.

I ended up staying out for three days." She then started going to a methadone clinic, riding with her father who was also taking methadone. She happened to come home on a Wednesday, and the clinic did intakes on Thursday. She was hesitant to go on methadone again, since the last time she did she had to detox in jail. Without access to a car, it "would be pain. It's not, up here, it's not like it is at home [Boston], where there's like MBTA, buses everywhere. Even in, like, suburbs, there's buses. But it's not like that up here. . . . I'm sure there's a way, but it's not something easy." Her mother gave her rides for her part time job cleaning houses. By the fifth interview, she was thinking about tapering down off of methadone. She said, "I just don't want to be on anything. I just don't. I remember—I just like going to sleep and waking up without having to have something to get me going every day." Sarah continued to use marijuana, "I like marijuana. It doesn't make me say, 'Oh, I want to go shoot a bag of heroin.' You know? Whereas drinking or something like that might make me want to use other drugs. . . . It helps me with the pain in my leg,[5] it helps with my anxiety, I don't know, I enjoy it." Because of this and the drug tests at the methadone clinic, she could not get approved to do "take homes," and so still needed to go daily to the methadone clinic.

Sarah described her town as boring, but also said "I'm kind of like a homebody anyway. As long as I have Netflix and my dogs." For a while, she got together with another woman who lived in the same town who had been her cell mate and friend in the House of Correction, until the woman moved to Dorchester. She maintained contact with other women she knew from the House of Correction via Facebook.

> Because you do, you know, I mean you're in there with these women, you know, every hour of every day. And it's hard not to forge relationships, you know. A lot of people will say, "Oh you know, you met her in jail, she's not a real friend." But I don't think that's true, because even more so, like what are you gonna do all day? Sit in there and have your coffee and you're going to talk and you're going to talk about your life and you know, your background and stuff. And you do, you get close with these women. And most of them, 95 percent of them, have kids, you know. And you bond over stuff like that, you know. Because you're all going through the exact same thing as that other person and you know, you both lean on each other to cope and deal with what you have to deal with there, you know? So you do, you get to know someone. I'm not going to say, like I didn't get out and meet up with a couple of these girls and they were totally different than how they were in jail. You know, just like, and you know that they're a good person because

that's what you really are when you're sober, but they do some fucked up shit, you know? . . . Like everyone's different when they use, aren't they?

While she was friendly with a few people she either saw at the methadone clinic or on the street, "I don't really have a social life up here. Kind of sucks, but it's better than being down there." She said she wished she were closer to Boston, but "it's a good thing, kind of, in a way, you know? . . . Not that I'd be down there using, but it could be a little less difficult to get high down there than it is up here if I wanted to. And just like being around certain people and areas, it's probably best." She also avoided the "Mass Cass" area.

> SARAH: I don't hang out on Mass Ave like girls from South Bay. I never frequented Mass Ave myself, but the few times I have been down there, it's bad. Like right around South Bay. It's really bad down there.
>
> AL: How so?
>
> SARAH: It looks like an episode of *The Walking Dead*. It's bad, it's just, blatant drug deals. Undercover cops everywhere. Like the Cumberland Farms on Mass Ave? Oh my god, it's just bad. Everyone down there. It's a mess, it's sad. It's really sad. People just like OD'ing at the bus stop. There's like three different methadone clinics over there, too.

She also sees "stupid" people on Facebook selling drugs, which she also avoids. For her, going to the methadone clinic in her town also restricted her movements, since she needed to go there daily. She spent much of her time at home, "During the week, I don't really do much, unless I have appointments or whatever, you know. I just go to the clinic, come home, we clean up a little, shower, watch TV, that's it."

Like the others living in smaller towns and trying to stay sober, Sarah spent most of her time at home. Her family did have a car, but she and her parents shared it and so her movements were restricted to where and when one of them could drive her. Unlike those returning to a hometown or other familiar area, Sarah also was new to her town. This made her feel more alone, which she both appreciated—as it provided distance from drug use and drug-using associates—and found isolating. She had her parents, a daughter she saw on weekends, and acquaintances she knew from the methadone clinic or other passing contacts. Her longtime friends, however, felt very distant to her. She maintained contact via Facebook with both her old friends and newer friends she met while incarcerated. This helped her bridge geographical distances and manage relationships with active drug users but was still a limited social circle.

CONCLUSION

This project was designed as a study of urban reentry, and so I did not anticipate having respondents who lived well outside the Boston metro area. Still, their paths to the House of Correction and to their current towns is illustrative of some issues and themes that are worth pursuing with more robust small town and rural samples. As criminologist Miriam Bohmert and colleagues (2017) have demonstrated, transportation is key to successful reentry. This can be taken for granted in urban areas, where not only is public transportation often more readily available but—at least in dense cities like Boston—more is accessible by walking. Some of the Boston-area participants walked significant distances as they accessed services and sometimes went to work and spent significant time on public transportation when walking was not preferred or desirable. These movements were important not only in accessing places, but in terms of the people they met and interacted with along the way. In smaller towns, public transportation was limited, at best, and there was often less to walk *to*. This might mean twice weekly twelve-step meetings in Donna's town, compared to close to fifty meetings a day in the immediate Boston area.[6]

Much like living in a high-crime area that is familiar, living in a smaller town was a double-edged sword for many. Those returning to a town they were familiar with were returning to social networks—for better and for worse. They might have a place to stay and social support and might also be returning to drug-using networks. This was like those returning to an old urban neighborhood, and yet these networks often were harder to avoid. Those moving to a new small town might be removed from problematic social networks but also from most other supports. There is no inherently good or bad place to live; rather, place is strongly shaped by people's histories and networks there and how they engage with others and the environment now. The relative lack of public transportation heightened these issues, for both supportive and problematic networks, and traveling to Boston or a different town was more challenging. Often people were also further disconnected from social services or supports, both because of a dearth of services and the relative inaccessibility of those that were there.

Finally, most of the people who were living in smaller towns were white, and most of them had significant histories of (self-reported) alcohol or drug use. Addiction was a common issue across the entire sample but was particularly pronounced in white respondents, and the experience of this was shaped by the local context, in terms of connections to drugs and drug treatment and related services. White respondents experienced incarceration and reentry differently than Black and Latinx people.

Conclusion

THIS STUDY WAS MOTIVATED by wanting to know more about how and why neighborhood and place matters in reentry from incarceration. As I've argued in the preceding chapters and develop in this conclusion, this project makes four overarching contributions. First, place matters largely through the relationships it fosters. Second, while the neighborhood in which one lives is one important place for many, it is not the only important place and, for some, residential neighborhood is either hard to define or plays a much less significant role than other places. Third, people have very different kinds and levels of engagement with the same places and these relationships are multifaceted. Fourth and finally, jails and houses of correction are important sites to understand the impact of mass incarceration on individuals and communities. In this chapter, I summarize these key findings. Then I discuss the policy implications.

The men and women who have served time in the House of Correction are often marginalized because of poverty, racism, and addiction, and then further marginalized because of criminal convictions. In many cases, they are at least partly detached from mainstream society and power structures. Drug addiction was prevalent, including several people who told me about multiple overdose experiences in the year I followed them. In addition to incarceration, a few had also been "sectioned," or civilly committed to drug treatment. Others were marginalized or perceived as threatening simply because they were young Black or Latino men. An extensive criminal history, when known, added to their "offensiveness." This was one of the ways in which they were trapped in a system that assumed they were guilty, making it that much more difficult to break out.

That the people we interviewed were incarcerated at the Suffolk County House of Correction meant that most were removed from and returned to the Boston area. When they returned, they returned to neighborhoods that include residents with varying levels of experience with crime and incarceration. This is an obvious point, and yet rarely do we consider perspectives of both returning prisoners and their neighbors, despite them living in the same neighborhoods and occupying the same spaces. Similarly, we rarely engage with the experiences of those who are particularly unstably housed upon their release from prison. Through repeated interviews with men and women being released from the House of Correction along with interviews and observations with other residents of three Boston neighborhoods, we can begin to see how and why place matters for people as they exit correctional facilities.

OVERARCHING THEMES ON NEIGHBORHOOD CONTEXT AND REENTRY

1. *Place matters through the relationships it fosters.* Researchers have long focused on some key relationships, like those with families of origin, children, and romantic partners. An often underappreciated aspect of life is the fleeting interactions those leaving incarceration have with people in public places. Those relationships may develop into recognizable forms, like a friend or romantic partner. They also may stay superficial or limited, but important—a source of information or someone who attracts the attention of the police. Those who rely on public transportation or walking may be particularly exposed to these types of encounters, and those trying to avoid these connections may avoid public places. The methods used in this project allowed even some of these fleeting connections to become visible. By listening to people describe their days, we can see fleeting encounters and perceptions of others that likely would not come up otherwise.

Most obviously, people returning from prison or jail to an old neighborhood, or traveling to or through one, will likely encounter people that they knew before. This can be, but is not always, a bad thing. For those who encounter people they know through offending or drug using pasts, these encounters can present temptation, expectations of wrongdoing, and heightened surveillance, so they are also an exchange to carefully navigate. At the same time, these encounters can include sharing of valuable information about resources and (re)establishing close relationships. In addition, many are returning to family members who support them and people with whom they have a shared history. There can be both a need to return to certain neighborhoods and also benefits of doing so. Those moving to a new neighborhood may lack temptations and heightened surveillance, at least initially, but also lack familiarity and social connection. They may trade familiar risks for a sense of isolation. That place is important to the development of positive and negative relationships also suggests how we may approach crime, punishment, and their aftermath more effectively—by fostering healthier and more supportive relationships and considering the role of neighborhood and transportation in them.

Many of the participants interviewed for this book talked about their connection to neighborhoods in which they grew up. This was most evident for those with ties to Dorchester (where many returned and continued to live) and South Boston (which none could now afford but was remembered fondly). At the same time, a number of people also talked about the value of getting away, either moving to a new neighborhood or to social services removed from the city on Long Island (see also Kirk 2020). These are not entirely opposing perspectives and considering them together might lead to more effective and supportive policies. In the examples of David Kirk's interview respondents, who left New Orleans after incarceration but also after the displacement that resulted from Hurricane Katrina, they often moved with or to relatives or loved ones. While they may be somewhat isolated in their new location, they were not alone (Kirk 2020). Neither neighborhoods nor people are uniformly good or bad. The people who felt a part of their neighborhood were connected to people in it and they knew how to navigate it, including "problematic" residents and the police (Miller 2001; Sharkey 2006; Clampet-Lundquist et al. 2011). For some, the concentration of "problems" was too great to navigate. Long Island was a place that felt safe to some, as it removed them, temporarily, from the risks, while also providing supports, like housing and counseling.

Nikki Jones (2018: 164) emphasized the social nature of redemption and argued that while people with histories of incarceration or criminal involvement need to find a new place in their neighborhood, others in the neighborhood need to validate these efforts. Rather than look merely at where people are living, we should be looking at how they engage with their neighbors, neighborhoods, and activity spaces, and how others engage with them. These relationships are not only about those with whom one is in close contact. Fleeting acquaintances or familiar faces can inspire both a sense of belonging or fear. A number of people we talked to emphasized the importance of being a familiar face and being able to recognize others as part of their neighborhood as a key part of their sense of safety. When they were in a new area, they would intentionally seek out these connections, however superficial they may be. For some, recognizing stigmatized others inspired fear, even if they were part of the neighborhood, particularly when they were too concentrated in a group or in a location. For residents of the South End, service users and others who congregated near the House of Correction, the Southampton Shelter, and the area methadone clinics, inspired discomfort, disdain, or fear, especially when they spread out into South End streets. It was not just that they were there, but how many were there, how visible they were, and how much they encroached on the "good" South End. Indeed, many South End residents considered the shelters and services a part of the fabric and character of the neighborhood, up to a point that was crossed after Long Island programs were shuttered.

2. *Residential neighborhood is one important place for many people, but other places and activity spaces should also be considered to understand their lives more fully.* For people returning from prison, this is particularly true, as many are extremely unstably housed and may go through periods of couch surfing, sleeping on the street, staying in shelters, or renting rooms. I began this study interested in neighborhood context, and I quickly learned how insignificant a concept this was for many of the people I was talking with. In addition to residential neighborhoods, the importance of place is reflected in the activity spaces created by people engaging in their daily activities and, for many, was largely distinct from their residential or contact address (Browning and Soller 2014; Browning et al. 2017a, b, c; Sugie and Lens 2017). For privileged residents, their activity spaces may be large, as they orient key aspects of their lives outside of their residential neighborhood. In these cases, a large activity space may reflect less engagement with their residential neighborhood. For example, some residents lived in South Boston, but shopped, socialized, and worked outside of their neighborhood. The same was true of young white residents in Dorchester, who perceived a dearth of amenities in their neighborhood and so looked outside, also giving them relatively fewer opportunities to engage with their neighbors. For less privileged residents, a larger activity space may be created by a need to access services outside of their residential neighborhood, living in one

neighborhood out of necessity while maintaining affective ties to another, or a lack of residential stability that necessitates "bouncing" from place to place.

Activity spaces highlight how people use and move about space, which is particularly important for an often highly transient population like people returning from incarceration. In some cases, activity spaces are similar to neighborhoods. In other cases, they include key additional areas that reflect daily patterns and lives not captured by any neighborhood measure. They also encourage us to go beyond questions of *if* neighborhoods matter to *how* and *why* they matter. Much the way Harding, Morenoff, and Wyse's (2019) typology considers both neighborhood dimensions (e.g., safe, chaotic) and individual engagement (detached, connected), this research highlights that people can experience the same neighborhood in very different ways, both because of their position within the neighborhood and their engagement with it. We should ask not just where they are living but how they are navigating place and space and how others are responding to them (Jones 2018). This is neither uniform nor static. Different people can engage with the same place differently, and individuals can change their engagement with places over time. Neighborhoods can also change over time, and thereby change residential composition and shape resident engagement.

For all, activity spaces also are shaped by access to transportation. Particularly for those who walk or take public transportation, being in transit provides its own opportunities for connection and risk. A key theme, both for the Boston-area participants and those who were living farther out in smaller towns, was the importance of transportation and mobility. In a densely populated urban area, people could access public transit and could travel more places on foot. While doing so, they crossed paths with others. These travels were not uniformly beneficial or problematic. Through these encounters they found roommates, met romantic partners, and learned about resources. They also encountered police, people who had taken out restraining orders on them, and people who may tempt them into illegal activity or behaviors that attracted police attention. Those living in small towns were—for better and worse—much more constrained in their movements. They typically had the same options—public transit and walking—as urban residents, with much more limited public transit and less dense areas that meant that fewer needs could be met within walking distance. This protected them from the dangers of being in public, but also meant they were more socially isolated and more disconnected from services.

3. *People who live in the same area may have very different kinds and levels of engagement with it and these relationships to place are multifaceted.* These experiences are shaped by individual motivations, but also by interlocking systems of power that criminalize poverty and addiction and see young Black men as inherently suspicious.

Three neighborhood case studies illustrate these dimensions of place and people's engagement with it, and how they reflect people's experiences exiting prison. The section of Dorchester I focus on is the stereotypically high-crime, high-incarceration neighborhood that researchers typically argue are detrimental to people's post-incarceration success. There is evidence of that in these interviews, but there is also evidence of the benefits of living in the neighborhood. People navigated their neighborhood carefully, to avoid both acquaintances that might draw them into trouble and police surveillance. But they also had important social ties in the neighborhood, who provided emotional support, a place to stay, and access to resources. They also felt a sense of belonging in Dorchester. Even those who now lived outside of Dorchester often retained an emotional connection to it. Many residents who did not have direct experience with incarceration had a level of tolerance and acceptance for those who did.

The South End similarly has strong ties to incarceration and related social problems, like homelessness and addiction. For people returning from the House of Correction, many experienced the neighborhood through this lens, and saw it as a neighborhood of threat, risk, and despair. Some of them appreciated its convenience, not only to services but to every other aspect of Boston life. For other (not formerly incarcerated) residents of the South End, some services were a component of their sense of neighborhood and place. However, when the presence of people struggling with drug use and homelessness crossed a threshold they were not willing to tolerate, some encouraged law enforcement crackdowns and sweeps. The South End also illustrates the interconnectedness of neighborhoods, both adjacent and more removed. The South End was intimately tied to what was happening on Long Island, the Boston Harbor island that housed many services that historically also existed in the South End and were expanded once access to the island closed. Police surveillance both near the shelters and clinics and in nearby public spaces like Boston Common also shaped the behavior of people in those places, sometimes pushing them in to residential areas of the South End.

South Boston, at the time of this research, had smaller numbers of people returning from the House of Correction (both in general and in terms of our interview sample). A few had ties to public housing in the neighborhood, but the neighborhood was unaffordable to people leaving the House of Correction and there was a relative lack of social service organizations or supportive housing options. Those who had grown up there had often been displaced before their incarceration and they found it inaccessible, both financially and socially. It was no longer a place *for* them. South Boston also reflects the highest level of privilege of place in which crime or violence is perceived as unusual and unacceptable. Yet those who remembered an earlier South Boston, when it was associated with gangs, drugs, white working-class insularity, and clear racial divides, also lamented the loss of a strong sense of community.

Through each of these neighborhood case studies, in addition to seeing different characters of place and different neighborhood dynamics, we can see varying perceptions of each neighborhood based on one's position within it. This is evident in differences between races, genders, and classes in how people experienced life in their neighborhoods and how they navigated space. Wealthy South Enders emphasized its amenities, while people exiting the House of Correction described it in dark terms, emphasizing the dangers for them. Many residents in Dorchester highlighted the presence of crime and violence, though it was primarily the newer white residents who perceived danger from racialized "others." Even those who had themselves once been involved in neighborhood offending described the neighborhood as quiet when not actively and intentionally engaging in street life. Many also emphasized the strengths and sense of community in their neighborhood. In contrast, many longtime South Boston residents lamented a loss of community, as they perceived a lack of commitment to the neighborhood among their newer neighbors. People exiting the House of Correction now found South Boston both socially and financially inaccessible. Across neighborhoods, there was not a single "neighborhood context," but rather this was shaped by one's place and role within it. And, at least to some degree, that role is changeable over time, as individual engagement and as the neighborhood itself changes.

Men and women also experienced different forms of vulnerability, which was further shaped by their race and ethnicity. White women expressed more physical vulnerability and concerns of navigating public spaces by themselves. Young white women living in Dorchester and the South End talked about feeling like outsiders and avoiding places with larger numbers of Black people. People of color and some longer-term white residents intentionally sought out at least superficial connections to their neighbors and area businesses to strengthen their sense of community and safety. Men generally did not talk about their sense of physical vulnerability. In contrast, they were very aware of being the target of police surveillance. They talked about avoiding trouble, but this too was often two-pronged—avoiding illegal activity but also avoiding the police attention that would likely follow both the perception and reality of illegal activity. White men expressed a sense of vulnerability when they perceived themselves as out of place (e.g., a white man in a Black neighborhood) or when they were known to the police and so also experienced heightened surveillance. Even then, in at least some cases this was minimized if they were not engaging in any behaviors that would draw attention to themselves.

4. *Jails and houses of correction matter in understanding the effects of mass incarceration on individuals and communities.* Those who served short sentences faced different challenges and different dynamics than those who served long sentences and so were removed from their communities for longer periods.[1] Short sentences, misdemeanor charges (Kohler-Hausmann 2018), and probation (Phelps and Ruhland 2021) are coercive and can trap people into cycles that are difficult to break out of (Sered and Norton-Hawk 2014; Leverentz 2018). The lives of many of the people we interviewed belie the idea that low-level charges mean an easier transition back to the community. While they may have served short sentences on minor charges, these charges might reflect lives that include extreme poverty, heavy drug or alcohol use, and/or unsupported and un/undertreated mental health issues, and rarely does incarceration help with any of these problems. That said, their removal from the community was for a shorter period, and so relationships were likely less attenuated—because of incarceration alone—than those serving longer sentences, and relatively less had changed in their absence. This also shaped how people approached their sentences, often rejecting visits and choosing to serve time incarcerated if it meant avoiding or minimizing community supervision or end their sentence faster. And some did talk about a jarring reentry because of what they had missed and what had changed.

Although it is an empirical question that I do not directly test here, I expect there to be parallels between the experiences of people exiting the House of Correction and others returning to different urban areas after short sentences. There are, however, a few key regional or historical factors to this study that shaped their experiences. The Houses of Correction house a larger percentage of incarcerated people than do prisons in states with a jail/prison system. Particularly in an urban area in a small and compact region and state, it was not hard to pick up charges from multiple court jurisdictions and from multiple counties. Visits were easier in terms of distance and accessible transportation, but often not in other senses.

During this research, the Long Island bridge, and the services located there, closed. This had a dramatic impact on those who were using services provided on Long Island. Several people talked about the benefits of being at some remove from the city while they tried to recover from drug use. A dramatic shift in services away from the island also meant a visible change in the presence of drug users in the South End, in particular. Even residents who embraced homeless shelters and halfway houses as parts of their community were overwhelmed and distressed by the volume of drug use and drug users on their streets. As of this writing, the city of Boston is still fighting Quincy for access to rebuild the bridge.

Another notable event during the period of data collection was the winter of 2015. Boston received record amounts of snowfall that closed businesses, restricted movements, and generally made life challenging for everyone. For people reliant on transient or service work, reliant on public transportation, and somewhat socially isolated even in the best of circumstances, it was particularly challenging.

Given these findings, what can we do to meet the needs of both incarcerated populations and their neighbors? In the final section, I discuss policy recommendations based on this research.

IMPLICATIONS FOR POLICY

A recent report found that Black and Latinx people are overrepresented in the Massachusetts criminal legal system and received harsher sentences (Bishop et al. 2020). Black and Latinx people are overrepresented in criminal caseloads, are less likely to have their cases resolved through less severe dispositions, and receive longer sentences among those sentenced to incarceration (Bishop et al. 2020). Much of these disparities reflect race/ethnic differences in the nature and severity of the initial charges (Bishop et al. 2020). We see evidence of that here by looking at the severity of the paths that led people to be incarcerated. Many of the white participants had very troubled histories with long periods of drug use, sometimes mental health issues, and related criminal activities. Some of the Black and Latinx people had similar histories, while others had much more limited illegal behavior in the lead up to their incarceration. The research in this book was not designed to test how someone comes to be incarcerated, so it is possible that these differences are a coincidence or an artifact of our recruitment strategies. But the patterns are both suggestive and consistent with other research (e.g., Harding and Harris 2020). On the one hand, this often meant that white respondents had substantial barriers to work through in their own lives when they were released. On the other hand, Black and Latinx respondents had considerable external constraints that shaped their efforts. Both are significant but lead to different responses to better support them and foster their success.

When I first learned of the House of Correction, it sounded promising to me. That it was a local facility should make visits and maintaining ties to friends and family easier. It houses people sentenced to short sentences who do not need to be sent across even a small state like Massachusetts. It sounded like a simpler, more humane, approach to punishment. When I began this project, I quickly learned the limitations of this framing. Even as the incarcerated population in Suffolk County dropped dramatically in the years leading up to data collection, it quickly became apparent how many of the people incarcerated at the House of Correction were there primarily because they were poor. Maybe they had a history of addiction or mental illness, or both. And maybe they were just young Black or Latino men in the wrong place at the wrong time, and so automatically suspect. And this was the *reduced* population—the ones who remained locked up as the overall incarcerated population shrank. Communities are not being kept safe with this approach. To be sure, some of the people I met had very real problems that they needed help addressing. And others were disadvantaged because of who they were, and so faced heightened barriers. Problems are not being adequately addressed—in spite of some dedicated and well-intentioned staff. This should not come as a surprise, and yet we maintain these seemingly intractable systems because often we—as the general public and many community and political leaders—assume they are necessary. They are not.

Some people who have been incarcerated have gone on to do extraordinary things. These accomplishments should be celebrated, and their voices should be heard in developing policy. Yet, extraordinary accomplishments should not be a standard expectation for what one must do to rejoin society. Reentry successes are not only about people's attempts to do so, but our willingness to let them. A number of the people interviewed for this project had difficulties to overcome. Some cited periods of incarceration as positive turning points for themselves, as a break from the "street" and drug use or problematic relationships. That does not mean, however, that incarceration is serving their (or our) needs. And in some cases, their current challenges were a result of previous and current interactions with other state institutions. Reducing—or eliminating—incarceration ultimately also means improving structures to support children, families, and communities, dismantling racist systems, and developing new ways to respond to harms. Scholars and activists have long warned us that reducing incarceration by lowering sentences, reducing the incarceration of those convicted of drug charges, or relying on community-based sentences will not have as much effect as we would like and will shift forms of coercion rather than eliminate them (Gottschalk 2015; Pfaff 2017; Kohler-Hausmann 2018; Phelps and Ruhland 2021). These changes may be a first step but cannot be the last one.

Reuben Jonathan Miller wrote, in his recent book *Halfway Home*, "I've found no easy answers; a five-point plan for policy reform can't save us from the society we've made" (Miller 2021: 19). There are not easy solutions to problems created or exacerbated by incarceration. In addition, it is not just a problem of "incarceration," but rather a more fundamental and far-reaching problem of society. Narrow reforms have limited effects and more radical reforms are criticized by some for being unrealistic. Yet over the course of the year in which I was writing this book, more widespread attention has been given to debating the idea of police and prison abolition. Our current level of reliance on incarceration as punishment is recent history and a reminder that our current approach is neither inevitable nor "natural." David Garland has argued that we resort to penal solutions to deal with marginalized populations because they are "immediate, easy to implement, and can claim to 'work' as a punitive end in themselves even when they fail in all other respects" (2001: 200). At the same time, Ruth Wilson Gilmore wrote that "prison is not a building 'over there' but a set of relationships that undermine rather than stabilize everyday lives everywhere" (Gilmore 2007: 242). She cautioned that many proposed reforms rely on the same logics, and thereby end up reinforcing prison's hold. Incarceration seems like a "commonsense" solution that does not target fundamental social and economic forces, but rather further marginalizes already marginalized people.

Scholars and activists have been arguing for years that we should instead move toward prison abolition (e.g., Gilmore 2007; Davis 2011). Nothing about the research I did for this book made me believe that the people we interviewed needed to be incarcerated, either from a public safety perspective or to help them with their problems. Not only did their situations not improve through incarceration, but also, many feared seeking help because of the likely punitive responses they might encounter (Brayne 2014), and they developed an understandable and deep cynicism about the state that further undermined compliance. Similarly, probation and parole are not necessarily "easier" sentences to endure, particularly when sentences could be easily extended in unpredictable ways (Phelps and Ruhland 2021). Other residents were concerned about crime, particularly violence and the disorder that came with poverty, homelessness, and drug use, but while they did rely on the police in some cases, this was more about a lack of alternatives than a sense that incarceration was a goal or necessity, particularly for more minor forms of disorder. Monica Bell (2020) has argued that "*security*, both objectively and subjectively, may not be solely or even primarily related to policing." People want to feel safe, and many have a hard time imagining a world with less reliance on police and prisons. That does not mean that such a world is not possible, just that we have not yet done it. And when we study issues related to the criminal legal system and responses to crime, we need to focus at least some of these studies more broadly, to allow alternative ideas and strategies to emerge. Rather than continuing to invest in coercive controls like prisons, jails, and community supervision, we would be better served with non-carceral investments in individuals and communities.

Prison abolition is a long-term project. Key to its success is not just dismantling our current systems but building new structures (Kaba 2021). Even for those for whom this sounds impossible now, abolitionist ideas provide an important framework through which to think about more incremental reforms to work toward these larger goals of building up communities and developing new and more effective ways to respond to harms. For example, during this research, I met multiple people who had been involved—as children and as parents—with the child welfare system. Several young Black men expressed understandable anger because of their experiences in these systems as children and multiple parents (white and Black, men and women) were frustrated by the extreme difficulties of reconnecting with their children in foster care or group homes. For young Black men, outward expressions of anger were often directly connected to their involvement with the criminal legal system and their distrust of other government institutions. An abolitionist approach would focus on better supporting children and families, which would in turn reduce young people's anger and distrust of systems. This does not mean relying on our current child welfare systems, which have their own substantial failures and limitations (Roberts 2009). It also does not mean ignoring harms done by those young men, but rather focusing on community accountability rather than state punishment. Harm-reduction approaches to drug use—including providing clean needles, safe injection sites, and overdose prevention education and tools—can reduce harms and dangers associated with drug use, and reduce barriers to treatment for those who want it (Schenwar and Law 2020; Hart 2021).[2] Providing housing, food, transportation, and health care to those who need it would also reduce crime more than punishing those who break the law because they lack them.

In working toward these goals, we must avoid reforms that redirect more money toward the current criminal legal system and individualistic "bad apple," rather than systemic, framings of the problems (Kaba 2021). Journalists Maya Schenwar and Victoria Law (2020) caution us against popular alternatives to incarceration or prison reforms that—at best—replicate the status quo or widen the net of the criminal legal system. Instead, we should focus on strategies that provide real alternatives, strengthen communities, and produce the safety and security that people want.

The focus of this book is neighborhoods and place and how people navigate them. How, then, do the findings speak to policy changes around neighborhoods? One, related to the above, is the need to invest in neighborhoods and fostering connections within those neighborhoods. As we shift money away from the criminal legal system, we can shift it toward community development. People engage with their neighborhoods, and the people in them, in complex ways that belie merely moving people out of their old neighborhood into a new or better neighborhood. People have social ties and social supports in neighborhoods that might also provide temptations or negative influences. Rather than trying to prevent any negative influences, we can help people learn to navigate them. We can also work to reduce these negative forces in neighborhoods altogether, which would not only improve the well-being of those returning from prison but also everyone living around them. Another investment that would benefit all residents is public transportation. What that may look like in different contexts may vary, but would provide access to job opportunities, social services, and social ties. In urban areas with existing public transportation infrastructure, this might mean ensuring that those who need access have it through, for example, free or discounted transit passes. In rural areas or small towns, it might mean a ride share program so that people can access what they need. Public transportation expands possible activity spaces (by choice and by meeting needs), extends job opportunities, and makes programs and services more accessible. Being in public, walking and on public transportation, is also a social experience, and it can lead to new or reignited friendships, romantic partnerships, and sharing of key information. Note that these strategies need not, and should not, be narrowly focused around "crime control," but rather on building community and equitable opportunities.

Sometimes people do want a fresh start or a temporary break from a neighborhood, and that should be supported. In Boston, one such place to provide a break was Long Island. Since the bridge was closed, many people have been frustrated by the alternatives. People who stay at the shelters or social services in the South End appreciate the convenience, but otherwise describe the area in grim terms. Drugs are rampant, conditions generally poor, and threats abound. Other South End residents also are frustrated, as their level of tolerance has been far surpassed. There is some value to a concentration of services, for the convenience it offers their users and because it may make any individual service user less conspicuous in the area. At the same time, it also makes them easy targets for both drug sellers and the police. People accessing services, including supportive housing, also are typically tolerated by neighbors until they become too visible in any one area. Long Island, or similarly removed service campuses, are less convenient than those more centrally located, but they can potentially provide a respite. One key to the success of Long Island services and other drug treatment facilities, sober homes, halfway houses, and the like is that they are separate from the criminal legal system and do not rely on the threat of coercive control. While many, regardless of their legal status, felt shame when they used drugs, a fear of going back to prison drove many to exacerbate their problems by avoiding reporting to court, leaving supportive housing, and going on the run. They may need case management or mentoring or assistance navigating services, but these supports should also be distinct from the criminal legal system. Another key to success is that decisions about the placement and nature of drug treatment and homeless services should be driven by the needs of potential clients and not a Not In My Backyard (NIMBY) influence of potential neighbors. That extends to a wide range of affordable housing options, including permanent supportive and affordable housing. Securing stable and affordable housing is an important first step to gaining stability in other areas of their lives.

Many of these are not straightforward suggestions. People who are struggling with avoiding drug use might not want to be near others who are actively using. Some people who are struggling with mental health issues or drug use may be disruptive, and so unappealing or threatening to neighbors. Many people who have been incarcerated have experienced extensive harm and trauma and would benefit from help processing this trauma. While some may benefit from merely opening prison gates, for others, this would likely shift the problem, not eliminate it. And yet we also have compelling evidence that incarceration and other punitive responses to poverty and disadvantage have a marginal effect, at best, on public safety. At most, it gives people some sense that "something is being done," without impacting crime or safety. In time, by investing in individuals and communities and experimenting with non-carceral alternatives, we can lessen or eliminate our reliance on incarceration and positively impact the lives of those who have been incarcerated, those who would be under our current systems, and the communities in which they live.

APPENDIX A

Methods

INTERVIEWING MEN AND WOMEN
IN THE HOUSE OF CORRECTION

The research team included me and graduate research assistants. Together, we interviewed one hundred people being released from the House of Correction.[1] The plan was to have each researcher be responsible for a group of participants, so each participant would always be interviewed by the same person and would, ideally, develop a stronger connection to that interviewer. In several cases, a research assistant left the university before completing all of the interviews; in these cases, I took over the remaining interviews (usually after the first or second interview). In all, I interviewed forty-three people at least once, including seven who were first interviewed by a research assistant (see Leverentz 2020a for a more detailed discussion on retention).

Everyone who was scheduled to be released during our recruitment period (late January 2014 through June 2015) was eligible to participate. Our goal was to interview them once shortly before their release and four times after. This allowed us to follow them through a key period of transition, and to see how their plans and goals unfolded over time. We were able to recruit a diverse group of participants in terms of their age, race, and offending and incarceration histories. Our intent was to sample for range—that is, to have sufficient respondents in key subcategories of people (Weiss 1994; Small 2009). This included oversampling women and interviewing people with ties to our three target neighborhoods.

Women were about 11 percent of the release population at the House of Correction during our recruitment period. Because of their relatively small numbers, we were able to recruit them directly. We arranged to go to the women's unit often, sometimes every week, and talk one-by-one with the women scheduled to be released in the next few weeks.[2] We explained the project to them and invited their participation. These initial conversations took place in a private classroom or a relatively open common area; interviews were conducted in private classrooms. We interviewed thirty-nine women.

To recruit men, staff posted fliers in the housing units explaining the project and inviting participation. Those who were interested told their case worker, who passed the information along to a central contact, who contacted me. We would then arrange to go in. When we got to the institution, we got a list of interested men, which we passed along to the security staff working in the lawyer visitation area. Staff then called the men down one by one. We went through the consent process with each man, made sure they were still interested, and interviewed them. We can't know if we missed any interested men through this passive recruitment. In a few cases, men we talked to described being quite determined to reach us and persistent in their efforts. In one case, I was called in the same day to meet with a man the day before his release. In total, we interviewed sixty-one men.

House of Correction staff did not participate in interviews with men or women.[3] Respondents were paid thirty dollars in cash for each interview. We paid them for the first and second interview at the time of the first post-release interview.[4] This eased the bureaucratic hurdle to compensating them while incarcerated, gave participants cash when many needed it most, and provided a slight additional incentive to do a post-release interview. I used cash so as not to attach any strings to their compensation. In one case, a participant asked to get his sixty dollars split between a gift card and cash, because he was struggling with drug use and feared having that much cash on him. We went together to a convenience store to try to buy a gift card, but they did not have one. I offered to hold some of the money for him, but he ultimately decided to take it.

The House of Correction does not systematically collect release addresses and so we did not limit recruitment to those with ties to our target neighborhoods. I did not want to turn down any potentially interested participant. This limitation proved fortuitous, as we also gained insight into important and prevalent reentry experiences, including those of housing instability and reentry to small towns, that otherwise would have been missed.

Our goal was to interview people once prerelease and four times post-release. In each interview we asked for direct contact information and information on loved ones who would know how to get in touch with them. Not surprisingly, release was a key time that we lost contact with people (see table 3 in appendix B). In some cases, people were being released to another institution to serve an additional sentence. Others had no known contact information or plan when we talked to them, and so we were reliant on them reaching out to us. This occasionally happened, but we lost track of most people in this situation.

Choosing an interview location can be a complex process, for both participant and researcher. There is much to say about both the choice of interview location and the social dynamics that unfold during an interview that I do not have the space to go into here. The interview location and interview dynamics are as important a part of the interview process as the conversation that unfolds. Post-release interviews took place in a variety of locations, including their homes, public libraries, and coffee shops. We always asked participants if they had a preferred location and traveled to their town or neighborhood (unless they requested to meet elsewhere). Our goals were to make the interviews as convenient and comfortable as possible for participants. Some participants welcomed me into their homes, while others preferred to meet elsewhere. In apartments, we sat at kitchen tables, in bedrooms, and on back porches. Sometimes this also gave me the opportunity to meet roommates, romantic partners, and family members. Some consciously saw the interview location as a reflection of themselves. Several commented on not wanting me to see a certain area, or meet their people, or see how they were living. Others just did not have a private space to meet, and so preferred to meet in a public space. Then, we met in public libraries, Dunkin' Donuts, restaurants, or coffee shops. When we went to a restaurant, I offered to buy them a meal or a drink. In libraries, I asked staff for access to a community meeting room; when that was not possible, we sat in a corner. Meeting in public also gave me the opportunity to see how people responded to them and how they engaged with others. I also met people at the shelters at which they were staying, in residential drug treatment facilities, and in correctional facilities. Here I tried to ensure that my presence and the cash stipend were not violations of the facility rules. Meeting in correctional institutions involved getting institutional approval, from the Massachusetts Department of Correction and the individual prison for state facilities.

We interviewed sixty-four people at least once post-release, three people four times, and thirty-six people five times. For those that we interviewed at least four times, we followed them for an average of 14.5 months (ranging from nine to twenty-eight months). One participant (that I know of) died over the course of the year, after our second interview. In two cases, people were reincarcerated for lengthy periods, and so we interviewed them once while incarcerated, but did not follow them after. In most cases, we lost contact and so cannot know for sure what was going on in their lives. Sometimes, their official criminal histories provide clues in new charges or convictions, as did conversations with loved ones as we tried to reach participants. Those we did maintain contact with reflect a range of experiences, including (occasionally) smooth transitions to post-incarceration life and often major struggles, particularly with addiction and mental illness. Each interview included some repeated questions about how their lives were going and some unique questions, including questions about their childhoods and their histories of offending and criminal legal system involvement.

The core of the data is the interviews. We asked to digitally record the interviews, though this was not mandatory and a few declined. In addition to interviews, we asked participants for permission to access their official criminal records. This also was not mandatory to participate, though ninety-three of the one hundred participants agreed to let us access their background checks, and we ultimately secured ninety-one of them.[5] These records provide a snapshot of the people's court involvement, and sometimes gave us stunning stories of the complexities of court involvement. Some of our participants had hundreds of charges over the course of their lives, mostly minor and often ultimately dismissed (see Kohler-Hausmann 2018 for a detailed account of the use of open cases to control defendants). These records tell an interesting, if limited, story. They should not, however, be read as a sign of the "badness" of the people captured in them. In most cases, the records demonstrate vulnerability and disadvantage, more so than "criminality" or "danger."

RESIDENT INTERVIEWS AND OBSERVATION

The research team conducted targeted participant observation and interviewed residents of the three neighborhoods. The goals of participant observation were to gain a sense of the neighborhood, its residents, and the issues important to them, particularly around crime issues. Most of the participant observation was of community meetings that, at least in part, focused on crime issues (e.g., police-community, resident association, task force meetings). The meetings we attended functioned like peer-group discussions in that the meeting attendants had existing relationships, the researcher role was minimized, and participants were free to interact and to cooperatively create meaning (Sasson 1995). Although the participant observation remains influenced by context, the researcher has a minimal role in shaping the discussion, allowing themes, language, and issues to emerge relatively independently. Often individual meetings drew a particular segment of the neighborhood, which collectively gave us a sense of some of the tensions in the neighborhood. For example, resident association meetings in the South End were primarily of wealthier homeowners. Public housing residents attended their own meetings, but did not attend the neighborhood meetings. The meetings also highlighted non-crime issues, like development and parking, that were of concern to residents.

Participant observation in Dorchester and the South End first began in 2008 and continued for approximately two and a half years. This initial participant observation was a part of an earlier study of community perceptions of crime (Leverentz 2011, 2012; Leverentz and Williams 2017). This field work informed the current project, and I occasionally draw on the data here to provide a sense of the ongoing nature of some of the issues. Participant observation in all three of the current target neighborhoods resumed in 2013 and continued through mid-2017.

We interviewed eighty-four residents across three neighborhoods (twenty-seven in Dorchester, thirty-eight in the South End, and nineteen in South Boston). As detailed in the introduction, we adopted a case-based, rather than a sample-based, logic to recruitment (Small 2009). A major goal of interviews was to capture the perspectives of key groups in the neighborhoods. For example, the South End and South Boston have experienced several waves of gentrification, and so we wanted to include residents from each of these waves. To achieve this range of respondents, we also used snowball sampling. This included asking interview participants for additional suggestions of people to interview (particularly people they knew who were less involved in community groups), emailing listservs and resident lists, and inviting participation through a variety of existing social networks. Participants were paid forty dollars in cash for their participation.[6]

In terms of their personal involvement with the criminal legal system, just under 20 percent had been arrested and almost half had been victimized. Two-thirds reported knowing someone with criminal legal system involvement, and just over half know someone who works in the criminal legal system. About two-thirds had called the police, just over half think the police do a good job, 14 percent reported feeling harassed by the police, and about a third report knowing police officers that work in the neighborhood. About 60 percent reported that they did not believe the prison system does a good job.

Research assistants conducted the semi-structured interviews. As with the interviews with people leaving the House of Correction, interviews were scheduled for the convenience and comfort of participants. We began with an interview guide that included general questions about their perceptions of the neighborhood, their connections to others in the neighborhood (relationships and participation in community groups or meetings), time spent in the neighborhood, and their perceptions of safety, disorder, and social control. All interviews were conducted in English.[7]

RESEARCHER POSITIONALITY
AND INTERVIEWER EFFECTS

In qualitative research, the researchers are an important part of the data collection process. There is extensive debate among qualitative researchers about the value of being an insider or an outsider, and the complexities of these statuses (e.g., McCorkel and Myers 2003; Twine and Warren 2000; Horowitz 1986). On one dimension, our incarceration status, we were clearly outsiders (McCorkel and Myers 2003).

Race and gender of interviewers and participants may shape recruitment and retention. Race and gender "matching" may improve recruitment and rapport building through a presumed sense of closeness, though outsider status may also be useful in fostering an "acceptable incompetent" identity (Lofland and Lofland 1994). In addition, identities are multifaceted and, in part, enacted in the field. Given the nature of our recruitment strategies, the demographic and experiential diversity in the institution, and the available interviewers, matching participants and interviewers along race, gender, or age lines was not possible. As with other studies of diverse populations, it is also difficult to know which dimensions of sameness or difference will be most important in different interactions (Stuart 2016). The two primary interviewers of people being released from the House of Correction were both white women (myself and a research assistant) and the two primary interviewers of neighborhood residents were a white woman and a white man. Over the course of the project, the research team included five white women, one Black woman, and two white men.

Among the people recruited from the House of Correction, men who participated did not know the race or gender of the interviewer until they had expressed interest and met with the interviewer. No men declined to participate in the first interview at this stage. Women on the other hand, first learned of the study through direct interaction with the interviewers, and so may have been influenced by researcher characteristics when choosing whether to participate. These exchanges were brief, and so provided little opportunity to overcome initial barriers to trust and rapport. When a woman declined to participate, we asked why she was not interested, but no woman who declined to participate offered reasons, and we did not systematically track the race or age of those who said no. I suspect there was greater suspicion on the part of Black women contacted by a white interviewer. The nature of our recruitment and the racial politics of both a correctional institution and Boston make this plausible. Still, ethnographic work in women's prisons suggests that the salience of race for female prisoner organization is more subtle and complex, and is shaped by characteristics of the institution (McCorkel and Myers 2003; Kruttschnitt and Hussemann 2008).

The breakdown of our sample, at least in terms of Black and white women and men, was comparable to the total release population (see table 1 on page 23). In addition, we were slightly more likely to lose contact with white participants than Black participants (see table 3 in Appendix B). White respondents were also more likely to have a history of drug or alcohol addiction, which shaped retention success. Looking at patterns of retention across researchers also suggests that other interviewer characteristics and interview dynamics were more important in retention than just race. For example, the primary research assistant lost contact with nearly 50 percent of her interviewees at release, compared to about 14 percent for me. Those proportions were reversed for the percent of participants we interviewed five times. I interviewed 70 percent five times, compared to just 15 percent for the research assistant (see Leverentz 2020a). These discrepancies in retention likely reflected skill as an interviewer, including developing rapport, experience interviewing, and experience interviewing similar populations. It is likely that the relative naiveté of early career researchers can also hinder rapport and retention (McCorkel and Myers 2003). In addition, the principal investigator is likely to be more invested in the project, and therefore be more diligent in following up.

Continuity of interviewer and developing rapport with participants is not enough to maintain contact, particularly with highly disadvantaged and mobile participants. With some of the more marginalized people we talked to, they often distanced themselves from loved ones if they relapsed into drug use. Still, the importance of the therapeutic aspect of interviews highlights the importance of a skilled and empathetic interviewer. While this is always important in interview-based studies, formerly incarcerated people are so frequently judged, dismissed, and feared that it is that much more important in terms of both retention and research ethics to not perpetuate this through interview dynamics. In addition, while single-interview studies can withstand occasional bad interviews (and all will have some), the cost is greater in repeated-interview designs.

Only female interviewers interviewed women. This was at the request of the institution, because of the common history of violence and trauma, often at the hands of men, among women prisoners (Owen 1998; Chesney-Lind 2002; Leverentz 2014). Since most of the research team was women, women interviewed most of the men as well, though the one male interviewer initially interviewed a few. While this may have shaped what men said and how they talked, the men did not seem inhibited talking with women. Occasionally a man was flirtatious with a female interviewer, but our social positionality and the interview context also made it easy to enact non-sexual roles with the men (Lofland and Lofland 1994; Pini 2005; Mazzei and O'Brien 2008; Soyer 2014). That we were doing one-on-one interviews also shaped this dynamic, as there was less need for the men to publicly perform masculinity or intimacy (Orrico 2015) and we could take on more therapeutic roles.

The challenges were different with neighborhood resident interviews. We conducted onetime interviews that were generally less sensitive and less holistic than the interviews with people who had been incarcerated. One of our greatest challenges was trying to reach different segments of the population, which we did by adopting a variety of recruitment strategies discussed in the previous section. Interviewers had varying levels of familiarity with the neighborhoods they were interviewing about, which is another dimension of insider-/outsiderness. They also were interviewing a diverse group of participants, along race/ethnicity, gender, and age lines. For the most part, they too were able to adopt acceptable incompetent roles during the interviews (Lofland and Lofland 1994).

ANALYSIS

I coded and analyzed the transcripts using abductive techniques (Tavory and Timmermans 2014). Abductive analysis involves an iterative engagement with existing literature and data to explain unexpected findings. This approach to analysis, combined with the repeated interviews with people released from the House of Correction, also allowed me to adjust the interviews as we went, to ask more directly about emerging themes. As one example, the idea of activity spaces and their relevance emerged over the course of data collection. In the final interviews, we asked more explicitly for people to describe a typical day, including where they went and how they got there. Some of this came up in earlier interviews, indirectly. I used multiple approaches to identify patterns in the data, including coding the interviews and transcripts in NVivo and sorting notecards that summarized each interview respondent.

Research Participants

TABLE 3 Retention, House of Correction Sample

	Prerelease Only N = 36		4–5 Interviews N = 39		Total N = 100	
	Men (N = 21)	Women (N = 15)	Men (N = 25)	Women (N = 14)	Men (N = 61)	Women (N = 39)
White %	43	73	32	64	38	75
Black %	29	27	60	36	44	2
Latinx/Hispanic %	29	0	8	0	18	3
Age (years)	34.9	35.9	40.2	38.1	37.7	36.5
Time served (months)	6.1	3.1	6.7	4.5	6.3	3.9
Average length of follow up			14.5 months (9–28 months)			

TABLE 4 Quoted Participants from House of Correction

Pseudonym	Race/ Ethnicity	Gender	Age at First Interview	Number of Interviews
Adam	Black	Male	40	5
Alfredo	Latinx	Male	44	3
Amanda	White	Female	39	5
Arturo	Black	Male	37	5
Bruce	Black	Male	32	5
Cathy	Black	Female	25	5
Charles	Black	Male	26	5
Christine	White	Female	44	3
Christopher	White	Male	44	4
Corey	Black	Male	18	3
Daniel	Black	Male	27	5
Donald	Black	Male	58	5
Donna	White	Female	53	5
George	White	Male	34	5
Gillian	White	Female	38	1
Jackie	White	Female	30	1
Jackson	Black	Male	29	1
James	White	Male	49	5
Jarrod	White	Male	43	1
John	Black	Male	38	5
Jose	Latinx	Male	41	5
Julio	Latinx	Male	34	5
Kayla	White	Female	30	1
Kevin	White	Male	28	5
Kristina	White	Female	28	5
Lena	White	Female	52	5
Lillian	Black	Female	27	5
Melissa	White	Female	35	1
Michael	Black	Male	31	5
Netta	Black	Female	38	5
Pablo	Black	Male	50	4
Philip	White	Male	35	3
Richard	White	Male	52	5
Sandy	White	Female	36	5
Sarah	White	Female	34	5
Sharon	Black	Female	42	1
Stephen	Black	Male	28	5
Theresa	White	Female	43	5
Tina	White	Female	32	5
Tom	Black	Male	42	5
Wallace	White	Male	44	5
William	White	Male	49	5

TABLE 5 Quoted Participants from Target Neighborhoods

Pseudonym	Neighborhood	Years in N'hood	Race/Ethnicity[1]	Gender	Age
Candace	Dorchester	1.5	White	Female	25
Deidre	Dorchester	47	Black	Female	54
Duane	Dorchester	40	Black	Male	55
Evandro	Dorchester	33	Cape Verdean/ Portuguese	Male	39
Greta	Dorchester	11	Afro-Latina	Female	45
Hector	Dorchester	46	Latinx	Male	69
Johnna	Dorchester	32	Black	Female	35
Karen	Dorchester	1	White	Female	23
Katherine	Dorchester	9	Black	Female	68
Ken	Dorchester	50	Black	Male	47
Millie	Dorchester	36	White	Female	67
Aaron	South End	21	White	Male	49
Andy	South End	22	White	Male	
Derek	South End	20	White	Male	55
Jane	South End	3	White	Female	34
Jeremy	South End	33	White	Male	58
Joan	South End	50	White	Female	75
Joe	South End	8	White	Male	34
Kathy	South End	2.5	White	Female	50
Linda	South End	40	Black	Female	59
Lisa	South End	26	Black	Female	25
Ronald	South End	26	Black	Male	57
Sally	South End	4	White	Female	25
Sandra	South End	53	White	Female	70
Timothy	South End	10	Black	Male	47
Crystal	South Boston	47	White	Female	76
Dylan	South Boston	.2	Asian	Male	43
Elsa	South Boston	50	White	Female	
Garrett	South Boston	21	White	Male	66
Jennifer	South Boston	3	White	Female	39
Joanne	South Boston	60	White	Female	74
Joshua	South Boston	4	White	Male	29
Keith	South Boston	2	White	Male	53
Kelsey	South Boston	28	White	Female	26
Leslie	South Boston	32	White	Female	
Linda	South Boston	20+	White	Female	64
Mark	South Boston	3	Black/White	Male	40
Mary	South Boston	43	White	Female	74
Sheila	South Boston	62	White	Female	70
Susan	South Boston	67	White	Female	65

1. All demographics self-reported.

TABLE 6 Resident Respondent Involvement with
and Perceptions of Criminal Legal System

	Dorchester N = 27	South Boston N = 19	South End N = 38	Total N = 84
Ever arrested? (% yes)	19	32	13	18.6
Ever harassed by police? (% yes)	22	5	13	14
Call police? (% yes)	63	68	66	64
Ever victimized? (% yes)	48	27	58	47
Know someone involved with criminal legal system? %	78	58	66	66
Know someone working in criminal legal system? (% yes)	52	53	63	56
Prison does a good job? (% disagreeing)	63	74	58	62
I would rent to someone with a criminal record (% it depends)	78	70	88	76
I would hire someone with a criminal record (% it depends)	59	81	67	68

NOTES

ACKNOWLEDGMENTS

1. All names of individuals interviewed are pseudonyms.

PREFACE

1. A white-majority rural area adopted a "community problem" approach as well. However, although they very much saw the legal system as something that could be invoked, when necessary, distance made it unreliable (Leverentz and Williams 2017).

INTRODUCTION

1. These are not all unique individuals. A small number of people may account for a disproportionate number of jail admissions, if they are arrested and detained multiple times over the course of a year. Nevertheless, more people are spending time in jail and for longer periods (Subramanian et al. 2015).

2. Some counties' pretrial detainees and county-sentenced prisoners are in the same facility.

3. In Massachusetts, a felony potentially carries a state prison sentence, though also may allow for a county sentence. A misdemeanor cannot result in a state prison sentence. See https://www.Mass.gov/orgs/district-court.

4. In FY 2013, the overall rate of incarceration for convictions was 41.6 percent (38 percent in District Courts and 81 percent in Superior Court). Survey of Sentencing Practices, FY 2013, https://www.mass.gov/doc/survey-of-sentencing-practices-fy-2013/download. FY 2013 is the most recent public sentencing report that includes district court cases. A 2018 report includes only Superior Court. In that report, 58 percent of those convicted were sentenced to state prison (including life sentences)

and 24.8 percent were sentenced to a House of Correction. See https://www.mass
.gov/lists/surveys-of-massachusetts-sentencing-practices. Accessed July 21, 2021.

5. In 2018, 23 percent of the Massachusetts DOC population (N = 594) were
women, which reflects the fact that MCI-Framingham, the state's only women's
prison also houses county-sentenced and pretrial women from counties that do
not have facilities for women. Overall, 19 percent of those released from DOC
facilities were women (https://public.tableau.com/profile/madoc#!/vizhome
/MADOCReleasestoCommunity/ReleaseToCommunity, accessed July 8, 2019). As
of December 31, 2017, 21 percent of women in DOC custody were county-sentenced
(31.7 percent of all sentenced women in DOC custody; compared to .00024 percent
of men in DOC custody or .00026 percent of sentenced men). In the same snapshot, 32 percent of women at MCI-Framingham were pretrial detainees (https://
www.mass.gov/files/documents/2018/01/05/QtrJurisdiction-Jun2017-Dec2017.pdf,
accessed July 7, 2019).

6. Data from the Suffolk County House of Correction. Similarly, 9 percent of MADOC releasees to Suffolk County were women (https://public
.tableau.com/profile/madoc#!/vizhome/MADOCReleasestoCommunity
/ReleaseToCommunity).

7. In 2014, the year data collection for this book began, the Massachusetts
Department of Correction housed 8,600 people sentenced on criminal charges.
The same year, 3,302 criminally sentenced people were released from state prisons in
Massachusetts. This was from a high of 3,901 releasees in 2010, and amid a decline
that continued to 2,305 people in 2020. Numbers went up slightly in 2012 and 2015,
during an overall downward trend (https://public.tableau.com/profile/madoc#!/,
accessed July 7, 2019, August 10, 2021).

8. This estimate is based on data provided by the House of Correction on all
people released during the seventeen months of recruitment (N = 2057). This aver-
ages to approximately 121 a month. About 1,600 people were released in the first
twelve months of recruitment (February 1, 2014–January 31, 2015). If a person was
incarcerated and released more than once during this period, they are counted only
once. In contrast, typically 20–25 percent of DOC prisoners were released to Suffolk
County, or approximately 750 people in 2014 (https://public.tableau.com/profile
/madoc#!/, accessed July 7, 2019).

9. Data from the Suffolk County House of Correction.

10. Survey of Sentencing Practices, FY 2013, https://www.mass.gov/doc/survey
-of-sentencing-practices-fy-2013/download.

11. Ibid.

12. Mears et al.'s (2008) sample was men released from Florida prisons in a 3.5-
year period. In their sample, 91 percent of nonwhite men were Black and 9 percent
were Hispanic. They excluded women from the analysis because of their small numbers in the sample (Mears et al. 2008).

13. Abra is referring to Alcoholics Anonymous (and related twelve-step programs) admonitions to stay away from "people, places, and things" related to your
drug use.

14. The Moving to Opportunity program was a randomized housing mobility experiment funded by the US Department Housing and Urban Development. Families were placed in one of three groups: a control, offered a housing voucher to move to private-market housing in less distressed neighborhoods, or offered a traditional Section 8 voucher. The program has since been extensively researched; some of the reports and papers written about the program are here: https://www.povertyactionlab.org/evaluation/evaluating-impact-moving-opportunity-united-states.

15. In both places, neighborhood meetings were often led by the credentialed class (Jones 2018) and in neither case do the voices represented necessarily reflect the full range of perspectives in the neighborhood. They were, however, the dominant public voices in each and they were distinct across places.

16. scsdma.org/south-bay-house-of-correction/. Accessed May 31, 2021.

17. Long Island has been a site of a homeless shelter since 1928 and addiction treatment services since 1940. abandoned spaces.com.

18. In 2007, weight limits were imposed on the bridge, limiting transportation to the island.

19. At the time of its closure, approximately one thousand people used services on Long Island at the homeless shelter, Boston Public Health Commission programs, several transitional housing programs, a "stabilization program," and several privately run residential treatment, recovery, and detox programs. Mayor's Office Press Release, November 26, 2014. "Mayor Walsh provides update on the Long Island Bridge," https://www.cityofboston.gov/news/Default.aspx?id=17885, accessed July 20, 2020. As of this writing, the island and bridge remain closed, with significant resistance by the residents and political leadership in Quincy to allowing necessary access to rebuild the bridge. See Mary Whitfill, "Quincy Has Spent $400,000 Fighting the Long Island Bridge. And More Is Coming," *The Patriot Ledger*, February 17, 2020

20. There are many definitions of gentrification that focus on both its causes and outcomes (Brown-Saracino 2013). Using the definitions of the National Community Reinvestment Coalition—neighborhoods were considered eligible for gentrification if they had populations of over five hundred, the median home value is less than the fortieth percentile, and the median household income is under the fortieth percentile—the South End and South Boston were both ineligible for gentrification because they were too wealthy. The western section of South Boston was classified as gentrified by 2012. Only some of the target sections of Dorchester were eligible for gentrification during this period but did not experience gentrification (defined by NCRC as an increase in the median home value to above 60 percent of the regional median, an increase in college educated populations to above the sixtieth percentile, and an increase in the median household income). While eastern sections of Dorchester did experience gentrification during this period, several sections in the target areas saw declines in median household income and percent of the population with a college degree between 2010 and 2017 (Richardson, Mitchell, and Edlebi 2020). Of course, measures like this do not account for variation within

the neighborhood or how people experience or perceive their neighborhoods. This perception is the focus of these chapters.

21. https://www.boston.gov/neighborhood/roxbury, accessed December 11, 2020.

22. This report is based on 2013 data, and so predates the opening of the Southampton Shelter.

23. All aspects of the study were approved by the university IRB and the facility.

24. A small number of participants declined to be recorded for one or more interviews. In these cases, the interviewer wrote notes during the interview, and elaborated on them afterward. Unless indicated otherwise, all quotes are direct quotes from recorded transcripts.

25. A 2000 survey found slightly over 23 percent of the US population reported involvement in a neighborhood association. Research has also documented a proliferation of such groups in the past fifty years (Ruef and Kwon 2016).

CHAPTER 1. CRIMINALIZING DISADVANTAGE

1. Intersectionality as a framework originated in Black feminist theory and critical race theory. Black feminist theory places the lived experiences of Black women at the center of the analysis and recognizes that Black women are typically oppressed both in society and within the Black community because of their subordinate race, ethnicity, sex, and gender statuses (Crenshaw 1991; Potter 2013, 2015). Some argue that intersectional perspectives can also be applied to the experiences, identities, and power matrices of men of color, white men, white women, and other women of color. They can also be used to consider the impact of other key aspects of one's identity, such as class and sexuality (Burgess-Proctor 2006).

2. Historically, women's reformatories were an opportunity for upper- and middle-class women to educate poor and working-class women on morality (Rafter 2017; Sue 2019). Reformatories and women's prisoners were implicated in the politics of gender, and definitions of appropriate gender roles (Rafter 2017).

3. Not all drug users, and not all people who break the law, go to prison or jail. Those that do are more likely to be marginalized, particularly in jail settings.

4. https://www.mass.gov/doc/districtmunicipal-court-rules-for-probation-violation-proceedings/download. Accessed July 11, 2017.

5. A section 35 is a court order to civilly commit and treat someone involuntarily for a drug or alcohol disorder.

6. One challenge is that roughly 90 percent of the population at the House of Correction are men. Some staff suggested that the idea that men had more resources and access was an inaccurate perception based on the relative sizes of the populations. Other times, the smaller numbers of women could make participation a challenge, such as if they wanted to be part of work crews but they needed to remain gender segregated.

7. I gave everyone my office and cell phone numbers on the consent form when they first agreed to participate. While some did call, in most cases I had to call them and many lost the numbers along the way. Tom said he had a photographic memory. And indeed, he called me from the House of Correction after almost surely not retaining the paper with my phone number. In addition, Christopher told me that he ran into Tom on the street and Tom gave him my number, after he had lost the paper.

8. ATR, Massachusetts Access to Recovery. This was one of the more commonly, and favorably, mentioned programs.

9. This estimate likely underestimates the prevalence of this experience among a House of Correction release population. A number of the people we did not connect with post-release had no plans and no contacts for when they got out. While we did manage to keep in touch with people who struggled a lot in their first year or two out, no doubt we disproportionately lost touch with people who were similarly struggling.

10. Pablo did not have access to a phone. My only way to reach him was to send letters to a day shelter where he received mail or to leave a voice mail on a shared voice mail at the same shelter.

CHAPTER 2. BOUNCING AND THE BLACK BOX OF REENTRY'S NEIGHBORHOOD EFFECTS

1. I focus here on individual activity spaces, but we might also consider the significance of eco-networks, or the collective structure of activity spaces. These may show where a group of people crosses paths in the same spaces that are characterized by extensive overlap in conventional routines, increasing familiarity, weak ties, and collective efficacy (Browning and Soller 2014; Browning et al. 2017c). Activity spaces and eco-networks need not be limited to conventional neighborhood boundaries, yet may be important parts of ecological communities, or activity locations and actors that intersect at higher rates (Browning and Soller 2014).

2. Much of the research on activity spaces has used survey data (Krivo et al. 2013; Jones and Pebley 2014; Browning et al. 2017b, 2017c) and GPS data, either through smart phones (Sugie and Lens 2017; Cagney et al. 2020) or social media with embedded GPS positioning (Wang et al. 2018; Phillips et al. 2021), which can provide detailed information on patterns of movement (Cagney et al. 2020). Using interviews to explore activity spaces is less precise in its measurement but provides more richness in *why* people go where they go.

3. Michael did not want to be recorded, so this is a paraphrase from written notes. In this case, at least, he was also right about Arturo's whereabouts. I talked to him a week later, in the House of Correction.

4. I was in court with Wallace the day he requested to have the ankle monitor taken off, and heard the judge confirm that he had worn it voluntarily.

5. Since this interview, in 2019, Dudley Square has been renamed Nubian Square, after the ancient African civilization of Nubia and to recognize the importance of the area for the Black community of Boston. Nik DeCosta-Klipa, "Boston officially changes Dudley Square to Nubian Square," *Boston Globe*, December 19, 2019.

6. See Clair (2020) for similar discussions of people (especially poorer people of color) with extensive criminal legal system experience, their frustrations with their lawyers, and the dismissal of their experiential expertise.

7. Until I met Pablo and Kevin and others who used the services on Long Island, and heard their impressions, I had been very skeptical about putting such services on an island in Boston Harbor. It seemed stigmatizing to the people who used the services and reflected an apparent desire to pretend that problems of homelessness and addiction did not exist in Boston. While I remain ambivalent about the "best" way to organize and place similar services, Pablo, Kevin, and others' perspectives tempered my own perspective on the value of the island to those who used its services.

8. While I do not know the nature of the motel Sandy stayed at, motels can be housing of last resort for formerly incarcerated and other disenfranchised people. See Dum's (2016) *Exiled in America* for one account of a residential motel in New York that served as housing of last resort.

CHAPTER 3. DORCHESTER

1. See also Vargas (2016) for similar dynamics in 2010s Little Village in Chicago.

2. Reviewing her criminal record confirmed the open cases Netta talked about. For much of the rest, I have only her version of events.

3. https://ncrc.org/qualified-opportunity-zones-2018-gentrified-neighborhoods -2000-2017/

4. See, for example, Walker (2016) on how racial politics justify racial categories at the institutional level and how they can be used as a management tool. The "racial projects" operate both at an institutional and at a micro-interactional level, in a reciprocal relationship. Patrick Lopez-Aguado (2018) also talked about the "spill-over" of carceral identities, including the racial sorting in prison.

5. Our first interview was not recorded, so these quotes are from written notes. Subsequent interviews were recorded.

CHAPTER 4. THE SOUTH END

1. "South End Landmark District," City of Boston, https://www.boston.gov /historic-district/south-end-landmark-district.

2. Boston Medical Center is a private not-for-profit hospital affiliated with the Boston University School of Medicine. It is the largest safety-net hospital and business trauma and emergency services center in New England. See bmc.org.

3. Woods and Kennedy's 1911 Handbook of Settlements says that the South End House was first established in 1891 and called the Andover House until 1895. https://socialwelfare.library.vcu.edu/settlement-houses/south-end-house-boston-ma/.

4. Miranda Suarez, "Alexandra Hotel Not Actually in South End, as City Thought," WBUR, April 17.

5. Ibid.

6. Nestor Ramos, "Store at epicenter of Boston's Addiction Problem Closes," *Boston Globe*, January 9, 2017.

7. Note: this was after the interviews with people exiting the House of Correction were completed, so we do not have their perspective on this period.

8. "Vicious Attack on Corrections Officer on Methadone Mile Caught on Camera," WCVB, https://www.wcvb.com/article/corrections-officer-attacked-in-boston-on-way-to-work/28578675

9. Felice Freyer, Milton Valencia, and Danny McDonald, "Tensions Flare as Homeless and Drug Users Spread into the South End," *Boston Globe*, August 8, 2019.

10. Jerome Campbell, "Operation Clean Sweep Arrest Reports Show Most Arrests Were for Drug Possession," WBUR, September 19, 2019.

11. Campbell, "Operation Clean Sweep."

12. Christina Prignano, "They Cannot Be 'Swept' Away: DA Rollins Criticizes South End Police Sweep," *Boston Globe*, August 8, 2019.

13. Campbell, "Operation Clean Sweep."

CHAPTER 5. SOUTH BOSTON

1. Bulger was on the run between 1995 and 2011. Arrested in 2011, he was convicted in 2013 on thirty-one of thirty-two counts of racketeering (including eleven murders) and firearms possession. He was killed in federal prison in 2018.

Shelley Murphy, Milton J. Valencia, and Martin Finucane, "Whitey Bulger, notorious Boston gangster, convicted in sweeping racketeering case; jury finds he participated in 11 murders," *Boston Globe*, August 12, 2013; Ray Sanchez, "Boston gangers James "Whitey" Bulger killed in West Virginia prison a day after transfer." CNN, October 30, 2018.

2. The water came from Lake Cochituate in Middlesex County via the Cochituate Aqueduct. The area was a reservoir for about fifty years, until it was filled in and South Boston High School was built on the site in 1901.

3. The Racial Imbalance Act of 1965 defined any school that was more than 50 percent Black as "imbalanced" (Vale 2002).

4. Harold C. Schonberg, "South Boston Schools Shut in Clashes over Stabbing," *New York Times*, December 12, 1974, https://www.nytimes.com/1974/12/12/archives/south-boston-schools-shut-in-clashes-over-stabbing-south-boston.html, accessed May 29, 2020.

5. In 1989, Charles Stuart, a white man from West Roxbury, killed his pregnant wife, Carol. He told police they were the victim of a carjacking attempt by a Black man in Mission Hill in Roxbury as they returned from a childbirth class at a nearby hospital. The police relied on their recently implemented stop-and-frisk policy to find a suspect. Stuart's allegations eventually unraveled.

6. Adam Nagourney and Ian Lovett, "Whitey Bulger Is Arrested in California," *New York Times*, June 23, 2011, https://www.nytimes.com/2011/06/23/us/23bulger.html, accessed May 11, 2020.

7. Hilary Sargent, "Map: Whitey's Boston," Boston.com, 2013, http://archive.boston.com/news/specials/whitey/whitey_bulger_map_boston/, accessed May 11, 2020.

8. Andrew Ryan (as part of the Spotlight Team), "A brand New Boston, even Whiter than the old," *Boston Globe*, December 11, 2017, https://apps.bostonglobe.com/spotlight/boston-racism-image-reality/series/seaport/, accessed May 28, 2020.

9. The problems of school choice and its connection to white flight is well documented and not unique to South Boston (Saporito and Lareau 1999; Logan et al. 2008; Kimelberg and Billingham 2013). In Boston, federal control over school desegregation lasted from 1974 to 1989. Today, Boston public school students are predominantly students of color (41% Hispanic, 36% Black, 9% Asian) and low income (approximately 75% qualify for free or reduced lunch) (Kimelberg and Billingham 2013).

10. According to the US Census American Community Survey estimates, 80.5 percent of South Boston residents lived in the same house one year ago. Of just those living in rental housing, 77 percent lived in the same house one year before.

11. This seems borne out by census data. Those under age 20 make up about 14 percent of South Boston's population. While South Boston is over 75 percent white, only 25.9 percent of youth aged 10–14 are white and less than half of those 15–19 are white. In contrast, nearly 90 percent of those between 25 and 34 are white and these age groups also make up the largest portion of the population. Given segregation patterns within South Boston, this suggests that most of the children live in the public housing developments, and not in large numbers in the private housing in the rest of the neighborhood. See https://statisticalatlas.com/neighborhood/Massachusetts/Boston/South-Boston/Race-and-Ethnicity (accessed July 3, 2020).

12. According to a *Boston Globe* article on the Fort Point Channel Historic District, Fort Point consists of Boston's largest collection of late nineteenth- and early twentieth-century industrial loft buildings. Bridges were built in the late nineteenth century to connect the area to downtown and to South Boston. Artists began using the warehouses for studios and residences beginning in the late 1970s, and eventually negotiated leases with the Boston Wharf Company. The area was designated a landmark district in 2009. Megan Turchi, "Boston's Former Industrial Mecca: Fort Point Channel Landmark District," Boston.com, http://realestate.boston.com/news/2015/03/26/bostons-former-industrial-mecca-fort-point-channel-landmark-district/ March 26, 2015, accessed July 3, 2020. See also Boston Landmarks Commission 2008.

13. Old Colony and D Street are two of the public housing developments in South Boston.

14. Jeremy C. Fox, "Two Dead in South Boston in Apparent Double Homicide," *Boston Globe*, May 6, 2017, https://www.bostonglobe.com/metro/2017/05/05/two-dead-south-boston-apparent-double-homicide/ute7IgEnWXQmwDHmlcTF7J/story.html, accessed May 9, 2020. The man ultimately convicted of the murder was a former security guard in their building and was arrested at the scene.

15. David Abel and Travis Anderson, "Police Detail How Amy Lord Died," *Boston Globe*, August 3, 2013, https://www.bostonglobe.com/metro/2013/08/02/police-report-details-how-amy-lord-died/lrHHPETw1qyDXB93Wx9QyN/story.html, accessed May 10, 2020.

16. This also happened in the lead-up to the mayoral election that followed five-term mayor Thomas Menino's final term. A dozen candidates were in the primary, and several (including the eventual winner Marty Walsh) were also in attendance.

17. Laura Crimaldi, "Prosecutors Describe Murder of South Boston Woman in 2012," *Boston Globe*, September 24, 2015, https://www.bostonglobe.com/metro/2015/09/24/prosecutors-describe-murder-south-boston-woman/7TjxW8UaCLoZrbZSjIm5lN/story.html. Retrieved May 10, 2020.

18. Colin A. Young, "Man Charged with Killing South Boston Woman: Victim Found in a Sober House; Officials Question Regulation," *Boston Globe*, June 27, 2013, https://www.bostonglobe.com/metro/2013/06/27/south-boston-man-charged-murder-former-girlfriend-sober-house/MqRWTbxXsqPDoVQxqVDpXI/story.html, accessed May 10, 2020.

CHAPTER 6. SMALL TOWNS, POVERTY, AND ADDICTION

1. Narcan, or naloxone, is used to treat a known or suspected opioid overdose.

2. This, of course, was not unique to those in small towns. Several people talked about experiencing multiple overdoses in a short time span. Lillian, a Black woman who was from a mill town outside of Boston, described her experience of overdosing about five times in five months:

> One time one of my good friends, she gave me CPR. After Narcaning me once, other—one time I was in the Brockton neighborhood health center bathroom. They found me because I guess they were closing. They found me. I woke up in the ambulance. . . . The ambulance said that they Narcaned me four times and that was my second overdose. They said I wouldn't live past another one. I continued to do it and I overdosed three times after that and still lived. By the end of my run, I have got so bad that I would do dope and I would tell them that I'm on a no-resuscitation policy. Do not call the police and do not resuscitate. Thank God I was always with somebody who cared enough to not even listen to what I was saying.

3. Our first four interviews were not recorded, so these quotes are based on my handwritten notes. The final interview was recorded.

4. Facebook also served an important function for a highly disadvantaged population, who often did not have a stable address or consistent phone number. While cell phones went in and out of service, their Facebook account could stay active. Some checked it (or email) at the public library, and others would temporarily drop off, but then access their Facebook account on their next phone. For some, it was the most reliable way to keep in touch.

5. Sarah hurt her leg while incarcerated, and it continued to bother her. She described the injury: "I fell while I was in Framingham on a sheet of ice.... You walk down a set of stairs and it was a sheet of ice. There's a ten-foot drop. I fell down the stairs and then I did the drop too. I broke my wrist too. And my leg, well, my femur. I broke the top of my femur, up where my hip is. It's pretty bad injury."

6. This estimation is based on a search of "aaboston.org" of meetings within five miles of Boston on a Thursday.

CONCLUSION

1. These distinctions are not necessarily straightforward. For example, Marie Gottschalk (2015), John Pfaff (2017), and others caution against making clear distinctions between "violent" and "nonviolent" offenders that often do not reflect varying levels of risk of reoffending or danger to the community.

2. Hart disagrees with the use of the term *harm reduction*, because it unnecessarily focuses on harms rather than pleasures of drug use. He does agree with providing education and strategies to keep people safe while using drugs.

APPENDIX A: METHODS

1. In one case, when we met for our second interview, one participant (Arturo) introduced me to someone (Michael) who said he had just been released from the House of Correction. I agreed to interview him even though I did not meet him in the House of Correction. In the other ninety-nine cases, we interviewed people first in the House of Correction shortly before their release.

2. We worked through the director of women's programming, and in a few cases, she decided a woman was not a good candidate, because of severe physical or mental health issues. It is also possible that we missed some women during our recruitment efforts because of the timing of our visits and their release, particularly as release dates could change on short notice.

3. The first day we interviewed, a research assistant and I were put in a classroom, with a case worker also sitting in the room. While she wasn't formally a part of the interview, it's possible she overheard some of our conversations. One of the men I interviewed that day occasionally engaged with her during the interview. Subsequent days, we used the lawyer visit rooms or were in classrooms in the women's unit and were alone with the interviewee.

4. This was at the suggestion of a grant reviewer. Doing this served two purposes: it simplified the bureaucracy of paying currently incarcerated people and it provided an additional incentive to meet with us outside. It was this transition to the street where we were most likely to lose contact with someone. In instances in which we conducted a follow up interview with someone who had been reincarcerated, we deposited a money order for them. The only time we did not do that was at the request of the interviewee, who said he preferred the money when he was outside.

5. The study and consent procedures were approved by the university IRB and by the facility. We used a three-stage consent process. The first was consenting to be interviewed and was the only mandatory stage. The second stage was consenting for these interviews to be recorded, which most agreed to. The third was consenting to let us access their criminal records. We then also applied to the Massachusetts Department of Criminal Justice Information Services to access these records. In some cases, we had to correct our own information (date of birth, name spelling) to get information back. For the two we did not find, it is possible we still had errors in our information. It is also possible that our respondents gave us and the courts inconsistent information.

6. The decision to pay resident participants forty dollars, rather than the thirty dollars (per interview) we paid people exiting the House of Correction, was a practical consideration. Since we were paying in cash, it was much easier to get twenty-dollar bills than ten-dollar bills. These interviews began after most of the interviews with formerly incarcerated people, so when we made this change, it was too late to do it for all participants.

7. It is a limitation that all recruitment and interviews were in English; 22 percent of the South End, 11 percent of South Boston, and 36 percent of Dorchester residents are foreign born and language barriers may have limited our reach to some of these residents.

REFERENCES

Abbott, Andrew. 2001. *Time matters: On theory and method*. Chicago: University of Chicago Press.

Adams, Richard E., and Richard T. Serpe. 2000. "Social integration, fear of crime, and life satisfaction." *Sociological Perspectives* 43 (4):605–629.

Alkon, Alison Hope, and Michael Traugot. 2008. "Place matters, but how? Rural identity, environmental decision making, and the social construction of place." *City & Community* 7 (2):97–112.

Anderson, Elijah. 1999. *Code of the street: Decency, violence, and the moral life of the inner city*. New York: W. W. Norton.

Baumer, Eric P., Steven F. Messner, and Richard Rosenfeld. 2003. "Examining spatial variation in support for capital punishment: A multilevel analysis." *American Journal of Sociology* 108 (4):844–875.

Beckett, Katherine, and Steve Herbert. 2009. *Banished: The new social control in urban America*. Oxford University Press.

Bell, Monica C. 2016. "Situational trust: How disadvantaged mothers reconceive legal cynicism." *Law & Society Review* 50 (2):314–347.

———. 2020. "Black security and the conundrum of policing." Just Security. https://www.justsecurity.org/71418/black-security-and-the-conundrum-of-policing/

Bishop, Elizabeth Tsai, Brook Hopkins, Chijindu Obiofuma, and Felix Owusu. 2020. "Racial disparities in the Massachusetts criminal system." Criminal Justice Policy Program, Harvard Law School.

Bohmert, Miriam Northcutt. 2016. "The role of transportation disadvantage for women on community supervision." *Criminal Justice and Behavior* 43 (11):1522–1540.

Bohmert, Miriam N., and Alfred Demaris. 2017. "Cumulative disadvantage and the role of transportation in community supervision." *Crime and Delinquency* 64 (8):1033–1056.

Boston Landmarks Commission. 1983. *The South End: District study committee report*. https://www.cityofboston.gov/images_documents/South_End_Study_Report_13_tcm3-32476.pdf.

———. 2008. "Fort Point Channel landmark district study report." https://www.cityofboston.gov/images_documents/Fort%20Point%20Channel%20Landmark%20District%20Study%20Report%20%23201_tcm3-51248.pdf.

Boyles, Andrea S. 2019. *You can't stop the revolution: Community disorder and social ties in post-Ferguson America*: Berkeley: University of California Press.

Brayne, Sarah. 2014. "Surveillance and system avoidance." *American Sociological Review* 79 (3):367–391.

Brooks, Lisa E., Amy Solomon, Sinead Keegan, Rhiana Kohl, and Lori Lahue. 2005. *Prisoner reentry in Massachusetts*. Washington, DC The Urban Institute.

Brown-Saracino, Japonica. 2013. *The gentrification debates: A reader*. New York: Routledge.

Browning, Christopher R. 2009. "Illuminating the downside of social capital: Negotiated coexistence, property crime, and disorder in urban neighborhoods." *American Behavioral Scientist* 52 (11):1556–1578.

Browning, Christopher R., Catherine A. Calder, Bethany Boettner, and Anna Smith. 2017a. "Ecological networks and urban crime: The structure of shared routine activity locations and neighborhood–level informal control capacity." *Criminology* 55 (4):754–778.

Browning, Christopher R., Catherine A. Calder, Lauren J. Krivo, Anna L. Smith, and Bethany Boettner. 2017b. "Socioeconomic segregation of activity spaces in urban neighborhoods: Does shared residence mean shared routines?" *RSF: The Russell Sage Foundation Journal of the Social Sciences* 3 (2):210–222.

Browning, Christopher R., Catherine A. Calder, Brian Soller, Aubrey L Jackson, and Jonathan Dirlam. 2017c. "Ecological networks and neighborhood social organization." *American Journal of Sociology* 122 (6):1939–1988.

Browning, Christopher R., and Brian Soller. 2014. "Moving beyond neighborhood: Activity spaces and ecological networks as contexts for youth development." *Cityscape: A Journal of Policy Development and Research* 16 (1):165–196.

Burgess-Proctor, Amanda. 2006. "Intersections of race, class, gender, and crime: Future directions for feminist criminology." *Feminist Criminology* 1 (1):27–47.

Cagney, Kathleen A., Erin York Cornwell, Alyssa W. Goldman, and Liang Cai. 2020. "Urban mobility and activity spaces." *Annual Review of Sociology* 46 (1).

Carr, Patrick. 2003. "The new parochialism: The implications of the Beltway case for arguments concerning informal social control." *American Journal of Sociology* 108 (6):1249–1291.

Carson, E. Ann. 2020. "Prisoners in 2019." *Bureau of Justice Statistics Bulletin*.

Chan, Dara V., Sucharita Gopal, and Christine A. Helfrich. 2014. "Accessibility patterns and community integration among previously homeless adults: A geographic information systems (GIS) approach." *Social Science & Medicine* 120:142–152.

Chesney-Lind, Meda. 2002. "Imprisoning women: The unintended victims of mass imprisonment." In *Invisible Punishment: The Collateral Consequences of Mass Imprisonment*, edited by Marc Mauer and Meda Chesney-Lind, 79–94. New York: The Free Press.

Chiricos, Ted, Sarah Eschholz, and Marc Gertz. 1997. "Crime, news and fear of crime: Toward an identification of audience effects." *Social Problems* 44 (3):342–357.

Chiricos, Ted, Ranee McEntire, and Marc Gertz. 2001. "Perceived racial and ethnic composition of neighborhood and perceived risk of crime." *Social Problems* 48 (3):322–340.

Christian, Johnna. 2005. "Riding the bus: Barriers to prison visitation and family management strategies." *Journal of Contemporary Criminal Justice* 21 (1):31–48.

Clair, Matthew. 2020. *Privilege and punishment: How race and class matter in criminal court.* Princeton, NJ: Princeton University Press.

Clampet-Lundquist, Susan, Kathryn Edin, Jeffrey R. Kling, and Greg J. Duncan. 2011. "Moving teenagers out of high-risk neighborhoods: How girls fare better than boys." *American Journal of Sociology* 116 (4):1154–1189.

Clear, Todd R. 2007. *Imprisoning communities: How mass incarceration makes disadvantaged neighborhoods worse.* New York: Oxford University Press.

Clear, Todd R., Dina R. Rose, Elin Waring, and Kristen Scully. 2003. "Coercive mobility and crime: A preliminary examination of concentrated incarceration and social disorganization." *Justice Quarterly* 20 (1):33–64.

Cobbina, Jennifer E. 2019. *Hands up, don't shoot: Why the protests in Ferguson and Baltimore matter, and how they changed America.* New York: New York University Press.

Cobbina, Jennifer E., Jody Miller, and Rod K. Brunson. 2008. "Gender, neighborhood danger, and risk–avoidance strategies among urban African American youths." *Criminology* 46 (3):673–709.

Comfort, Megan. 2008. *Doing time together: Love and family in the shadow of the prison.* Chicago: University of Chicago Press.

———. 2016. "'A twenty-hour-a-day job': The impact of frequent low-level criminal justice involvement on family life." *The Annals of the American Academy of Political and Social Science* 665 (1):63–79.

Conover, Ted. 2010. *Newjack: Guarding Sing Sing.* New York: Vintage.

Costelloe, Michael T., Ted Chiricos, and Marc Gertz. 2009. "Punitive attitudes toward criminals: Exploring the relevance of crime salience and economic insecurity." *Punishment & Society* 11 (1):25–49.

Covington, Jeanette, and Ralph B. Taylor. 1991. "Fear of crime in urban residential neighborhoods: Implications of between- and within-neighborhood sources for current models." *Sociological Quarterly* 32 (2):231–249.

Crenshaw, Kimberlé. 1991. "Mapping the margins: Intersectionality, identity politics, and violence against women of color." *Stanford Law Review* 43 (6):1241.

———. 2013. "From private violence to mass incarceration: Thinking intersectionally about women, race, and social control." *Journal of Scholarly Perspectives* 9 (1):23–50.

Cullen, Francis T., Bonnie S. Fisher, and Brandon K. Applegate. 2000. "Public opinion about punishment and corrections." *Crime and Justice* 27:1–79.

Davis, Angela Y. 2011. *Are prisons obsolete?* New York: Seven Stories Press.

Desmond, Matthew. 2012a. "Eviction and the reproduction of urban poverty." *American Journal of Sociology* 118 (1):88–133.

——. 2012b. "Disposable ties and the urban poor." *American Journal of Sociology* 117 (5):1295–1335.

Dilulio, John J. Jr. 1995. "The coming of the super-predators." *Weekly Standard* 1 (11):23.

Drakulich, Kevin M. 2013. "Perceptions of the local danger posed by crime: Race, disorder, informal control, and the police." *Social Science Research* 42 (3):611–632.

Drakulich, Kevin M., and Robert D. Crutchfield. 2013. "The role of perceptions of the police in informal social control: Implications for the racial stratification of crime and control." *Social Problems* 60 (3):383–407.

Dum, Christopher P. 2016. *Exiled in America: Life on the margins in a residential motel.* New York: Columbia University Press.

Eason, John M. 2017. *Big house on the prairie.* Chicago: University of Chicago Press.

Ellis, Rachel. 2020. "Prisons as porous institutions." *Theory and Society*, online first:1–25.

Fader, Jamie J. 2021. "'I don't have time for drama': Managing risk and uncertainty through network avoidance." *Criminology* 59(2):291–317.

Fagan, Jeffrey A. 2010. "The contradictions of juvenile crime and punishment." *Daedalus* 139:43.

Farrall, Stephen, Ben Hunter, Gilly Sharpe, and Adam Calverley. 2014. *Criminal careers in transition: The social context of desistance from crime.* Oxford: Oxford University Press.

Forman, Benjamin, Laura Van Der Lugt, and Ben Goldberg. 2016. "The geography of incarceration: The costs and consequences of high incarceration rates in vulnerable city neighborhoods." Boston Indicators Project. 1–24.

Gans, Herbert. 1982. *The urban villagers: Group and class in the life of Italian Americans.* New York: Vintage Books.

Garland, David. 2001. *The culture of control: Crime and social order in contemporary society.* Chicago: University of Chicago Press.

Gilliam Jr, Franklin D., and Shanto Iyengar. 2000. "Prime suspects: The influence of local television news on the viewing public." *American Journal of Political Science* 44 (3):560–573.

Gilmore, Ruth Wilson. 2007. *Golden gulag: Prisons, surplus, crisis, and opposition in globalizing California.* Berkeley: University of California Press.

Giordano, Peggy C., Stephen A. Cernkovich, and Jennifer L Rudolph. 2002. "Gender, crime, and desistance: Towards a theory of cognitive transformation." *American Journal of Sociology* 107 (4):990–1064.

Giordano, Peggy C., Ryan D. Schroeder, and Stephen A. Cernkovich. 2007. "Emotions and crime over the life course: A neo-Meadian perspective on criminal continuity and change." *American Journal of Sociology* 112 (6):1603–1661.

Girling, Evi, Ian Loader, and Richard Sparks. 2000. *Crime and social change in Middle England.* London: Routledge.

Goffman, Alice. 2014. *On the run: Fugitive life in an American city*. Chicago: University of Chicago Press.

Goffman, Erving. 1963. *Stigma: Notes on the management of spoiled identity*. New York: Simon and Schuster.

Gottschalk, Marie. 2015. *Caught: The prison state and the lockdown of American politics*. Princeton, NJ: Princeton University Press.

Gowan, Teresa, and Sarah Whetstone. 2012. "Making the criminal addict: Subjectivity and social control in a strong-arm rehab." *Punishment & Society* 14 (1):69–93.

Hairston, Creasie Finney. 2003. "Prisoners and their families: Parenting issues during incarceration." In *Prisoners once removed: The impact of incarceration and reentry on children, families, and communities*, edited by Jeremy Travis and Michelle Waul, 259–282. Washington, DC: Urban Institute Press.

Haney, Lynne A. 2010. *Offending women: Power, punishment, and the regulation of desire*. Berkeley: University of California Press.

Harding, David J. 2010. *Living the drama: Community, conflict, and culture among inner-city boys*. Chicago: University of Chicago Press.

Harding, David J., and Heather M. Harris. 2020. *After prison: Navigating adulthood in the shadow of the prison*. New York: Russell Sage Foundation.

Harding, David J., and Jeffrey D. Morenoff. 2013. "Home is hard to find: Neighborhoods, institutions, and the residential trajectories of returning prisoners." *The ANNALS of the American Academy of Political and Social Science* 647 (1):214–236.

Harding, David J., Jeffrey D. Morenoff, and Jessica J. B. Wyse. 2019. *On the outside: Prisoner reentry and reintegration* Chicago: University of Chicago Press.

Harris, Alexes. 2016. *A pound of flesh*. New York: Russell Sage Foundation.

Hart, Carl L. 2021. *Drug use for grown-ups: Chasing liberty in the land of fear*. New York: Penguin.

Heimer, Karen, and Stacy De Coster. 1999. "The gendering of violent delinquency." *Criminology* 37 (2):277–318.

Herbert, Claire W., Jeffrey D. Morenoff, and David J. Harding. 2015. "Homelessness and housing insecurity among former prisoners." *RSF: The Russell Sage Foundation Journal of the Social Sciences* 1 (2):44–79.

Hipp, John R. 2010. "A dynamic view of neighborhoods: The reciprocal relationship between crime and neighborhood structural characteristics." *Social Problems* 57 (2):205–230.

Hipp, John R., Joan Petersilia, and Susan Turner. 2010. "Parolee recidivism in California: The effect of neighborhood context and social service agency characteristics." *Criminology* 48 (4):947–979.

Horowitz, Ruth. 1986. "Remaining an outsider: Membership as a threat to research rapport." *Journal of Contemporary Ethnography* 14 (4):409–430.

Horton, Frank E., and David R Reynolds. 1971. "Effects of urban spatial structure on individual behavior." *Economic Geography* 47 (1):36–48.

Hummon, David. 1990. *Commonplaces: Community, ideology, and identity in American culture*. Albany: State University of New York Press.

Irwin, John. 1985. *The jail: Managing the underclass in American society*. Berkeley: University of California Press.

Jacobs, Jane. 1961. *The death and life of great American cities*. New York: Vintage Books.

Jones, Malia, and Anne R Pebley. 2014. "Redefining neighborhoods using common destinations: Social characteristics of activity spaces and home census tracts compared." *Demography* 51 (3):727–752.

Jones, Nikki. 2010. *Between good and ghetto: African American girls and inner-city violence*. New Brunswick, NJ: Rutgers University Press.

———. 2018. *The chosen ones: Black men and the politics of redemption*. Oakland: University of California Press.

Kaba, Mariame. 2021. *We do this til we free us: Abolitionist organizing and transforming justice*. Chicago: Haymarket Press.

Kaeble, Danielle. 2018. "Time served in state prison, 2016." *Bureau of Justice Statistics Bulletin*. Washington, DC: Office of Justice Programs, US Department of Justice.

Kennedy, David M., Anthony A. Braga, and Anne M. Piehl. 2001. *Reducing gun violence: The Boston Gun Project's Operation Ceasefire: Developing and implementing Operation Ceasefire*. National Institute of Justice. Washington, DC: US Department of Justice, Office of Justice Programs.

Kimelberg, Shelley McDonough, and Chase M. Billingham. 2013. "Attitudes toward diversity and the school choice process: Middle-class parents in a segregated urban public school district." *Urban Education* 48 (2):198–231.

King, Anna, and Shadd Maruna. 2009. "Is a conservative just a liberal who has been mugged? Exploring the origins of punitive views." *Punishment & Society* 11 (2):147–169.

Kirk, David S. 2009. "A natural experiment of the effect of residential change on recidivism: Lessons from Hurricane Katrina." *American Sociological Review* 74 (3):484–505.

———. 2012. "Residential change as a turning point in the life course of crime: Desistance or temporary cessation?" *Criminology* 50 (2):329–358.

———. 2020. *Home free: Prisoner reentry and residential change after Hurricane Katrina*. New York: Oxford University Press.

Kohler-Hausmann, Issa. 2018. *Misdemeanorland: Criminal courts and social control in an age of broken windows policing*. Princeton, NJ: Princeton University Press.

Krivo, Lauren J., Heather M. Washington, Ruth D. Peterson, Christopher R. Browning, Catherine A. Calder, and Mei-Po Kwan. 2013. "Social isolation of disadvantage and advantage: The reproduction of inequality in urban space." *Social Forces* 92 (1):141–164.

Kruttschnitt, Candace. 2016. "The politics, and place, of gender in research on crime." *Criminology* 54 (1):8–29.

Kruttschnitt, Candace, and Jeanette Hussemann. 2008. "Micropolitics of race and ethnicity in women's prisons in two political contexts." *British Journal of Sociology* 59 (4):709–728.

Krysan, Maria. 2003. "Community undesirability in black and white: Examining racial residential preferences through community perceptions." *Social Problems* 49 (4):521–543.

Kubrin, Charis E., and Eric A. Stewart. 2006. "Predicting who reoffends: The neglected role of neighborhood context in recidivism studies." *Criminology* 44 (1):165–195.

La Vigne, Nancy G., Cynthia A. Mamalian, Jeremy Travis, and Christy Visher. 2003. *A portrait of prisoner reentry in Illinois*. Washington, DC: The Urban Institute.

La Vigne, Nancy G., Christy Visher, and Jennifer Castro. 2004. *Chicago prisoners' experiences returning home*. Washington, DC: Urban Institute.

Laub, John H., and Robert J Sampson. 2003. *Shared beginnings, divergent lives: Delinquent boys to age 70*. Cambridge, MA: Harvard University Press.

Leverentz, Andrea. 2010. "People, places, and things: How female ex-prisoners negotiate their neighborhood context." *Journal of Contemporary Ethnography* 39 (6):646–681.

———. 2011. "Neighborhood context of attitudes toward crime and reentry." *Punishment & Society* 13 (1):64–92.

———. 2012. "Narratives of crime and criminals: How places socially construct the crime problem." *Sociological Forum* 27 (2):348–371.

———. 2014. *The ex-prisoner's dilemma: How women negotiate competing narratives of reentry and desistance*. New Brunswick, NJ: Rutgers University Press.

———. 2018. "Churning through the system: How people engage with the criminal justice system when faced with short sentences." In "After Imprisonment," edited by Austin Sarat. Special issue, *Studies in Law, Politics, and Society* 77: 123–143.

———. 2020a. "Interviewing the 'rabble class': Recruitment and retention in studies of prisoner reentry." In *Beyond Recidivism: New Approaches to Research on Prisoner Reentry and Reintegration*, edited by Andrea Leverentz, Elsa Chen, and Johnna Christian, 100–133. New York: New York University Press.

———. 2020b. "Beyond neighborhoods: Activity spaces of returning prisoners." *Social Problems* 67 (1):150–170.

Leverentz, Andrea, Adam Pittman, and Jennifer Skinnon. 2018. "Place and perception: Constructions of community and safety across neighborhoods and residents." *City & Community* 10 (3):311–324.

Leverentz, Andrea, and Monica Williams. 2017. "Contextualizing community crime control: Race, geography, and configurations of control in four communities." *Criminology* 55 (1):112–136.

Lofland, John, and Lyn Lofland. 1994. *Analyzing social settings: A guide to qualitative observation and analysis*. Belmont, CA: Wadsworth Publishing.

Logan, John R., Deirdre Oakley, and Jacob Stowell. 2008. "School segregation in metropolitan regions, 1970–2000: The impacts of policy choices on public education." *American Journal of Sociology* 113 (6):1611–1644.

Lopez-Aguado, Patrick. 2018. *Stick together and come back home: Racial sorting and the spillover of carceral identity*. Berkeley: University of California Press.

Lundman, Richard J. 2003. "The newsworthiness and selection bias in news about murder: Comparative and relative effects of novelty and race and gender typifications on newspaper coverage of homicide." *Sociological Forum* 18(3): 357–386.

MacDonald, Michael Patrick. 2000. *All souls: A family story from Southie*: Random House Digital, Inc.

Madriz, Esther I. 1997. "Images of criminals and victims: A study on women's fear and social control." *Gender & Society* 11 (3):342–356.

Maruna, Shadd. 2001. *Making good: How ex-convicts reform and rebuild their lives.* Washington, DC: American Psychological Association.

Maruna, Shadd, and Kevin Roy. 2007. "Amputation or reconstruction? Notes on the concept of "knifing off" and desistance from crime." *Journal of Contemporary Criminal Justice* 23 (1):104–124.

Massoglia, Michael, Glenn Firebaugh, and Cody Warner. 2013. "Racial variation in the effect of incarceration on neighborhood attainment." *American Sociological Review* 78 (1):142–165.

Mayorga-Gallo, Sarah. 2014. *Behind the white picket fence: Power and privilege in a multiethnic neighborhood.* Chapel Hill: University of North Carolina Press.

Mazzei, Julie, and Erin E. O'Brien. 2008. "You got it, so when do you flaunt it?" *Journal of Contemporary Ethnography* 38 (3):358–383.

McCorkel, Jill A. 2013. *Breaking women: Gender, race, and the new politics of imprisonment.* New York: New York University Press.

McCorkel, Jill A., and Kristen Myers. 2003. "What difference does difference make? Position and privilege in the field." *Qualitative Sociology* 26 (2):199–231.

McDermott, Monica. 2006. *Working-class white: The making and unmaking of race relations.* Berkeley: University of California Press.

McRoberts, Omar. 2005. *Streets of glory: Church and community in a Black urban neighborhood.* Chicago: University of Chicago Press.

Mears, Daniel P., Xia Wang, Carter Hay, and William D. Bales. 2008. "Social ecology and recidivism: Implications for prisoner reentry." *Criminology* 46 (2):301–340.

Merry, Sally E. 1981. *Urban danger: Life in a neighborhood of strangers.* Philadelphia: Temple University Press.

Miller, Jody. 2001. *One of the guys: Girls, gangs, and gender.* New York: Oxford University Press.

———. 2008. *Getting played: African American girls, urban inequality, and gendered violence.* New York: New York University Press.

Miller, Reuben Jonathan. 2021. *Halfway home: Race, punishment, and the afterlife of mass incarceration.* New York: Little, Brown and Company.

Mollenkopf, John H. 1983. *The contested city.* Princeton, NJ: Princeton University Press.

Oldenburg, Ramon, and Dennis Brissett. 1982. "The third place." *Qualitative Sociology* 5 (4):265–284.

Orrico, Laura A. 2015. "'Doing intimacy' in a public market: How the gendered experience of ethnography reveals situated social dynamics." *Qualitative Research* 15 (4):473–488.

Owen, Barbara. 1998. *"In the mix": Struggle and survival in a women's prison.* Albany: State University of New York Press.

Pager, Devah. 2007. *Marked: Race, crime, and finding work in an era of mass incarceration.* Chicago: University of Chicago Press.

Parker, Cory A. 2019. "Homeless negotiations of public space in two California cities." PhD dissertation, Geography, University of California, Davis.

Parrott, Scott, and Caroline Titcomb Parrott. 2015. "U.S. Television's "mean world" for white women: The portrayal of gender and race on fictional crime dramas." *Sex Roles* 73 (1–2):70–82.

Paternoster, Ray, and Shawn Bushway. 2009. "Desistance and the 'feared self': Toward an identity theory of criminal desistance." *Journal of Criminal Law and Criminology* 99 (4):1103–1156.

Pattillo-McCoy, Mary. 1999. *Black picket fences: Privilege and peril in the black middle class*. Chicago: University of Chicago Press.

Peterson, Ruth D., and Lauren J. Krivo. 2010. *Divergent social worlds: Neighborhood crime and the racial-spatial divide*. New York: Russell Sage Foundation.

Pfaff, John F. 2017. *Locked in: The true causes of mass incarceration and how to achieve real reform*. New York: Basic Books.

Phelps, Michelle S. 2013. "The paradox of probation: Community supervision in the age of mass incarceration." *Law & Policy* 35 (1–2):51–80.

Phelps, Michelle S., and Ebony L Ruhland. 2021. "Governing marginality: Coercion and care in probation." *Social Problems*, spaa060, https://doi.org/10.1093/socpro/spaa060.

Phillips, Nolan E., Brian L. Levy, Robert J. Sampson, Mario L. Small, and Ryan Q. Wang. 2021. "The social integration of American cities: Network measures of connectedness based on everyday mobility across neighborhoods." *Sociological Methods & Research* 50(3): 1110–1149.

Pini, Barbara. 2005. "Interviewing men: Gender and the collection and interpretation of qualitative data." *Journal of Sociology* 41 (2):201–216.

Pittman, Adam W. 2020. "Managing methadone mile: Dynamics of neighborhood change and social control in Boston's South End." PhD dissertation, Sociology, University of Massachusetts Boston.

Potter, Hillary. 2013. "Intersectional criminology: Interrogating identity and power in criminological research and theory." *Critical Criminology* 21 (3):305-318.

———. 2015. *Intersectionality and criminology*. New York: Routledge.

Quillian, Lincoln, and Devah Pager. 2001. "Black neighbors, higher crime? The role of racial stereotypes in evaluations of neighborhood crime." *American Journal of Sociology* 107 (3):717–767.

———. 2010. "Estimating risk stereotype amplification and the perceived risk of criminal victimization." *Social Psychology Quarterly* 73 (1):79–104.

Rafter, Nicole. 2017. *Partial justice: Women, prison, and social control*. New York: Routledge.

Richardson, Jason, Bruce Mitchell, and Jad Edlebi. 2020. "Gentrification and disinvestment 2020." *National Community Reinvestment Coalition*.

Roberts, Dorothy. 2009. *Shattered bonds: The color of child welfare*. New York: Basic Books.

Ruef, Martin, and Seok-Woo Kwon. 2016. "Neighborhood associations and social capital." *Social Forces* 95 (1):159–190.

Russell-Brown, Katheryn. 1998. *The color of crime: Racial hoaxes, White fear, Black protectionism, police harassment, and other macroaggressions.* New York: New York University Press.

Sampson, Robert J. 2012. *Great American city: Chicago and the enduring neighborhood effect.* Chicago: University of Chicago Press.

Sampson, Robert J., and Stephen W. Raudenbush. 2004. "Seeing disorder: Neighborhood stigma and the social construction of 'broken windows.'" *Social Psychology Quarterly* 67 (4):319–342.

Saporito, Salvatore, and Annette Lareau. 1999. "School selection as a process: The multiple dimensions of race in framing educational choice." *Social Problems* 46 (3):418–439.

Sasson, Theodore. 1995. *Crime talk: How citizens construct a social problem.* New York: Aldine de Gruyter.

Schenwar, Maya and Victoria Law. 2020. *Prison by any other name.* New York: The New Press.

Sered, Susan Starr, and Maureen Norton-Hawk. 2014. *Can't catch a break: Gender, jail, drugs, and the limits of personal responsibility.* Oakland: University of California Press.

Sharkey, Patrick T. 2006. "Navigating dangerous streets: The sources and consequences of street efficacy." *American Sociological Review* 71 (5):826–846.

Sharkey, Patrick, and Robert J. Sampson. 2010. "Destination effects: Residential mobility and trajectories of adolescent violence in a stratified metropolis." *Criminology* 48 (3):639–681.

Simes, Jessica T. 2018. "Place after prison: Neighborhood attainment and attachment during reentry." *Journal of Urban Affairs* 16 (1):1–21.

Small, Mario Luis. 2004. *Villa Victoria: The transformation of social capital in a Boston barrio.* Chicago: University of Chicago Press.

———. 2009. "'How many cases do I need?' On science and the logic of case selection in field-based research." *Ethnography* 10 (1):5–38.

Soyer, Michaela. 2014. "Off the corner and into the kitchen: Entering a male-dominated research setting as a woman." *Qualitative Research* 14 (4):459–472.

St. Jean, Peter. 2007. *Pockets of crime: Broken windows, collective efficacy, and the criminal point of view.* Chicago: University of Chicago Press.

Stuart, Forrest. 2013. "From 'rabble management' to 'recovery management': Policing homelessness in marginal urban space." *Urban Studies* 51 (9):1909–1925.

———. 2016. *Down, out, and under arrest: Policing and everyday life in skid row.* Chicago: University of Chicago Press.

Subramanian, Ram, Ruth Delaney, Stephen Roberts, Nancy Fishman, and Peggy McGarry. 2015. *Incarceration's front door: The misuse of jails in America.* New York: Vera Institute of Justice.

Sue, Kimberly. 2019. *Getting wrecked: Women, incarceration, and the opioid crisis.* Oakland, CA: University of California Press.

Sugie, Naomi F., and Michael C. Lens. 2017. "Daytime locations in spatial mismatch: Job accessibility and employment at reentry from prison." *Demography* 54 (2):775–800.

Suttles, Gerald. 1972. *The social construction of communities*. Chicago: University of Chicago Press.

Tach, Laura M. 2009. "More than bricks and mortar: Neighborhood frames, social processes, and the mixed-income redevelopment of a public housing project." *City & Community* 8 (3):269–299.

———. 2014. "Diversity, inequality, and microsegregation: Dynamics of inclusion and exclusion in a racially and economically diverse community." *Cityscape: A Journal of Policy Development and Research* 16 (3):13–45.

Tavory, Iddo, and Stefan Timmermans. 2014. *Abductive analysis: Theorizing qualitative research*. Chicago: University of Chicago Press.

Thernstrom, Stephan. 1973. *The other Bostonians*. Cambridge, MA: Harvard University Press.

Tissot, Sylvie. 2015. *Good neighbors: Gentrifying diversity in Boston's South End*: New York: Verso Books.

Travis, Jeremy. 2005. *But they all come back: Facing the challenges of prisoner reentry*. Washington, DC: The Urban Institute Press.

Twine, France Winddance, and Jonathan W. Warren. 2000. *Racing research, researching race: Methodological dilemmas in critical race studies*. New York: New York University Press.

Tyler, Tom R., and Robert J. Boeckmann. 1997. "Three strikes and you are out, but why? The psychology of public support for punishing rule breakers." *Law and Society Review* 31 (2):237–266.

Useem, Bert, Raymond V. Liedka, and Anne Morrison Piehl. 2003. "Popular support for the prison build-up." *Punishment & Society* 5 (1):5–32.

Vale, Lawrence J. 2002. *Reclaiming public housing: A half century of struggle in three neighborhoods*. Cambridge, MA: Harvard University Press.

Vargas, Robert. 2016. *Wounded city: Violent turf wars in a Chicago barrio*. New York: Oxford University Press.

Vivant, Elsa. 2020. "Naming the sites of the opioid crisis in Boston: A political issue." *EchoGéo* 53.

Walker, Michael L. 2016. "Race making in a penal institution." *American Journal of Sociology* 121 (4):1051–1107.

Wallace, Danielle, and Brooks Louton. 2018. "The disorder perceptions of nonresidents: A textual analysis of open-ended survey responses to photographic stimuli." *City & Community* 17 (1):21–43.

Wang, Qi, Nolan Edward Phillips, Mario L Small, and Robert J. Sampson. 2018. "Urban mobility and neighborhood isolation in America's 50 largest cities." *Proceedings of the National Academy of Sciences* 115 (30):7735–7740.

Warr, Mark. 1980. "The accuracy of public beliefs about crime." *Social Forces* 59 (2):456–470.

Weiss, Robert S. 1994. *Learning from strangers: The art and method of qualitative interviewing*. New York: The Free Press.

Western, Bruce. 2018. *Homeward: Life in the year after prison*. New York: Russell Sage Foundation.

Western, Bruce, Jaclyn Davis, Flavien Ganter, and Natalie Smith. 2021. "The cumulative risk of jail incarceration." *Proceedings of the National Academy of Sciences* 118 (16).

Williams, Seth A., and John R Hipp. 2019. "How great and how good? Third places, neighbor interaction, and cohesion in the neighborhood context." *Social Science Research* 77:68–78.

Wyse, Jessica J. B. 2013. "Rehabilitating criminal selves: Gendered strategies in community corrections." *Gender and Society* 27 (2):231–255.

Zeng, Zhen. 2020. "Jail inmates in 2018." *Bureau of Justice Statistics Bulletin*. Washington, D.C., Office of Justice Programs, US Department of Justice.

INDEX

research participants (Appendix B), 220*t*, 221*t*, 222*t*, 223*t*, 228n24
Richard, drug use of, 67, 186–87
Ronald, 126, 129
Roxbury, 89, 91, 126, 167; as the "heart of Black culture in Boston," 20; Lower Roxbury, 89

Sally, 126; interview with, 125
Sampson, Robert, 13
Sandra, 130
Sandy, 1–2, 82–83, 85; family ties of, 82; interview with, 82; living conditions of, 83–84, 230n8
Sarah, 40, 44–45, 174; attempts to get sober, 187–90; daughter of, 190; interviews with concerning her relapse, 190–91, 192; leg injury while incarcerated, 234n5; maintenance of contact with other women she knew from the House of Correction, 191–92; on "stupid" people on Facebook selling drugs, 192; use of Facebook by, 190, 191, 192–93
Schenwar, Maya, 207
security, 206
Sered, Susan, 34
Serenity, 35
Sharkey, Patrick, 13
Sharon, 46
Sheila, 155–57
Small, Mario, 123–24
small towns (rural towns), poverty, and addiction, 174–75, 225n1; addiction and support services in nonurban areas, 180–83; and managing life without a car, 176–80; reentry/starting over in a small town, 187–93
social anxieties, 16
South Boston, 3, 21–22, 26–27, 143, 200–201, 232n10, 235n7; in the 1960s, 150; annexation of to Boston, 149; crime in (including high-profile homicides), 165–67, 173; demographics of, 232n11; as a destination, 157–62; displacement of ethnic groups in, 150; experiences of living in South Boston, 152–57; gentrification in, 153, 170; history and development of, 149–52; long-term residents of,

155, 156–57; "old" South Boston, 162; population loss of after World War I, 150; problems of drugs, addiction, and gangs in, 163–64; reentry to, 168–72; relaxation of tensions related to racial integration in, 151–52; reputation of, 147–48, 188; school busing protests in, 151; school choice and the connection to White flight in, 232n9; small neighborhoods of, 159–60; and "Southie" narratives, 151–52; specific developments in (Old Harbor, Old Colony, McCormack Public Housing, and West Broadway), 150, 162; ties of to organized crime, drugs, and racial conflict, 148; treatment centers for institutionalized individuals in, 149–50; water reservoir of, 149, 231n2. *See also* Fort Point; City Point
South Boston District Court, 168
South Boston High School, 151
South End, 3, 20–21, 24, 26, 27, 120–22, 198, 201, 235n7; appeal of, 121; architecture and amenities of, 124–27; "Black Quarter" of, 89; clear divides between South End residents, 130–31; demographics of persons leaving the South End, 122–23; economic bifurcation in, 140; from the perspective of prisoner reentry, 121–22; high-income and professional residents of, 129–30; history and development of, 122–24; as a landmark district, 123; policing in, 140–45; Puerto Rican families in, 89; as a site of reentry, 134–40; tensions in due to assault on a deputy sheriff, 143–45
South End House, 122, 231n3
Southampton Street shelter, 140, 142
SPAN, 67, 68
split sentences, 6
Stephen, 46, 87; attempts to avoid trouble after his return from incarceration, 107; description of his Dorchester neighborhood, 108; drinking of, 108–9; return of from incarceration to his Dorchester neighborhood, 106–7
stigma and reputation, 34–36
Stuart, Charles, 151, 232n5

Sue, Kimberly, 35

Suffolk County House of Correction, 2, 5, 6, 20, 22, 27, 41, 42, 43, 44, 45, 78, 88, 99, 118–19, 122, 134, 141, 142, 145–46, 148, 162, 175, 198, 201, 204, 216; centrality to understanding incarceration in Massachusetts, 5; interviewing residents of, 212–14; marginalization of those housed in because of poverty, racism, and addiction, 195; number of persons released from (2014–2015), 5, 226n8; percentage of men in, 228n6; release population of, 229n9; return of those housed in to the Boston area, 196

Sugie, Naomi, 59–60

Supplemental Security Income (SSI), 54

surveillance, 2, 7–8 20, 59, 61, 65, 70, 86, 101, 107, 119; heightened surveillance, 37, 105, 196–97, 202; police surveillance, 32, 67, 136, 184, 200, 202; "surveilling institutions," 35

Tallahassee, Black residents of, 15

Ted, 158

Theresa, 50, 51

This Old House, 92–93

Timothy, 131–32

Tom, 46, 47

transportation, access to, 9, 44. *See also* reentry, in Boston, and transit issues

Turner, Susan, 10

United South End Settlements, 123

United States, 34

Urban Hub, 16

Vale, Lawrence, 34

Villa Victoria (Small), 123

Villa Victoria, 127, 131

violent/nonviolent distinction, 234n1

Wallace, 62, 64–65, 229n4

Warner, Cody, 11–12

West Dedham Street, 127

Western, Bruce, 7

William, 147, 169–70; experiences of living in Dorchester, 113–14

Wilson, Darren, 167

women, 234n2; prison experience of, 32–33, 42–43; percentage of women incarcerated in Massachusetts, 226n5; release of from Illinois prisons to Chicago neighborhoods, 10–11; vulnerability of, 201–2; white women, 201–2; women's reformatories, 228n2. *See also* Black women

Wyse, Jessica, 8

Founded in 1893,
UNIVERSITY OF CALIFORNIA PRESS
publishes bold, progressive books and journals
on topics in the arts, humanities, social sciences,
and natural sciences—with a focus on social
justice issues—that inspire thought and action
among readers worldwide.

The UC PRESS FOUNDATION
raises funds to uphold the press's vital role
as an independent, nonprofit publisher, and
receives philanthropic support from a wide
range of individuals and institutions—and from
committed readers like you. To learn more, visit
ucpress.edu/supportus.